Latin American Women On/In Stages

SUNY series in Latin American and Iberian Thought and Culture

Jorge J. E. Gracia and Rosemary Geisdorfer Feal, Editors

Latin American Women On/In Stages

Margo Milleret

State University of New York Press

Material from Chapter 1 on Consuelo de Castro's À prova de fogo was previously published in Hispania 82, no. 3 (2002): 658–664.

Material from the first section of chapter 2 originally published in Todo ese Fuego: Homenaje a Merlin H. Forster. Eds. Mara L. García and Douglas J. Weatherford. Universidad Autónoma de Tlaxcala, 1999. 135–147. Reprinted by permission of the editors and the press of the Universidad de Tlaxcala.

Material from chapter 3 on Mariela Romero's Esperando al italiano originally published in Revista de Estudios Hispánicos 34, no. 2 (2000): 247–260. Reprinted by permission of the editors.

Permission to quote from the unpublished scripts Amantíssima, Parque para dos, and Adorável desgraçada was granted by Susana Torres Molina, Teresa Marichal, and Leilah Assunção respectively.

Published by
State University of New York Press, Albany

© 2004 State University of New York

For information, address the State University of New York Press,
90 State Street, Suite 700, Albany, NY 12207

Production by Judith Block
Marketing by Susan Petrie

Library of Congress Cataloging-in-Publication Data

Milleret, Margo, 1951–
    Latin American women on/in stages / Margo Milleret.
        p. cm.
    Includes bibliographical references and index.
    ISBN 0-7914-6221-8
    1. Latin American drama—Women authors—History and criticism. 2. Latin American drama—20th century—History and criticism. 3. Women in literature. 4. Sex role in literature. 5. Motherhood in literature. I. Title.

PQ7081.5.M55 2004
862'.6093522—dc22   2003067307

10 9 8 7 6 5 4 3 2 1

For Miriam

In memory of LaMoyne

Contents

Acknowledgments

Given the scope and duration of this project, it would come as no surprise that I have been blessed with a large network of supporters. Funding for this project was initially granted by the Institute of Latin American Studies at the University of Texas, Vanderbilt University, and most recently by the University of New Mexico. Many colleagues helped me make contacts, collects plays, find criticism, and write about women dramatists in Spanish America and Brazil. My heartfelt gratitude for their generosity and helpful feedback goes to Merlin H. Forster, Russell Hamilton, George Woodyard, Vicky Unruh, Jackie Bixler, Ron Burgess, Margarita Vargas, Laurietz Seda, Kirsten Nigro, Yolando Flores, Diana Taylor, Adam Versényi, Cathy Larson, Judy Bissett, Michael Doudoroff, Angela Marino, David George, Jean Graham-Jones, Amalia Gladhart, John Lipski, Diana Rebolledo, Dorothy Chansky, and Judy Maloof. Special thanks to Patricia Rosas Lopátegui for her help with difficult translations and to Kimberle Lopez for her attentive readings of the chapters. Many students have contributed to lively classroom discussions about these plays and I appreciate their astuteness and enthusiasm.

I received help from critics, actresses, and women playwrights in Brazil and Spanish America to whom I say thank you for sharing your insights and your work with me. I would like to send a friendly *abraço/abrazo* to Leilah Assunção, Consuelo de Castro, Thais Erminy, Teresa Marichal, Susana Torres Molina, Maria Adelaide Amaral, Cristina Escofet, Malena Espinosa, Zenobia Azogue, Alberto Guzik, Sábato Magaldi, Mariangela Alves de Lima, Maria Theresa Vargas, Regina Zilberman, Elza Cunha de Vincenzo, and remember the late Décio de Almeida Prado and Yan Michalski.

My partner Vance Bass has debated many of my ideas with me over meals and has helped me in countless ways with my research and writing. I have been sustained by his loving care for me and his intellectual interest in the project.

INTRODUCTION

Domesticating Drama

The title of this chapter refers to two meanings for "domesticate" that apply to the relationship between theater in Latin America and women. The first definition implicates the theater as a site for the domestication or subjugation of women, while the second definition describes the actions of female dramatists to domesticate the theater, that is, to make it more accommodating to women. Traditionally Latin America's plays and playhouses have attempted to tame and subdue women with images and values that limit them to narrowly defined roles and behaviors. At the same time, Latin American theaters have not been friendly toward aspiring women dramatists or directors. Rather, their men in control of operations and aesthetics have scrutinized and questioned those of the "weaker sex" who ventured to enter there. As Brazilian actress and playwright Isis Baião (b. 1941) affirms: "O teatro é, na verdade, como tantas outras, uma casa patriarcal, onde as mulheres são as rainhas, mas os homens dão as ordens e a ideologia" ("A mulher" 1989, 26) [The theater is, in truth, like so many other places, a patriarchal house where women are the queens, but the men give the orders and make the ideology].[1]

Women have been seen in the theaters of Latin America since the early 1800s either playing roles on the stage or watching performances from the audience. We know that class differences and the unsavory reputation of the theater prevented any solidarity between the actresses and the ladies of *buena sociedad* (social standing) in the audience (Seibel 1990, 145). Nonetheless, these two groups had much in common since they shared the same socialization into the two reigning versions of womanhood: the morally virtuous Mary, the marriageable woman and future mother, or the immoral Eve, the prostitute and wanton woman. Both the women on stage and those in the

1

audience have been shaped by the behaviors that male dramatists have created for them in plays. Most of those dramatic roles have confined women to the peripheries of the stage as characters that were incidental to the plot or as sex objects to the actors and the audience. Women's actions on stage have been limited to supporting roles as helper or selfless enabler to the hero or, on the negative side, as barrier to the dramatic events unfolding.

Such images do not provide insights into women's lives but rather are prescriptions of what the men writing have wanted from or for women. That is to say, they are models designed to coerce women into the appropriate roles desired by a patriarchal culture. Beatriz Seibel, for example, has documented the monumental gap between real historical women, those from the conquest and colonial periods, who could have provided exciting material for the stage, and the female characters in the early days of Latin American theater who were portrayed as subordinated to the tutelage of husbands and priests (59). In these plays and others that have been written since, the theater's actions "to domesticate" women point to its social role as an enforcer of patriarchal norms.

The second meaning of domesticate used in this chapter refers to what happens when Latin American women dramatists bring their own perceptions of feminine reality to the stage. This alternative meaning for "domesticate" pertains to plays and theaters that make female audiences and performers feel comfortable and help them "to accommodate to surroundings or to an environment" (American Heritage Dictionary, 389). Women dramatists are turning the stage and its seating into more friendly places for women by making them truthful places in which to perform or watch a performance. Slowly plays by women dramatists are occupying Latin American stages and converting the theaters' houses (the term for the seating area) into more inviting places for women, that is, into real "homes."

Latin America's inhospitality to women is recorded in its theater history. The concepts of scarcity and exception that were introduced in the studies of the first woman dramatist in the Hispanic new world, Sor Juana Inés de la Cruz (1648?–95) dominate the accounts of dramatic activity. The Seminar on Feminism and Culture in Latin America points to the portrayal of Sor Juana as "a unique phenomenon, an iconographic feminist presence, rather than one of many women involved in a long tradition of engagement of Latin American culture"

(1990, 1). Sor Juana the playwright appears in the literary accounts as a writer who left no meaningful legacy and established no theatrical canon for female playwrights. It has been widely accepted that there were/are few women dramatists in Latin America. More than three hundred years after Sor Juana, women dramatists still are burdened by a label that marks them as deviations to the rule of male supremacy in theater arts. In an interview published in 1993, Griselda Gambaro, often presented as the only important Latin American woman dramatist of the twentieth century, remembers the demeaning terms, *joven damita* (young little lady) and *la mejor dramaturga mujer*, (the best woman dramatist) applied to her by critics and reviewers that called attention to her gender and age in patronizing and negative ways (Jabif 1993, 54). Literary histories and anthologies written in the twentieth century repeat the errors of the past, according to Marcela del Río, by failing to acknowledge women dramatists or include their plays in collections, even though more women were writing and staging plays in the 1980s–1990s than ever before (1999, 45).

The recent work of researchers Kathleen O'Quinn (1994), Lorena Pino Montilla (1994), Valéria Andrade Souto-Maior (1996), Frank Dauster (1999), Marcela del Río (1999), and Halima Tahan (1998) have brought to public attention hundreds of names of women playwrights and the titles of their plays that counter the notion of scarcity and exception. For example, O'Quinn has amassed a database of 595 playwrights who wrote an average of 2.6 plays each since Sor Juana's play *Los empeños de una casa* [The house of trials] written in 1683. According to her report, of these 1,560 known plays only 30 percent or 469 were produced. Dauster and del Río have called attention to women dramatists in the early twentieth century who were acclaimed at the time of their participation in the theater but since then have been taken out of literary history. Souto-Maior's search of over sixty-six scholarly and historical sources uncovered fifty-four women playwrights active in Brazil from the seventeenth to the nineteenth centuries. The majority of those, thirty-eight, were active during the nineteenth century, having written 156, or an average of four plays per person (1996, 25–44). Montilla's research in Venezuela reflects similar figures as those in Brazil, but refers only to the nineteenth and twentieth centuries. *La dramaturgia femenina venezolana* lists seventy-one active dramatists writing a total of 321 plays, or an average of 4.5 plays per person (1994, 352–62). More recent work conducted by

Tahan collected over nine hundred plays from two hundred women dramatists and performance artists in Argentina for the years 1965–1995 alone (1998, 14). All these efforts represent significant discoveries for women's literary history, and the history of women in drama in particular.

The recent history of twentieth-century women dramatists, which can be divided into three generations, has been recorded with a little more scholarly attention and somewhat less prejudice than the centuries preceding. Nonetheless, Kati Röttger points out in her introduction to a recent colleciton of essays about Latin American women's theater, that this subject matter has not yet gained recognition as a field of study. She notes the scholarly work done on women's theater, but not Latin American women; on Latin American women writers, but not women dramatists; and on Latin American theater, but not women dramatists (1999, 10). The collection of essays that Kati Röttger and Heidrun Adler have edited, contributes to a growing number of scholarly studies published in the last decade of the twentieth century and dedicated solely to the study of Latin American female playwrights. From this growing body of work will emerge a more truthful picture of the works women have written and staged in the Spanish American and Brazilian theaters.

In contrast to earlier versions of history, current accounts highlight the traditions being established by twentieth-century women dramatists. The oldest generation of women dramatists were born in the 1920s–1930s, according to Frank Dauster, and built a legacy for those who followed with their innovations in dramatic form (1999, 39). Many of these women, whom we might call the grandmothers of twentieth-century Latin American women's drama, have received critical recognition for their efforts. Some of the names Dauster mentions are the Mexican playwrights Luisa Josefina Hernández (b. 1928), Elena Garro (1920–1998), Rosario Castellanos (1925–1974), and Maruxa Villalta (b. 1931); the Chileans, Gabriela Roepke (b. 1920), and Isidora Aguirre (b. 1919); and the Argentine, Griselda Gambaro (b. 1928) (1999, 26). In addition, Marcela del Río calls attention to an important example of group work accomplished by the "Ateneo Mexicana de Mujeres," a women's theater collective founded in 1934 (1999, 43). Mentoring from both male and female playwrights and professors, as well as participation in creative theater groups, has been crucial to the emergence of the second generation of playwrights born in the post-World War II era. These playwright-mothers, who represent the largest group of women to engage in the profession of writing theater in the history of Latin America, are the subject of this study. Although some historians might present these baby boomer-aged women dramatists as an anomaly in the otherwise meager record of theater history in Latin America, the information outlined thus far should begin to dismiss that worn-out thesis. During the preparation of this manuscript, the third generation of women dramatists have written and staged their first plays. These are the granddaughters of the pioneering dramatists born more than eighty years ago. This group of young women will help to guarantee that the legacy of their grand-mothers does not disappear as easily as it did for their foremothers during the foundational years in Latin America.[2] (See Appendix 2 for a list of dramatists born since World War II.)

Beyond the acts of erasure by literary scholars and historians, we know that women in the Western world have had to overcome their own socialization and the cutthroat culture of the theater in order to write drama. Even then, the rewards for their accomplishments have not always been forthcoming. Consider the case of the Cuban writer Gertrudiz Gómez de Avellaneda (1814–1873). According to Naomi Lindstrom, Avellaneda was denied entry into the Royal Academy of Letters in 1853 in part because she was a woman writer, but especially because she had become a playwright, in addition to her already ac-claimed talents as poet and novelist. Avellaneda drew criticism not for the content of her plays, which Lindstrom describes as not inflammatory, but because "The occupation of playwright was held to be unsuitable for a woman" (1998, 120).

Comments by Michelene Wandor on theater in Great Britain and Patricia O'Connor on conditions in Spain outline the obstacles and considerations that have an impact on women's participation in theater as playwrights. Well into the twentieth century the image of middle-class femininity in Latin America emphasized passivity, sub-mission, and social roles as dutiful daughter and patient wife (Skidmore 1999, 203–04), characteristics that certainly are in conflict with the traditional combative style of drama and the competitive environ-ment of the theater production world. As O'Connor notes, the the-ater requires aggressiveness and verbal virtuosity, skills that culture attempts to socialize out of women (1990, 376). Wandor suggests that the masculine powers in the theater police the content of plays, and that both the aesthetics and economics of theater are risky (1986, 125), additional conditions that mediate against women dramatists. Both scholars point to the high visibility of the theater, with its marquees announcing titles and names and its actors dramatizing words and deeds, as a big inhibitor to women who are trained to be modest and retiring (Wandor 1986, 126; O'Connor 1990, 376).

Two other reasons that often are offered as barriers to women's participation as writers in the theater are the fact that there are few role models or mentors for aspiring dramatists and that there is no feminine theatrical tradition, beyond that of acting, to which neo-phytes can refer (O'Connor 1990). While it is clear from Kathleen O'Quinn's research that many of the dramatists she uncovered prac-ticed their art alone and left behind little legacy, the environment for women began changing during the mid-twentieth century. In the early 1960s, educational reforms and economic growth contributed to the appearance of greater numbers of women dramatists. Over the next twenty years the numbers of women writing theater slowly increased. Using numbers from Argentina as an example, only 4.4 percent of all plays produced were written by women during the decade of the 1960s, whereas by the 1980s that number had risen to 28 percent (Alvear 1998, 33). Tahan suggests that these numbers reflect the specific con-ditions of Argentina in its postdictatorship, postcensorship years (1998, 16). Yet, many other countries without those conditions— Venezuela, Puerto Rico, and Mexico, for example— also experienced an increased feminine presence during the same time period. This boom of women dramatists also can be attributed to the proliferation of theater festi-vals throughout Latin America during the mid-1960s to 1970s (Montilla 1994, 36) and to the important role of the theater as a tool for social and political consciousness raising. Proponents of social and political reform, based on the models of the Cuban Revolution and its Marxist thinking, participated in popular theater groups where they learned egalitarian and collaborative approaches to making theater (Bonilla and Vladich, 300). In spite of these events, the total number of women involved in the theater at the end of the twentieth century is difficult to calculate. The major obstacle to recognition that still presents itself is the ephemeral nature of the theater itself. Plays must be published and distributed in order for the critical world to discover them. The results from the aforementioned project conducted by Halima Tahan and Inmaculada Alvear in Argentina reveal that 50 percent of the more than nine hundred plays written by women and collected for the years 1965–1995 were never published (Alvear 1998, 34). Thus, while the total number of women writing for theater has never been greater, the record of their contributions easily could disappear if their texts are not preserved.

Much has been made of the social and economic barriers that keep women from participating in the theater world, however, little attention has been given to the strengths of women's socialization that contribute to their potential success as dramatists. For example, women in Latin America grow up within a strong oral tradition that includes storytelling, tales of advice and warning, and gossip (Andrade and Cramsie 1991, 17–18; Castello Branco 1989, 115). These forms of language are interactive, colorful, and dynamic resources for dialogue. Women witness and participate in struggles over power and control of financial resources, the interactions of age and gender, and the education of children, events that have dramatic conflict at their core. As the scholars in the Seminar on Feminism and Culture have observed, the terms "interior" and "private" do not truly describe where women spend their time, since they frequent public places such as the marketplace and church (1990, 6), all potential contexts for dramatic action. The most prized of dramatic goals, creating emotional impact, is an area in which women especially are encouraged to develop their skills in empathy and support of others and as communicators of their own feelings. Since the late nineteenth century when the naturalist/realist movement brought the setting for dramatic action inside the home, domestic settings have been accepted as worthy places in which to stage drama. For at least two centuries then, women within their so-called private spheres have been in training to write drama based on their own feminine abilities and experiences.

The last two decades of the twentieth century witnessed an unprecedented growth in scholarly attention to women playwrights in Latin America. More women were writing and more critics, both here in the United States and there, noticed when their plays were staged. A greater number of women's plays were published in professional journals and by editorial houses which allowed scholars better access to this ephemeral art form. Although finding copies of plays and reviews of performances is not easy, the accessibility of research materials has improved as women dramatists have gained greater visibility. Some of that visibility is due to the increased number of women playwrights, especially in Argentina and Mexico that have long-standing theatrical traditions. Some of it has been generated by North American scholars whose recognition of Latin American women dramatists has created a wider audience and further study.[3] Greater visibility and availability should not be interpreted as having achieved parity with male writers, however. Tahan presents the following disclaimer to any notion of equality: from 1995–96 sixty titles about the theater were published in Buenos Aires of which twenty-eight were plays and of those only five were written by women (1998, 19).

The efforts by Latin American women dramatists to present a woman's viewpoint on the stage have been labeled a re-writing of myths, a dismantling of cultural and gender stereotypes, a subversive movement to bring the marginal, the unofficial into the sacred space of the theater in order to undermine patriarchal order. Through their plays, women dramatists are searching for authentic language, themes, costumes, and gestures that reflect how women see themselves and others rather than how others wish them to be presented. Playwrights are also finding new ways in which to portray women as subjects or protagonists in drama. In this manner, women dramatists are giving birth to themselves by staging performances in which their own images of women are replacing the images created by male desire. In addition, they are giving value to the daily personal events of women's lives by moving the private, denigrated world of the feminine into the center of the stage. Beatriz J. Rizk confirms this notion when she identifies as a *leitmotif* of women's dramaturgy the "poder estética de la cotidianeidad, lo vernacular, del mundo femenino" [aesthetic power of the quotidian, of the idiomatic, of the feminine world] (100).

Scholarship to date has viewed Latin American women's theater as concerned with identity, described by Cristina Escofet (b. 1945, Argentina) as *mujer—proyecto inacabado* (woman—unfinished project) and by Ana Istarú (b. 1960, Costa Rica) as *la búsqueda de este ser auténtico femenino* (the search for this authentic feminine being) (Andrade and Cramsie 1991, 226). The idea of searching for identity not only resonates with Latin American women playwrights, but it also represents one of the major topics in Latin American literature since the colonization. Yet, the search conducted by women dramatists differs from that of their countrymen past and present in that it involves the specificity of their sex. Critics such as Beatriz J. Rizk and Nieves Martinez de Olcoz refer to a woman's body (2000, 94; 1998,

11), María de la Luz Hurtado to the feminine point of view (1998, 38), Marcela del Río to women's experience (1999, 43), and Kati Röttger to gender (1999, 102) when they delineate how women dramatists are showcasing the search for feminine identity in a world defined by men.

There also are similarities between the dramatic art of Latin American women writers and the fiction written by women novelists. One argument presented in studies about Latin American women's prose and poetry is that women's marginal condition as social being and as creative writer caused her to pursue subversive strategies designed to resist the imposed definitions of female identity (Quinlan 1991, 22). Prose writers adopt not only a resisting narrative, but also a subversive use of language to tell their stories. Amy K. Kaminsky states that Latin American women writers reinvent or assert language in order to codify new languages and myths (1993, 23). Women novelists also share concerns with female dramatists about disrupting gender categories that legitimize the division of the world into separate spheres. According to Deborah Shaw, female novelists critique gender as an organizing principle in the division of roles and labor (1997, 171), while Jean Franco points to gender as the supporting ideology behind old and new authoritarianism in Chile ("Margins" 1997, 205).

One difference between writers of poetry or prose and playwrights is that the latter not only can construct their stories with language, but also with the subversive use of bodies and space on stage. The stage becomes a laboratory in which the single most effective mode of repression—gender—can be exposed, dismantled, and removed, according to Sue-Ellen Case (qtd. in Austin 1990, 19). The theater is a place where the topic is immediate, the characters physical, and the reality present. Lynda Hart has pointed out that "women who enter this space are taking a much greater risk than novelists or poets, but they also have the greatest potential for effecting social change" (1989, 2). The stage can provide new examples of womanhood, models that confront the narrowly defined binary images of Mary/Eve that traditionally shape women's lives in Latin America. The stage also can become an outlet for expressing publicly the sexual and emotional needs and dreams that women feel in their private lives. Kirsten Nigro defines the praxis of Latin American women dramatists as transgressive and she states: "these transgressions are both destructive, in that they break down barriers, and constructive, in the way that they refocus, redefine fundamental issues concerning women's subjectivity—how women experience themselves; concerning their representation—how others, especially men, construct them; and concerning their self-representation—how they construct themselves" (1994, 138).

Latin American women playwrights are providing needed detail about women's lives in the special attention they give to the speech, costuming, and settings of their plays. Their female characters undermine the traditional image of Hispanic women's speech as compliant and trivial. Like women novelists, women dramatists use language as both the vehicle for and the sign of their struggle. Chilean playwright Isidora Aguirre identifies the language of women dramatists as possessing *una tendencia a la denuncia* (a tendency toward denunciation) [Andrade and Cramsie 1991, 71]. In fact, women dramatists create characters that resist the rules of proper women's speech by speaking in a colloquial, sometimes aggressive and profane manner. Others employ sexually explicit language to bring taboo subjects like women's sexual drive and desire into the dialogue. Humor, irony, and parody are also tools for unmasking society's expectations for women and for poking fun at stereotypes of gendered behavior. This rich language of women characters can initiate a liberating process both for the actresses speaking and the audience watching. Female bodies that are forthright with their words, expressing the truths of their lives, show the audience how to recognize and then express its own needs. Speaking meaningful sentences that make a difference in the action of the play also suggests that women have power, that they can intervene in and change the events of their lives and those around them.

Female playwrights also have gained attention for their use of costuming and its relationship to gender. Disguises and mistaken identity are long-standing theatrical conventions that Latin American women playwrights employ to examine the construction of gender. They utilize theatrical costuming as a masquerade in order to portray gender as a sexual costume and therefore variable rather than as evidence of identity. Performances may suggest a multiplicity of personalities associated with both sexes, a conflict between the gender of a costume and the body of a performer, or the mobility and variability of a trait normally associated with only one gender.

The dramatic settings employed by women playwrights move domestic activity that is assumed to occur offstage and behind the scenes onto center stage, making it an integral part of the play and its meaning. The dramatists showcase family spaces in order to question the traditional notion of the safety and sanctity of the family and home. Rather, women's plays reveal that the home is a training ground in which the vulnerable and weak are controlled by explicit or implicit laws of the father. Patriarchy and church ideology are shown exerting stifling control over women's sexuality and identity. The home is revealed to be an extension of male power and influence where women are coerced into self-destructive roles, where mothers train their daughters in values that are noxious to both, and where unequal and authoritarian family relations reproduce the political injustices of the nation. The peace of the home is broken as it becomes the site for conflict and rebellion against traditional values and doctrines.

Most Latin American women dramatists employ a feminist critique, even if they refuse to be labeled a feminist. As Naomi Lindstrom has pointed out, the term "feminist" can have negative connotations for women writers causing them to deny it. She notes that this move reflects a desire not to be associated with an activist agenda or a doctrinaire position rather than an opposition to women's equality or an indifference about women's issues (1998, 124). Many women dramatists define their approach as the practice of social criticism aimed at bringing justice to men and women. These women would agree with Jean Franco's statement that "it is precisely Third World women who have insisted not only that there are differences *between* women, but also that there are circumstances in which women's emancipation is bound up with the fate of the larger community" (*Plotting* 1989, xi). In fact, feminists in Latin America first participated in the social justice movements of the 1920s in which they attempted to press for economic, social, and legal equality within the larger context of reform (Seminar 1990, 4). In the twenty-first century some dramatists embrace the terminology and the feminist critique because they see it as associated with the broader context of social justice and at the same time specific to women's condition.

The three themes about women's lives that appear in the chapters of this book were selected from a sampling of 120 published plays collected in the United States in libraries, journals, archives, and through professional contacts. The themes that demonstrated the highest frequency in this corpus were male-female relations, mother-daughter relations, and aging. These topics represent three significant moments or stages of female development: adolescence, the childbearing years, and the postmenopausal years. Most importantly, they have been almost invisible on Latin American stages where sociopolitical topics concerning the public world of male power predominate or where women's presence is neither questioned nor of importance. The other topics that appeared in the corpus in lesser numbers were sexuality and eroticism, father-daughter relationships, women's friendships, the work place, and growing up.

The plays about these three topics were written by more than forty dramatists born between 1940–1960, who began staging their plays in the late 1960s, and represent ten Spanish-speaking nations and Brazil.[4] While the majority of the dramatists are active in Mexico and Argentina, there were numerous examples of women's dramaturgy about women from Brazil, Costa Rica, Venezuela, Chile, Puerto Rico, Cuba, Colombia, Perú, and Bolivia. Approximately one-half of the dramatists were born between 1942–1950; the remaining were born between 1951–1960. The corpus collected for this study represents the work of urban women working in Latin America's capitals and industrial cities. These are the locations of playhouses and publishing companies that can serve as venues for the work of female dramatists. Although some countries publish plays or reviews of play performances from the hinterlands, the vast majority of dramatic work that gains international attention is generated in large commercial centers.

Many of the playwrights included in this study entered the theater as actresses and then became dramatists and/or directors. Such a professional step would have been unusual and difficult before the 1960s, but university theater groups and collective creation groups nurtured women and exposed them to a wider range of opportunities than before. University-trained women were more aware of the stereotyping in the female roles they played and turned to writing their own versions as a method for creating more appealing and realistic characters for themselves and other women to perform. In addition to writing plays for adult theater, this generation has expressed itself creatively in children's theater, prose, and poetry, and as script writers for Latin America's popular *telenovelas*, or television soap operas.

From the standpoint of dramatic technique, this corpus of plays reveals some striking similarities in the choices of length, setting, characters, and approach. This generation of Latin American women dramatists prefer short plays (more than 50 percent are one act) with a preponderance of female characters, much like their sister playwrights in Great Britain (Wandor 1986, 123–25).[5] Their settings are both contemporary and domestic, with 50 percent of the plays taking place in an apartment or home. Only a quarter of the plays are comedies while the remaining are serious dramas or tragedies. The overwhelming starting point for portraying the issues of women's lives is realism, however, many plays incorporate a range of antirealist techniques that produce a heterogeneous theatrical style.

The twenty-four plays studied in this book present a sampling of women's dramaturgy by eighteen playwrights from Spanish America and Brazil. All of the plays refer to the specificity of women's condition as part of the family network. Chapter 1, "Reclaiming the Home," studies middle-class romance and marriage with its themes of confinement and convention, sexual politics, and gendered roles. The play were written by Ana Istarú (b. 1960, Costa Rica); Inés Margarita Stranger (b. 1957, Chile); Consuelo de Castro and Leilah Assunção (b. 1946, b. 1943, Brazil); Estela Leñero and Sabina Berman (b. 1960, b. 1953, Mexico); and Thais Erminy (b. 1947, Venezuela). I argue that in these plays female characters attempt to destabilize the traditional components of romance and patriarchal matrimony and the social and religious norms that underwrite them. The plays in chapter 1 critique the subordinate and passive status of women in patriarchal marriage, the false promises of romance, the imbalance of power between the sexes, and the constructions of gender that ensure opposition and inequality. In the process of confronting male partners, the protagonists attempt to reclaim and redefine their own identity and the domestic space that imprisons them.

Chapter 2, "Questioning Motherhood," investigates the representation of mother-daughter relations in plays by Ana Istarú (b. 1960, Costa Rica); Pilar Campesino and Rebecca Bowman (b. 1945, b. 1960, Mexico); Maria Adelaide Amaral and Isis Baião (b. 1942, b. 1941, Brazil); Susana Torres Molina and Diana Raznovich (b. 1946, b. 1945, Argentina); and Thais Erminy (b. 1947, Venezuela). I argue that Latin American women dramatists challenge the cult of motherhood by emphasizing antagonism between mothers and daughters. Instead of being drawn together by their common subservient condition, these mothers and daughters are split apart. The conflicts that entangle them reveal that the patriarchal family and society use mothers to inculcate daughters into their traditional, subordinate roles. The plays in chapter 2 offer two possibilities— either that motherhood in patriarchal society ruins mother-daughter relations and limits the subjectivity of women, or that mother-daughter relations offer an opportunity to negotiate a new sense of self for both women.

Sexuality figures prominently in the chapters on relations between mothers and daughters and between men and women. However, its appearance in the last group of works on aging is unexpected. Western society views aging women as neuters whose best years are passed and whose future years are programmed with only one acceptable role as grandmothers. Yet, the plays addressed in chapter 3, "Staging Age and Sexuality," confront head-on the negative stereotypes that associate age with loss of beauty and desirability. In these eight plays, I argue that Latin American women dramatists situate their characters as seekers of new roles who recapture their pasts in order to create their futures. In the majority of the plays only aging women occupy the stage and from there they provoke the audience's voyeuristic expectations for pleasing views of youthful feminine bodies. The playwrights whose works on aging are presented in chapter 3 are Mariela Romero, Carlota Martínez and Lidia Rebrij (b. 1949, b. 1949, b. 1948, Venezuela); Leilah Assunção and Isis Baião (b. 1943, b. 1941, Brazil); Teresa Marichal (b. 1956, Puerto Rico); and Gabriela Fiore (b. 1966, Argentina). The eight plays in this chapter affirm that aging in women is an activity worthy of dramatic treatment, not as a document to the decline of human life, but rather as a homage to its vitality.

These three chapters domesticate the traditional masculinist theater in Latin America by presenting a fuller range of individual feminine personalities, activities, and actions. In many of the plays the women characters are strong individuals who refuse to play the roles that others want or need them to perform. They are not victims of society's suffocating rules because they don't passively accept their situations. Instead, they engage in conflict, in self-examination, and in change. These alternative versions of womanhood have the potential to undermine the firm foundations of the Mary/Eve dichotomy common to Latin American theater, religion, and culture. They may even free the women in the audience to live fuller lives. (See Appendix 1 for a list of all plays by chapter and their dates of performance and publication.)

The plays affirm the interdependency of the social and familial network that supports individuals and proffer different models for family interactions. Unlike the modern Western dramatic structure that tends to focus on the individual in conflict, many of these plays analyze the primacy of emotional connections between characters. Women dramatists may question the real power that women wield in their roles as the centers of family life, but they do not question the need for supportive places and persons in order to live and grow. In fact, in their treatments of the search for a true sense of identity, women dramatists portray their protagonists attempting to create a better, safer place for themselves within the family and society. These plays suggest alternatives to the domineering paternal authority practiced in the home with their models of democratic relations based on equality, negotiation, and mutuality.

Finally, these women's plays replace traditional misogynist treatments from the Western canon that are/were designed to domesticate women into their subservient places. In a classic essay on the theater Hèléne Cixous asks: "How, as women, can we go to the theatre without lending our complicity to the sadism directed against women, or being asked to assume, in the patriarchal family structure that the theatre reproduces *ad infinitum*, the position of victim?" After presenting a lengthy list of the horrible fates of women characters in traditional masculinist theater, she concludes: "That is why I stopped going to the theatre; it was like going to my own funeral, and it does not produce a living woman or (and this is no accident) her body or even her unconscious" (1984, 546). Since the translation and publication of that essay in 1984 and even before, many Latin American women playwrights have staged their versions of women's lives that counter the masculine theatrical tradition Cixous describes. In fact, these writers have begun to establish a new tradition out of which many different feminine voices can grow. The number of plays written by women about women is of consequence since for the first time more of them are being staged and published than ever before. It is a promising beginning that invites women to come to the theater to appreciate versions of feminine reality that dignify women, their struggles, and their potential to engage patriarchal society in change. As more women are called to the theater and are rewarded with plays that speak of real issues, portray real women, and address real needs, the theater will be domesticated, and will become more welcoming and inclusive of feminine experiences.

CHAPTER 1

Reclaiming the Home

"The images of married life that are formed in childhood remain unwavering even when actual experience might betray them as false."

—Regina Barreca, *Perfect Husbands & Other Fairy Tales*

In her commentary on the status of marriage in the 1990s, Regina Barreca posits that Western culture teaches women that their natural state is within marriage, that Mr. Right is anyone who will wed them, and that they should marry as soon and as well as possible (1993, 6–34). This message encourages husband hunters to contort themselves physically, emotionally, or spiritually in order to make a match (8). Yet, once safely protected within marriage, wives often discover that they are disillusioned rather than elated by their accomplishment. The romantic notions of living happily ever after are replaced by feelings of suffocation and entrapment, as newlyweds determine that they have lost control over their lives. In exchange for the safety and security of home and husband, women are offered passivity. When feelings of emptiness, longing, and loneliness bubble to the surface, women are encouraged to fill the void with children. Rather than engaging in a search within the self, wives move forward to answer the social and biological call to reproduce. Yet while child raising and domestic duties are important, they do not necessarily lead to development of the self or one's gifts (Suplicy 1985, 235). Thus, in the rush to join hearts and lives, women abandon parts of themselves that are difficult to recover and they assume disguises that betray their real needs and desires.

Staging women caught in this socially constructed trap of romance and marriage was the specialty of theater practitioners of the naturalist/realist aesthetic in the late nineteenth century. Henrik Ibsen (1828–1906), one of the best known members of this school, transformed the staging of marriage by moving dramatic action into the

17

drawing room of the bourgeois family (Scolnicov 1994, 99). In *A Doll's House* (1879) and *Hedda Gabler* (1890) the Norwegian dramatist illustrated how the bourgeois ideology of marriage, portrayed in the elegant and detailed drawing rooms, was blindly internalized by his protagonists Nora and Hedda. Behind the apparent beauty and security of married life and family, each woman discovers the suffocating rules governing wives. Ibsen's psychological analysis and realistic treatment of his protagonists' conflicts within the economic, sexual, and even emotional constraints of marriage make manifest each protagonists' resolve to escape her fate. Nora refuses to accept her inferior and dependent status, especially once she learns that her husband values money not love. Hedda cannot find any allowable form of self-expression, including motherhood, that meets her personal needs. While Nora walks out of her "doll house," leaving behind the status of marriage and access to her children, Hedda takes her own life and that of the baby she is carrying. In these two plays and others, Ibsen employed the scenery inside the house to elaborate a portrait of women as socially confined and personally stunted. Rather than fulfill its ideological purpose as a refuge, the drawing room provided yet another stage on which women were required to perform their feminine roles (94, 96).

In this chapter, I will discuss plays by Spanish American and Brazilian dramatists that examine male-female relations within romance and marriage. This is the theme that appeared in almost one third of the plays in my sample and that engaged the largest number of dramatists representing the greatest number of countries. In these dramas, the playwrights address romantic love, the gendered division of labor, relations of power and dependence, and sexuality and infidelity in marriage. I will argue that the protagonists in these plays attempt to redefine their traditional inferior status by reclaiming domestic theatrical space. In provocative words and actions, the female characters endeavor to assert themselves as individuals, achieve an equitable relationship, and question the reigning model of patriarchal marriage.

While many of the plays begin with a realistic setting reminiscent of Ibsen's time, they differ from that tradition by offering a feminine perspective that involves both theatrical and thematic variations. From a theatrical standpoint, these plays venture into comedy, parody, the symbolic, and abstract treatments of women's lives. Most of the protagonists have a greater variety of choices than the self-destructive ones exercised by Ibsen's protagonists. In order to achieve their personal goals, the protagonists in these plays destabilize the traditional components of romance and matrimony and the social and religious norms that underwrite them. That is, they build on Ibsen's concerns about patriarchy by engaging with rather than escaping from the intricate network of social and cultural practices that operate within Latin America today.

The eight plays that serve as examples for this analysis are divided into three thematic sections: romantic love, sexual politics, and gender bending. The first group of plays composed of Ana Istarú's *El vuelo de la grulla* (Costa Rica, 1984), and Inés Margarita Stranger's *Cariño malo* (Chile 1990), explores the ways in which romantic love and marriage can lead to the loss of self.[1] These two plays communicate the deception of women when they discover the unequal exchange they have made for love. The second group of plays about sexual politics treats the imbalance of power in relations between the sexes and the role of political activism in raising awareness about that inequity.[2] The settings re-create two key moments in the history of Latin America: the politically contentious period of the 1960s–1970s and the fall out from those movements twenty years later in the late 1980s and 1990s. The two plays in this second section are *À prova de fogo* (Brazil, 1977) by Consuelo de Castro and *Boca molhada de paixão calada* (Brazil, 1988) by Leilah Assunção. The last group of four plays questions traditional sex roles and gender divisions in marriage through role reversal, parody, and ambiguity.[3] In these plays, Latin American women characters demonstrate "unseemly" behavior when they transgress the rules of femininity within romantic relationships. The first two plays in which protagonists outmaneuver their partners by becoming dynamic defenders of their right to enact "masculine" privileges are *Casa llena* (Mexico, 1986) by Estela Leñero and *Whiskey & Cocaína* (Venezuela, 1984) by Thais Erminy. The final two plays of the chapter, *Roda cor de roda* (Brazil, 1977) by Leilah Assunção and *Uno/El bigote* (Mexico, 1985) by Sabina Berman, venture even further into unstable gender terrain by presenting characters who appear to fuse, exchange, and/or parody each other's sex roles, but from within the confines of the traditional romantic triangle.

In order to analyze these eight plays on romance and marriage, I will employ both social science research on women and family in Latin America and a critical framework on the gendered meaning of theatrical space. Social science research provides insights into the division of power and responsibilities in the family, the separation of worlds into the masculine public and the feminine private, and the social and religious norms that cooperate to enforce gender difference. In addition, an understanding of the relationship between the space portrayed on stage (mimetic) and that referred to beyond the stage (diegetic) is particularly useful for treating relations between the sexes, since society and the theater alike associate each gender with a separate domain.

All but two of the eight plays focus on a couple or couples, while the remaining two place a group of students and a trio of women on center stage. Unlike Ibsen's homemaker protagonists, here the majority of the main characters are educated, professional women who participate in the work-world outside the home. Most of these characters, who could be alter egos of the dramatists, are strong, independent women rather than passive, long-suffering and dependent wives commonly held as the stereotypical image of married women in Latin America. Moreover, these protagonists, who aren't afraid to challenge the rules of traditional male-female relations, are seen as threatening equals to the men in their lives. In their conflicts they attempt to rewrite the rules that have governed male-female relations and thus to make their homes more nurturing for themselves.

A quick review of the keyword *matrimonio* (marriage) in Spanish language reference sources *Libros en venta* and the *Hispanic American Periodicals Index (HAPI)* confirms the popularity of this topic in scholarly and journalistic writing in Latin America. *Libros en venta* reported over seven hundred citations of books with sociological, economic, and religious themes. *HAPI* listed ninety-five records of articles with similar approaches to the topic. Both databases registered the ubiquitous presence of the Roman Catholic Church whose numerous publications serve to advise and prescribe about matrimony and family life.

The church began its role as moral educator in the earliest days of the colonization, and it continues to exercise this function more than five hundred years later. Patriarchal marriage came to the New World with the Spanish and Portuguese religious and civil authorities who imposed it as a method for policing the sexual relations of a heterogeneous racial population. Elizabeth Dore defines this marriage relationship as, "the particular family/household type in which the senior male controls and protects everyone in the household—male and female" (1997, 105). Virginia Wright Wexman adds to the definition that patriarchal marriage rests on the idea of separate spheres for each of the sexes (1993, 13). Marriage was a colonizing vehicle for imposing European concepts of lineage, social class, and social order and for establishing the family as an important unit for transmitting customs, norms, and traditions (Lavrin 1989, 13–24). Laws governing marriage made women and children property of husbands. In addition, legal inferiority for wives was butressed by a network of moral injuctions that divided and separated human behavior by gender. Men were placed in a priviledged position and women were further regulated by equating their viriginity or chastity with their moral virtue, a concept expressed with the terms "honor" and "honesty." Catholic religious doctrine has justified the supression of women since the sixteenth century with its three precepts of "matrimonial morality"— monogamy, exogamy, and the repression of pleasure (Cicerchia 1997, 123). These European rules for marriage and for the moral behavior of each sex were never equally enforced, however, leading to the development of the double standard, as Pilar Gonzalbo Aizpuru and Cecilia Rabell have observed (1994, 13).

The current popular image of marriage in Latin America was shaped by romanticism, civil legislation, and secularization during the nineteenth century. European romanticism with its emphasis on individualism and its idealization of romance as a key to domestic harmony, changed the nature of relations between the sexes. Romanticism influenced marriage in North America by turning it into an environment for personal fulfillment, rather than an extension of family needs or religious dictates (Wexman 1993, 12). Similar changes occurred in Latin America when, for example, the Portuguese court arrived in Rio de Janeiro in the early 1800s bringing along new values, such as romantic love as the means to and reason for marrying (Núcleo de Estudos Sobre a Mulher 1984, 32). Romanticism also helped advance the myth of complementary relations: that each partner was incomplete before finding the other and that the two together made one whole being (Vaitsman 1994, 160). Romantic love also obscured the fact that women had few alternatives but to marry if they were not self-supporting (Barreca 1993, 231). In its promise of fulfilling individual emotional aspirations, romantic love seemed to provide the answers to many problems—loneliness, poverty, fear, and the need for sexual expression (Núcleo de Estudos Sobre a Mulher, 35).

Laws governing the family were altered during the nineteenth century to grant individual freedom from parental authority to grown children, although wives remained subordinated to their spouses and daughters transferred guardianship from father to husband when they married (Dore 1997, 108). The church lost most of its legal control over the family to the state as civil society established its own rules during the years of independence, according to Ricardo Cicerchia (1997, 122). During this slowly evolving but consolidating practice of married life, the division of the world into private feminine spaces and public masculine spaces was reinforced by the transition from rural to urban life. Farm life had required involvement of family members in the production and consumption of essential goods. However, the move into the city where industrial jobs prevailed eventually took women and children out of the labor force. Children went to school and women went home to the isolation of the domestic terrain where their labor was seen as an individualized expression of affection and nurture rather than as an economic contribution to society (Bonaparte 1997, 55; Durham 1991, 58).

The first half of the twentieth century saw suffragette movements in the United States and Great Britain marking the beginning of the great struggle for civil rights. However, only in the last half of the twentieth century did the model of patriarchal marriage, that had survived with some modifications since colonization, begin to be seriously questioned in Latin America. It was socioeconomic, political, and educational changes instigated by governments, international organizations, and women themselves that initiated this process. The Cuban Revolution (1958), the declaration of the International Decade of the Woman (1975–1985), and the Sandinistas in Nicaragua (1980s) contributed to a re-evaluation of the status of women in marriage and in the work force. Fidel Castro began a movement for greater human rights for women by introducing a restructuring of society that valued women and their work outside the home and supported them with social services, reforms, and efforts to create equality in their home lives. The United Nations drew attention to and thus legitimized the idea of equality between men and women with its initiative "Equality, Development and Peace" (Schutte 1993, 211, 223–24). The Sandinistas adopted a liberating stance toward women in their revolutionary theory and practice in which women were active inside and outside the party (Bose and Acosta-Belén 1995, 7).

In addition, conditions in Latin America following World War II encouraged economic expansion and the establishment of postsecondary institutions forever changing the landscape of opportunities for women. In Brazil, for example, educational reforms set up separate but equal facilities for men and women in 1943 and then later, in 1961, gave women the same access to a college education as men. According to June E. Hahner, from the early 1960s to the early 1970s, the number of women attending universities in Brazil increased tenfold, while the number of male university students only quadrupled, so that by 1980 women came to comprise close to half the nation's university students (1990, 187). The university experience not only encouraged women to pursue career opportunities beyond the most common training as a primary school teacher, but it also provided them with the critical framework to question the reigning political, social, religious, and sexual values. Marxism provided the liberating model and ideal for many young people while the theater became an important place for discussing the values of autonomy and equality that Marxism espoused (Vaitsman 1994, 108–10).

By the 1980s, dictatorships in the Southern Cone countries and widespread economic hardship throughout Latin America provoked the most recent challenge to the hierarchical and authoritarian practices of patriarchal marriage. In Brazil, Chile, and Argentina the repressive military regimes established during the mid-1960s and 1970s induced a range of collective responses that called women from different social classes away from their homes to defend democratic principles as well as "women's" issues. When the economic downturn threw many industrial laborers out of work, their wives responded by forming collective kitchens, clubs, and other self-help groups to support their families and others in lower-class communities (Jelin, "Citizenship" 1990, 188). Given the time spent away, some women encountered problems at home that led them to question the traditional division of labor and relations of power (Acurio 1994, 90–97). All these forms of public activism, often independent of political parties or union movements, opened up new spaces for women's self-development by making them "actors" in their own and society's transformation (Jelin, "Citizenship," 189–94; Soares 1998, 35). Lourdes Arizpe describes their efforts this way: "What do so many types of women have in common? They are all involved in actions which through protesting, defending and demanding, make them the active subjects of social change" (1990, xvi).

Democracia en el país y en la casa (democracy in the nation and in the home), a Chilean feminist slogan from the years of the Pinochet dictatorship (Trevizan 1997, 49), expresses the realization that freedom for women is a dual goal that must take place in- and outside the home in order to bring real equality. Arizpe reports that in this call to action there is an implied struggle against all forms of domination, and she compares women's double workday (economic and domestic) to their double militancy (in politics and in marriage): "In one the woman struggles as worker and mother at the same time; in the other as citizen and wife" (xix). This call for equality means that feminists and activists want to remake marriage into a new, more democratic union. Ofelia Schutte has noted the family-oriented aspect of Latin American feminism stating that "the major characteristic in the region is that women hold on to their identity as mothers/family members at the same time that they participate outside the home" (1993, 234). After decades of dictatorship in the Southern Cone and Central America, the idea of democracy in marriage carries significance in Latin America where the efforts to establish a democratic political system are as nascent as those to bring about equality in matrimony. Unlike the traditional divisions between private and public worlds, the goals of democracy and equality unite the personal with the political.

However, while women's opportunities for change have increased steadily since the 1980s, the social imaginary for men, and especially for husbands, remains fairly stable. Regina Barreca declares that little has altered the notion in the United States which maintains the "invisible and static image of the husband as provider, protector and patriarch" (1993, 113). Later she expands this cultural context when she remarks that "Many studies suggest that the primary role of the husband as provider of food and shelter is strikingly cross-cultural and surprisingly unchanging, given the rapidly evolving role of the wife. Husbands are seen as instrumental to survival instead of simply important in our intimate lives" (227). Many men and women still uphold this image of the primacy of husbands in socioeconomic terms. The Argentine sociologist Héctor Bonaparte suggests at least three factors that contribute to the durability of the role "male head of household." First, he notes that many women defend the status quo because they are benefiting from it: "*lo pasan bien* porque los ingresos familiares les permiten toda clase de servicio doméstico, comodidades, y un standard de vida con aspectos gratificantes" [*they live well* because the family income provides for domestic service, comforts, and a standard of living with gratifying aspects] (1997, 204). He proposes that men resist changes to patriarchal marriage because of what they would have to give up: "desde el ser y la identidad viril, hasta a los privilegios, ventajas, protecciones, indulgencias, justificaciones y ritos susten-tadoras" [not only their identity as males, but also the privileges, advantages, protections, indulgences, justifications and sustaining rites] (1997, 203). Lastly, he argues that the work-world contributes to the status quo by reinforcing the dominator role. Thus, men become blind to their own subordination as workers because they are busy with and satisfied by their role as dominator of all the women around them in their work and family life (120).

Regina Barreca and Héctor Bonaparte suggest that patriarchy and patriarchal marriage are so firmly implanted in the social imaginary and so crucial to the capitalist economic system that changes take place only at the individual level, while the traditional structures remain in place. According to Bonaparte, capitalism, racism, and patriarchy are so closely intertwined that they cannot be separated or changed individually (1997, 186–91). Some women have made considerable advances in the work-world, but without altering significantly either that world or the one at home, as Pat M. Keith and Robert B. Schafer point out (1991, 51). While the ideals of democracy and equality in the home represent lofty goals, they are enmeshed in an intricate and complex web of familial and political relations. Elizabeth Jelin explains that this tight association between networks of personal and political relations makes it a formidable task to reform or democratize the sociopolitical environment since it cannot be easily disconnected from family ties. She also indicates the reverse is true, that family ties tend to subordinate individual interests in order to maintain political advantages ("Introduction," *Women and Social Change* 1990, 2). To summarize, the forces at work to reform the traditional ending of the romance/marriage scenario must engage with powerful institutions in commerce, politics, the church, and with social conventions that have changed little since colonization.

Among the historians and social scientists consulted for this book, several describe marriage in colonial households and in modern day Latin America using dramatic terms. For example, Asunción Lavrin "sets the stage" for her readers in the introduction to a collection of essays on sexuality and marriage in colonial Hispanic America with the title, "El escenario, los actores y el problema" [The setting, the actors and the problem] (1989, 13). Pilar Gonzalbo Aizpuru and Cecilia Rabell open their edited collection on the family in Ibero-America with "Diálogo abierto sobre la familia iberoamericana" [Open dialogue about the Iberoamerican family] (1994, 9) calling attention to their efforts to make public and reciprocal a topic that long has been considered private and monologic.[4] Lourdes Arizpe's foreword to a collection of essays on women and social change, "Twentieth-century Women: Characters in Search of an Author" (1990, xiv), utilizes the title of Pirandello's most famous play to compare the unfinished status of being female but without models, to that of the play's characters who are unable to finish their play performance and their lives without a dramatist to complete the script.

Why is it so tempting to turn to theatrical analogies when discussing romance and marriage? Marriage represents the most important human relationship between the sexes, because it is charged with the burdensome responsibility of reproducing, socializing, and educating the species while at the same time juggling individual autonomy, sexual desire, and solidarity. As a romantic ideal, marriage exemplifies the best virtues of human behavior—devotion, generosity, kindness, and altruism. At the same time the weight of social norms, gender role expectations, and economic demands can transform affection and dedication into anger, distrust, and guilt. Western culture expects romantic love to fulfill two contradictory and conflictive purposes, as Wexman points out, since it is both a "short, compelling and consuming passion" and the "cornerstone for lifelong monogamous marriage" (1993, 8). Given these obligations, expectations, and complications, it is easy to see that modern marriage contains the key elements for good drama —action, a drive for autonomy, conflict, and resolution.

Romance and marriage generate opportunities for internal conflict not only because they are the site of many varied activities, but also because they are highly controlled by moral imperatives and social norms while at the same time being especially vulnerable to outside forces. Inside the home family life is dynamic, involving relations between generations and sexes that are held together by emotional bonds, economic dependence, and obligation. At the same time forces outside the home such as changing economic conditions, social norms, and politics can put pressures on the family as individuals and as a unit. As the epigraph of this chapter suggests, the ideal of married life is a solid, unchanging picture in the mind, but in reality it can be vulnerable and fragmenting in response to both internal and external demands (Jelin, "Everyday Practices," 33). In Latin America, family life defines itself as a refuge from the chaotic and dangerous influences outside the home, a concept that is demonstrated by the affluent in gated communities, high walls, security gates, and watchmen, and in social rules governing who may enter.[5]

Romance and marriage are dramatic and theatrical in Latin America because of the cultural importance of couples and families. Having a steady relationship is an important part of growing up and modeling adult behavior for young people. Strong emotions of possessiveness and jealousy drive relations between the sexes and ensure that social life remains divided and regulated, although not equally, as we have seen.[6] As Ibsen demonstrated, marriage can be suffocating since individuals must attempt to hold on to a sense of self within a human and physical environment that perpetuates narrowly defined gender expectations. Within the confining space of the home, tension between individuals can quickly provoke physical action and emotional display. Whereas romantic films made in the United States during the golden years of Hollywood featured the couple finding a happy ending to their travails (Wexman 1993, 3–8), the Western theatrical tradition of staging romance and marriage tends toward the unhappy and tragic. Since Shakespeare's *Romeo and Juliet*, dramas about love and marriage have served to highlight conflict between individuals, families, and societies. Consuelo Morel Montes has observed "el teatro muestra muy pocos amores logrados" [theater shows very few successful loves] (1996, 236). Because their representation of love and marriage usually serves to critique rather than reaffirm social values, few plays find a happy resolution, if a resolution is suggested at all.

Feminine socialization has employed romantic love as the only means girls can use to gain a sense of self, albeit through the love of someone else. Thus, love and marriage are made to appear desirable and appealing to girls. Héctor Bonaparte cites the common wisdom that teaches the importance of love to girls—"lo más que puede esperar una niña es ser amada por un hombre" [the most that a young woman can hope for is to be loved by a man] (1997, 135). Love functions as a validation for women of their desirability and femininity (Barreca 1993, 106), creating a sense of need for women to seek it out in order to reaffirm their identity and value. Romance penetrates the feminine psyche more easily since looking to others is reinforced as a trait of importance to girls in all aspects of their lives. But as Regina Barreca notes, this kind of romance takes it toll: "Romance is like nuclear waste—it creeps into other aspects of our lives even when we think it is contained. In romance women give up independence and a sense of self slowly not realizing what it will mean in the long run" (128). Romantic love transforms girls into servants once they take their vows of marriage as Bonaparte confirms in this commonly heard saying *Esposa—mujer a su servicio* (Wife—a woman at your service) (43). Confined to their homes, married women accept the domestic domain as their place to exercise some small measure of control. But given the material and cultural power of men, women's resources are limited to affective ties while men impose their dominance through government, civil laws, and religious authority (Barreca, 108).

When women dramatists stage plays that make public the private world of the home, they question romance and its power to control women and convert them into submissive servants. In their versions of women in marriage, they emphasize the possibility of new emotions and new selves based on more egalitarian values. The home dramatized on stage, which has often been described as a womb or a haven, becomes what Liliana Trevizan calls in her description of women's fiction of the 1980s *espacios desafiantes* (defiant spaces) (1997, xii), that is, places where women directly challenge the status quo and attempt to enact democratic versions of male-female relations. As women longing to be free of emotional and physical servitude in the home, these characters are searching for new versions of being female that contradict the traditional passive and subservient image of Latin American women. In their journeys, the protagonists must confront the fact that masculine power controls domestic space, divides its inhabitants according to sex roles, and organizes their opportunities accordingly. The challenge becomes, then, how to reclaim and remake space so that it serves purposes of nurture and growth rather than confinement and repression.

In order to examine these plays about marriage and the home, I will employ a framework about the meaning of space in the theater. Michael Issacharoff calls attention to the nuances in dramatic space by comparing narrative space with its one-dimensional imagined world to dramatic space with its multidimensional world that is represented on stage and imagined to exist beyond it (1981, 211). The dynamics of the theater often rest on the conflict between these two domains (215). Hanna Scolnicov employs this multidimensional relationship of dramatic space in *Women's Theatrical Space*, her feminist study of plays from the Greek, Roman, and European masculinist theatrical canons. She claims that both in society and on the stage women have been identified with the house which in turn defines their social rank, body, and sexuality (1994, 7). Scolnicov argues that in the development of Western theater the male viewpoint is directed toward entering female space, whereas the female point of view, in modern times, is how to escape the space of the home (8). Thus, Ibsen's Nora, of *A Doll's House*, rebels against her domestic prison by walking out the door in the climactic closing scene. Scolnicov shows that in contemporary theater the equation of woman with home comes to an end and she declares that "Space is no longer a woman" (154). However, in her final chapter, the critic notes that today's feminist playwrights have not transcended that space, but rather are employing it critically since it still contains many unresolved questions about feminine identity (155). In these observations, Scolnicov refers to well-known British playwrights Maureen Duffy and Caryl Churchill, but she could be speaking about Latin American women dramatists as well. In the realist tradition of using the home as a battleground and the marriage partners as warring parties (Scolnicov 1994, 133), all of the plays studied here involve a space marked as feminine. But unlike Ibsen's Nora, who wants to regain her sense of self by leaving the home, what Scolnicov calls "her sacred duty to herself" (98), these Latin American women characters are fighting to reclaim their bodies and their identities by taking back the home on their own terms.

In all of the plays analyzed in the three sections of this chapter, home is the site where the values of autonomy and equality intersect with the values of sexual difference and division. In the sections on romantic love and sexual politics, homes ruled by patriarchal values suffocate and circumscribe the dreams and identity of female protagonists who challenge those traditions and norms. The four plays discussed mark the beginning and the end of a forty-year period of tremendous political and social upheaval that initiated a restructuring of relations between the sexes in Latin America. In the last section with its four plays on gender bending, the home continues to operate as the organizing space for relations between men and women. However, it is a home where sex roles and gender are either redefined by reversing their traditional characteristics, or by making them mobile and variable.

Romantic Love and the Loss of Self

El vuelo de la grulla and *Cariño malo* are one-act plays and first works by their authors that demonstrate the conflict between women's idealized notions of romantic love and their encounters with real-life men. Of the two plays, *El vuelo de la grulla* [The flight of the crane] by Ana Istarú has received less scholarly attention. It was first performed in 1984, the same year it was published in the Costa Rican theater magazine *Escena* as an example of the dramaturgy of the author, then a recipient of a national scholarship. The definitive version was performed by the Compañía Nacional de Teatro in 1994 under the direction of Remberto Chávez (Rojas and Ovares 2000, 315).[7] *Cariño malo* [Bad love] has attracted considerable attention for its experimental form and unusual theme. It was first performed in 1990 at the Teatro de la Universidad Católica de Chile after two years of rehearsals by the dramatist, Inés Margarita Stranger, the director, Claudia Echenique, and a group of actresses.[8] The play appeared in the *Revista Apuntes* published by the Universidad Católica de Chile in 1990 as well.

Both plays employ poetic language to communicate the loss of the feminine self in romantic love, as María de la Luz Hurtado has proposed for *Cariño malo* (1998, 37). Together these pieces demonstrate that romantic love should not constitute the only life project for women, because it often prevents the formation of a complete person, which is a more worthy life goal. In her comments on *Cariño malo*, Morel Montes states: "ser mujer no necesariamente pasa por el proyecto amoroso sino que es un trayecto que vale la pena recorrer" [being a woman does not necessarily require passing through love, it is a trajectory that is worth following in itself] (1996, 219). Both plays aim to influence and educate the audience, as the director of *Cariño malo* stresses in an interview when she states that her objective was: ". . . comunicarme, lograr una difusión masiva y modificar estructuras sociales y familiares" [. . . communicate my message, reach a large audience and change social and familial structures] (Rojo 1991, 257).

El vuelo de la grulla is a metaphoric title that refers to the efforts a young married woman makes to work outside the home at something more fulfilling than keeping house. In his introduction to the translated version of the play, Timothy J. Rogers summarizes the situation as: "Her immediate world is founded in a patriarchal value system that stifles any questioning of self-fulfillment on her part . . . but now she is determined to transform her dreams into reality, to become free from her unrewarding status and to escape like the symbolic unfettered crane of the title" (1989, 7). When she expresses these needs to her husband he opposes any change in the distribution of responsibilities. Worse yet, he and his mother intimidate her and force her to abandon her dream and comply with their version of wifely duties.

Cariño malo's abstract and minimalist setting portrays three women who represent the division of self caused by an unhappy love affair. During the course of the play, the women undertake a journey of healing that involves enacting rituals of male-female relations until the three become one again and that one woman prepares to relive her childhood. In her analysis of the play, Morel Montes describes it in these terms: "La obra investiga en zonas de la mente femenina que nunca en nuestra dramaturgia habían sido tratadas como tales y que son importantes de reconocer" [The play investigates areas of the feminine mind that have never been treated before and that are important to acknowledge] (1996, 224).

I will argue that in both plays the protagonists act to affirm themselves, in symbolic and real ways, and to gain agency over a love that has caused them a loss of reason and a surrender of self. María Luisa of *El vuelo de la grulla* attempts to assert herself in a series of escalating actions that begin when she goes on strike and refuses to do housework, then argues with her husband and threatens to move out, and finally tries to force her mother-in-law to leave. When her actions provoke her husband's violence and recriminations instead of understanding and support, she feels abandoned and defeated. She grieves the loss of her dreams and herself in exchange for a love that offers her little self-expression. Her attempts at affirmation and agency are foiled by those who claim to want the best for her.

Cariño malo portrays the loss of dreams to love as well, but also the need to recapture and rebuild a new female identity. There are no real masculine bodies on the stage, but the power of men to control women in love is always present in the words of the protagonists and in the skits they perform. Whereas Istarú's play starts with the optimism of its protagonist who believes in love, in her husband, and in the possibilities for change, Inés Margarita Stranger's play starts at the opposite point, with a loss of love and the pain of disbelief. But while the Costa Rican playwright plots a course of failure for her protagonist, the Chilean offers a more promising ending.

Both plays question the importance and power of romantic love for/over women. Traditional socialization teaches women to place romantic love at the center of their lives and to commit their resources and energies to pursuing men to love and marry. Sara Rojo calls love "la meta creada para todas las mujeres" [the goal created for all women] (1991, 127). If this is true, then when love goes bad, women lose their center, their purpose and their goal, that is, they lose their sense of identity. Consuelo Morel Montes explains that "Siempre se supone que el odio destruye y eso lleva al dolor y la reparación, pero cuando lo que destruye es el amor se queda en una situación sin salida" [We have always assumed that what destroys is hate and this leads to pain and atonement, but when it is love that destroys, one is stuck in a situation with no exit] (1996, 222).

The title *Cariño malo* refers to a negative force that "somete, anula y culpabiliza e impide que las mujeres se constituyan en seres integrales" [submits, voids and blames, and keeps women from becoming complete beings] in Rojo's words (1991, 128). If love can be bad, as the title of the play implies, then there can also be such a thing as good love, one that does not handicap or stunt women. *El vuelo de la grulla* appears to present an example of "good love" in its domestic setting with a young couple, happily married in their own home. Yet this love is destructive for María Luisa who has suffered an identity crisis, because she is no longer comfortable with her routine as a housewife. Unfortunately she learns that change in one partner does not guarantee adaptation by the other. María Luisa discovers that she participates in a traditional patriarchal marriage that is not an equitable relationship, but rather one that accords separate but "complementary" spaces and jobs to each and subordinates women to men. Sociologists Pat M. Keith and Robert B. Schafer comment on situations like María Luisa's in which one person is under benefited and they note that this situation may be disappointing, distressing, and may make the individual feel victimized (1991, 158). Certainly this description applies to Istarú's protagonist.

In *El vuelo de la grulla*, Esteban and María Luisa come into conflict over the meaning of "love" in their marriage. For Esteban the love he gives is defined in terms of fulfilling his duties and anything outside of this definition cannot be love. He tells María Luisa that his love is *recto* (correct), because he works to maintain the house and he is faithful to her. He sees their relationship as an exchange and he reasons that because he performs his role she should fulfill hers. For him, any change in her indicates a loss of love for him and a lack of loyalty, since patriarchal marriage requires wives to give unquestioned support to their husbands. As Esteban remarks:

> "—¡Una esposa sigue a su marido, porque así debe ser, y no hay una ley humana que lo cambie!" [A wife follows her husband, because that is the way it is, and there is no human law that will change that] (17).

From his perspective the "natural" arrangement that he accepts cannot be questioned, but if it is, then the questioner not the relationship itself becomes the problem. The system is in balance according to Esteban and he blames María Luisa for upsetting it by not wanting to have children, and by wanting to change the work load inside and outside the home.

María Luisa harbors a different definition of love that has evolved since she first married Esteban while still in high school. According to her when she was young,

> "no tenía juicio" [she had no judgment] (17),

however now she has outgrown her younger ideas and expects her love and her marriage to do the same. She reasons that love makes them equals in everything, which means in work both in- and outside the house. María Luisa:

> "—¿No serías capaz de barrer el piso solo por el inmenso amor que me tenés?" [Wouldn't you be able to sweep the floor just because you love me so much?] and "¡No quiero sirvientes, quiero compartirlo todo! ¡Las responsabilidades, los problemas, las ollas sucias!" [I don't want servants, I want to share everything! The responsibilities, the problems, the dirty dishes] (17).

What is clear throughout the lengthy argument between the couple is that María Luisa has many illusions about what their love and marriage could mean that go beyond its current definition. Because she can imagine another kind of love, she sees her present situation as a slave; she feels resentful and suffocated at home. From her perspective she is asking for so little, just a chance to try something to use her potential. Esteban has only one answer to her reasoning:

"Tengo una casa y allí quiero a mi mujer" [I have a house and I want my wife in it] (17).

He is determined to resist her while at the same time she has made up her mind to find a convincing argument to change him.[9]

El vuelo de la grulla is a tragedy in which María Luisa creates a standoff with her husband until, in complete frustration, he loses control of himself, threatens her, and then hits her. However, the factor that changes the equation in his favor is not, surprisingly, his abuse of his wife, but rather the arrival of his mother for Sunday lunch. She immediately agrees with her son regarding María Luisa's malaise and seizes the opportunity to offer her services to prepare lunch and even to move in with them. Doña Berta is an invader who quickly takes possession of the kitchen and begins throwing away María Luisa's treasures. Worse yet, María Luisa discovers in a phone call in the closing moments of the play that her own mother reaffirms the position taken by her husband and her mother-in-law. Thus, the play concludes with a defeated protagonist who has no power to win against such overwhelming obstacles that destroy her will.

The setting reinforces the divisions that María Luisa wants to renegotiate and Estaban wants to maintain. The opening scene with its realistic, domestic surroundings of a kitchen and dining room, is so familiar and mundane that it is difficult at first to see its divisions and inequalities. For the audience and for Esteban the opening scene represents the normal image of married life. The play begins with each person working, even though it is Sunday. She cleans the floor while he sits at the dining room table doing calculations related to his sales job. Her simple clothing, apron, standing position, and broom reinforce her image as the person who performs the physical labor of keeping up the house. His conservative dress and his location at the table mark him as the worker outside the house. He is not participating in the cleaning of the home, rather his location at the table reinforces his role as the patriarch whose status and gender identify him as worthy of being served. This division in dress, in location, and in task not only associates the couple with two separate jobs and two different places in the house, but also with the ideology of complementary marriage. Such an arrangement accords tasks for each that are separate and different from the other and at the same time necessary for the marriage to maintain its balance. Both husband and wife complain about the difficulty of their jobs: hers is boring and physically exhausting, while his is demanding and demeaning. Yet he accepts the divisions and exercises the benefits that his traditional superior role accords him while María Luisa questions both the divisions and the limitations. Esteban is a prime example of Héctor Bonaparte's contention that "varones sometidos en el terreno económico y político, pueden actuar como 'patrones' y 'jefes' en la casa" [men oppressed in the world of economics and politics can act as bosses in the home] (1997, 182).

All the action of the play takes place within the mimetic space of the home. Access to that home is controlled by Esteban, who serves as its jailer. His mother comes in, she and her son go out, but María Luisa cannot leave. She is isolated by her responsibilities and place within the home as wife and isolated from the world outside the home by the same condition. María Luisa longs to leave the labor of the home in order to develop herself in the work-world, but Esteban expects to come home to a refuge from those work demands. In this refuge, María Luisa is reduced to the condition of slave, a point she makes in her argument with Esteban. Her real strengths as a person are intellectual and creative, but neither of these are fulfilled within the confines of the home she occupies on stage.

To escape her boredom, María Luisa builds an imaginary world of fantasy and dreams of doing something productive in the work-world. During the play, Istarú's protagonist attempts to bring her imagined world of fantasy and work into the space of her home. She employs poetic language to describe the world of her alter ego Leandra whose story she enacts at the beginning and end of the play. Leandra, who rescues her lovers, leads a flock of birds, and has adventures, portrays characteristics of strength, leadership, and heroism. María Luisa dramatizes Leandra's actions with the hope of winning her husband's sympathy when she asks him for permission to work (16). However, Esteban is more amused and aroused than convinced that her performance in some way speaks about his wife's aspirations. María Luisa also imagines possible jobs for herself, especially after hearing a radio program about a former classmate who has just defended a thesis in anthropology. She compares herself to that classmate and she dreams of opportunities beyond the home. However, a house defined by Esteban as a refuge from work, an unchanging and stable abode, cannot nurture María Luisa's dreams, because they would alter the balance inside the home. Her imagined opportunities that may or may not exist somewhere beyond the home in a space she can only imagine, are a fantasy that she has created to cultivate her needs. But they are in conflict with her husband's definition of himself and of their shared space.

The tension between an unseen force in diegetic space and a visible force on stage is a common theatrical model, according to Michael Issacharoff (1981, 210). In *El vuelo de la grulla* both Esteban and his mother argue that the outside world is an unfriendly, corrupt place, where María Luisa is not qualified to work, and that her place is in the safety of the home. As such María Luisa's imagined world beyond the home in diegetic space is no more than a fantasy, easily discounted by others and unsubstantiated by experience or example. As a fragile alternative reality it cannot constitute a threat against the strong forces within the home. The change purse, which she grabs as she tries to walk out the door, represents her inadequate preparation to be a real threat. Its few coins cannot buy her food or shelter, a point her husband relishes in making, just like her dreams and fantasies cannot come true if they exist only in an imaginary world.

The fragility of María Luisa's dreams, and of her self, reappear in the final scene of the play as she gives a second performance of the adventures of Leandra after her husband and mother-in-law have left to collect Doña Berta's belongings. Alone in the home María Luisa expresses her feelings of hopelessness and despair. This moment projects a more familiar image of woman as the Pietá, but the being she cradles and describes is not a child but her broom that she addresses as if it were her alter ego Leandra. Her imagery of clipped wings refers to the taming of birds and is an apt comparison for her own sense of being confined.

The final erasure of María Luisa and any illusions of another life outside the home will occur after the play ends when Doña Berta and Esteban return with the mother-in-law's belongings. María Luisa cannot expand her existence beyond the home and at the same time she cannot even be the woman of the house anymore since her mother-in-law will also occupy that role. What's more, husband and mother-in-law are pressuring her to have children as an alternative to finding work, in order to fulfill her sense of longing, and to satisfy them as well. Thus, the audience is left with the feeling that even more bodies soon will crowd into María Luisa's already shrinking space.

In the conflict over reclaiming home and self, María Luisa is the loser since she cannot escape the home. At the same time, her husband's physical threats and her mother-in-law's pending occupation mean that she is now confined to a place that has become even more foreign and hostile. Her disappointments multiply because not only does she not gain access to the work-world, but also she has learned that her husband cannot attend to her needs. He is trapped within his own preconceived notions of love and marriage. She reads correctly his attachment to his mother as greater than that to her, especially if she won't act like a married woman, but she incorrectly assumes that her wishes might be important to him. He shows her that her wishes will only be important to him if they are the same as his own. María Luisa's idea of love and marriage as growing, flexible, and based on mutual affection is defeated by Esteban's model of complementarity that depends on maintaining a balance between two separate worlds. The arrival of Doña Berta guarantees that the old ways will survive, since she will provide domestic help to María Luisa and aid her in fulfilling her expected duties as wife and mother. The change desired by María Luisa, to leave the home in order to find herself, provokes an overwhelming response to keep her there. Worse yet, María Luisa's attempt to request more for herself, more from love, and more from her marriage has produced a response that will leave her with even less than when she began.

The three protagonists of Stranger's *Cariño malo*—Victoria, Amapola, Eva—engage in a more successful bid to reclaim the self by uniting their fragmented voices into one woman at the play's end. These three characters portray a history of women's experiences in love beginning with the biblical story of Eve. But unlike María Luisa's direct and open challenge of her subordinate status in the home, these three make use of metaphorical language and a series of allegorical skits in order to question existing paradigms of love.

Critics have identified each of the three voices as dominated by a single characteristic or personality trait that comes into conflict with the others and debates the importance of love in their lives. For example, Sara Rojo describes the three this way: "Amapola reflejaba las culpas, la búsqueda de un amor idealizado; Victoria era la lucha por la identificación; Eva, la necesidad de reír que se pierde con la infancia" [Amapola reflected guilt, the search for an idealized love; Victoria was the fight for identification; Eva, the need to laugh that is lost with childhood] (1991, 127). Consuelo Morel Montes agrees with Rojo's view of Amapola stating: "Amapola cree que el amor es el único proyecto de vida y continúa añorando a su compañero" [Amapola believes that love is the only project for life and continues to yearn for her lover], but she adds these characteristics to the others: "Victoria aparece como la más decidida y amarga; Eva encarna el arquetipo de lo femenino con sus contradicciones vitales" [Victoria appears as the most determined and bitter; Eva incarnates the archetypal feminine with all her contradictions] (217). Hurtado suggests the most succinct portrait of the three "la pasión, el romanticismo y el intelecto o razón" [passion, romanticism and intellect or reason] (1998, 38).

The skits in the play put love on trial when the three women, who assume positions as defenders and critics of romantic love, stage an emotional replay of past love affairs. Amapola argues for love as a positive influence using the literary and cultural clichés with which women have been inculcated since romanticism, that love is the be-all and end-all of their lives. Victoria, on the other hand, points to the negative aspects of love, that is, the real costs to women who accept the promises of love and then lose themselves in an unequal exchange. The point the play emphasizes is that for women all love is *Cariño malo* [bad love] because it demands too much of the self in exchange for too little.

The play's three parts may be characterized as a ritual that Graciela Ravetti and Sara Rojo propose "recupera a tradição da cultura popular de morrer para renascer, atualizando as metamorfoses sociais e individuais" [recovers the tradition of popular culture of dying in order to be reborn, bringing about a social and individual metamorphosis] (1996, 125). This idea of finding one's identity or cleansing oneself is introduced in the opening moments of the play when Victoria enters saying

"Quisiera encontrar la niña que fui" [I would like to find the girl I was] and outlines in simple words her intent to make a change: "Voy a separar sus cosas de las mías y romper los lazos" [I am going to separate his things from mine and break the lover's knot] (128).

In the stories that are re-enacted on stage the characters first outline in words and actions the distortions of body and soul that women adopt in order to attract love and then how they suffer when in love. By uncovering these cultural traps of love—the image of union with the other, of two becoming one, of realizing one's dreams through another—the play challenges love's seductive power over women. But it does more than simply expose its audience to the problems of love, it takes them on a journey of healing.

The play's skits, performed by Victoria, Amapola, and Eva, constitute a ritual of death and rebirth, and thus a return to health or to psychological wholeness. Part 1 provides several examples of bad love identified in the playtext as "El mal del amor" (The illness of love) that culminate with the metaphoric "death" of the lover. Part 2 features the suffering of the protagonists in a jail setting where they experience feelings of guilt associated with their crime. They all become ill, suffer, and then recover. Part 3 features a recital of the three voices unified into one that tells how to forget the lost love and then return to childhood.

The skits move seamlessly from one idea to the next as the characters change clothes and pull props to set up the scenes. Several skits stand out for their striking visual images and/or powerful words about women and love. In part 1, the "mating game" is presented as a boxing match, but it is a game that must be won with seduction not with strength. In spite of her name, Victoria is not victorious even though Eva, her coach, teaches her how to win a man by seducing with her body, her makeup, and her youth and warns her of the negative consequences if she doesn't:

"No pierdas la fe, te puedes poner vieja, fea, flaca y amargada" [Don't lose hope, you could become old, ugly, skinny, and bitter] (1996, 132).

After Victoria loses her fight, Coach Eva speaks of the importance of winning the battle and the necessity of pursuing another fight. She even attempts to explain a loss in love as the result of making a bad choice. But Victoria suggests a more realistic reason, that loneliness causes women to settle for anyone (*el primer huevón que encuentra*) with little attention to his qualities (132).

In the wedding dress skit that ends part 2, the protagonists, dressed as men, uncover a wedding dress representing a deceased bride in her bed. The three conduct a funeral procession that is described as melodramatic and expressionistic in which they cry and sing spirituals as they take the wedding dress to be buried. They bury the "bride" along with her bier, funeral candles, and their costumes. As they stand in their underwear, the three protagonists close the trap door in the floor that marks the tomb. This skit without dialogue offers a strong image of the destruction of the romantic dream of a *príncipe azul* (Prince Charming) and the illusion of marriage as a life of "happily ever after" (1996, 136).

In the third part of the play the characters present a series of statements and explanations that justify why it was necessary to kill the lover. These are presented in a repetition of phrases that becomes a form of incantation. The playtext advises that the lines should be spoken together *(Se sobreponen los textos)* so that each gains power as it is spoken again. Amapola attempts to explain her actions of murdering her lover (represented by the dropping of a watermelon) while Victoria and Eva justify her reasons for acting. The three then join together in harmony with each other but independent of the power of the lover whom they defy with the words

   yo no te sigo (I will not follow you) [138].

This one voice then explains how she will remove all the trappings that connote female sexuality, bathe herself, and then return to her mother to recover her virginity and begin again (138). In this recital of unity, represented by the Christian Trinitarian model of three becoming one, the repeating voices reject society's views that women need to find a man at any cost.

The setting for the first and third parts of the play presents an open, desolate space with a bleached bone, beach sand, and a dying tree. The second part takes place in a jail that contains a bed, sink, chair, pitcher of water and cup, and a toilet. Whereas in El vuelo de la grulla the home became a jail for María Luisa, here there is a real jail that is used to house the three protagonists after the symbolic murder of the lover. Both settings are stark, even harsh and unwelcoming to the protagonists. Consuelo Morel Montes has called this space internal, symbolic, and unrealistic (1996, 217) and Graciela Ravetti and Sara Rojo associate it with the interior feminine self, deserted and without vegetation or life (1996, 122). All of the costumes and properties are held inside several trunks that Victoria pulls onto the stage with Amapola sitting on top. The text notes that Amapola holds a box of memories that Eva also handles (127–28). Even though the trunks serve a practical function in the play, they also can be identified as containers of memories that associate the characters with the many roles they have dressed up to play as women in love. The properties from the box also support this idea since they are clearly linked to images of romance. One skit involves a love letter while another makes use of the icons of romantic love: a candelabra, a wine glass and wine, a tablecloth, and a flower. These trunks, much like Pandora's box, let out the pain and suffering associated with previous romantic roles that women have played for centuries. In a ritualistic sense, though, once the contents have been employed to bring about the cleansing and unity of the protagonists, they no longer serve any purpose and can be discarded and left behind. In fact, the flower, the wine glass, and the love letter are placed on the tomb of the wedding dress by the protagonists as they leave the stage at the end of the performance.

In *El vuelo de la grulla*, the mimetic space was a real home that María Luisa was unable to wrestle back from Esteban's control, because her imagined world in diegetic space was too weak to support her efforts to gain subjectivity. *Cariño malo* offers a mimetic space that is symbolic and multireferential, not realistic. Nonetheless it is a space that the characters leave behind after their transformation. The desolate setting of the first and third parts of the play refer to both an internal emotional world of emptiness and an external world of lifelessness. The jail setting of the second part communicates a place for atonement where internal feelings of pain and suffering are expressed externally as an illness. These two mimetic spaces of the play, the open, desolate space (parts 1 and 3) and the closed, confining space (part 2) could be seen as a binary that divides the world into two opposing places. As a site for a ceremony of cleansing, these spaces permit a process to take place in which inner and outer selves pass through hardship and then are united. But, since neither of these spaces serves to nurture the characters, we could conclude that these opposite worlds cancel each other out. The fact that the characters leave the stage and their properties behind, that is, they abandon mimetic space, implies the hostility of both worlds that require the protagonists to leave in search of another, alternative space in which to cultivate another, new version of the self.

As suggested earlier, both *Cariño malo* and *El vuelo de la grulla* use the mimetic space on stage to communicate an unfriendly environment that negates support and nurture to its characters. María Luisa escapes the home through her world of fantasy, but her imagination alone cannot bring about the changes she desires. In contrast, the protagonists of *Cariño malo* use their imaginations and their actions to produce a change in themselves and thus they are able to leave their space behind. They are more successful than María Luisa, in part, because of their solidarity, they work together. Graciela Ravetti and Sara Rojo refer to the protagonists and their actions as *una hermandad o cofradía de mujeres* (a sorority or sisterhood of women) [1996, 124], who are bound together by their task of gaining wholeness and wellness.

The skits that the protagonists of *Cariño malo* portray require them to adopt different personalities or roles and different costumes. These role-playing moments are fictions taken from the real world of bad relationships between men and women. In the skits, the characters speak familiar lines about love, but in unusual contexts, such as a boxing ring or a jail. They also perform familiar actions but with symbolic content, such as the funeral of the wedding dress, or the "death" of the watermelon/lover. That is, they defamiliarize romantic cultural notions and language so these normal components of womanhood can be seen and heard more critically. The women treat love and romance as concrete substances that can be spoken of and acted upon,

> "Puedes romper su reflejo. Puedes matar ese amor" [You can break its reflection. You can kill this love] (132–33).

As a poetic and ritualistic experience, the purpose of the events on stage is evocative but also dramatic since the play moves toward a unifying and optimistic resolution. In these "archetypal moments" from the lives of women, as María de la Luz Hurtado has called them (1998, 39), the words and worlds referred to by the protagonists are not inevitable nor are they necessary, as the characters demonstrate. They can be acted upon allowing women to free themselves from the trap of bad love. Each of the skits marks an attempt to expose women to and separate them from the cultural idealizations that turn them into victims of love. The episodic construction of the skits encourages the audience to think about each situation, evaluate its application to real life, and decide if there is common ground where personal experience meets with and reveals itself in the scenes on stage.

Cariño malo explores the loss of self and its restoration by building a bridge between the abstract setting on stage and the audience with the powerful words and skits of the three characters. In this manner, the play reaches out to a feminine audience, who, in Rojo's words: "deseaba ver y escuchar hasta la identificación catártica sus propios conflictos ante el amor" [wanted to see and hear their own conflicts with love even to the point of cathartic identification] (1991, 128). The image of dreams is repeated throughout the skits and serves as the common denominator for the stories of women and romantic love. For example, women have their own goals or dreams, but then men and love interrupt them and distract the women (131). The love of men becomes a traitor to women's dreams, because it replaces them with the many masks men wear (133). Women use their dreams to create a lover who does not correspond to reality and they live in those dreams with that imagined lover until love goes bad (135). The persistence of the characters in clinging to those dreams can be seen in the structure of the play as well. It is only toward the end of part 3 that Amapola decides to let go of the dream, the man, and love in order to attend to her own growth and self (137).

Cariño malo and *El vuelo de la grulla* communicate strong criticisms of the traditional notions of love and marriage. The plays argue that women must reject society's message that they have value only when loved and desired by men (Barreca 1993, 36). Both plays question the importance women place on love since it often leads them to commit their energies to others rather than to themselves. Love is constructed as the dream-come-true for women, the fulfillment of their every need. Yet, as *El vuelo de la grulla* suggests, love is not a limitless dream but rather a constraining relationship when governed by the rules of patriarchal marriage and the self-centered expectations of husbands. The plays suggest that as human beings women must recognize romantic love and lovers for what they are rather than what they are hoped for in dreams. This means developing personal goals from childhood that focus on the importance of the feminine self or feminine completeness, before looking beyond the self to others. Such a transformation of the expectations for women begins in Inés Margarita Stranger's *Cariño malo* where the protagonists try to establish "un nuevo paradigma discursivo e imaginario, en el cual sea posible creer, reflejarse para construir una identidad" [a new discursive and imaginary paradigm in which it is possible to create and reflect in order to construct an identity] according to Ravetti and Rojo (1996, 121).

Sexual Politics

À prova de fogo by Consuelo de Castro and Boca molhada de paixão calada by Leilah Assunção refer to real events and experiences of the playwrights and their compatriots during the years of the Brazilian dictatorship 1964–1985. À prova de fogo [Trial by fire] marks the beginning of the most repressive years of the dictatorship while Boca molhada de paixão calada [Moist lips, quiet passion] signals its end.[10] Both plays weave together the personal and political lives of the characters who as student activists attempted to instigate change in Brazil's educational and political institutions. Castro's first play is based on her involvement in the conflicts between the leftist students of the Universidade de São Paulo's Faculdade de Filosofia, Ciências e Letras located on the Rua Maria Antônia and the rightist students at the Mackenzie Business School across the street just a few months before the imposition of Institutional Act No. 5.[11] The play was being rehearsed by the Teatro Oficina theater group in 1969 under its original title, Invasão dos bárbaros [Invasion of the barbarians], when it was closed down by censors. Almost ten years later, it was performed secretly at the USP's Cidade Universitária (where the classes were relocated after the building on Maria Antônia burned) and then published with prefaces by Sábato Magaldi, Décio de Almeida Prado, and Guilherme Mota. Finally, in October 1993, it was performed in the newly reopened building on Rua Maria Antônia where its events originally took place.

The action in À prova de fogo begins as a group of students discuss their options now that they have received a police ultimatum to leave the campus building they have occupied for almost a month. They decide to defy the police by staying and vote to engage in more confrontational politics against the dictatorship. Later the president of the students, Zé, is deposed by his exgirlfriend Júlia and another male student who also convince their classmates to participate in a citywide demonstration. After this march in which students are injured, taken into custody and tortured, and one is even rumored to have been shot and killed, the remaining students gather again to await the arrival of the police forces. As soon as the armed forces give orders for the students to abandon the building, they begin to walk out peacefully. But when one grieved woman refuses to leave and throws Molotov cocktails down from the rooftop on the forces below, the police return fire. The play ends as Zé carries her body out of the building while the voice of the police commander repeats that they have orders to shoot to kill.

Boca molhada de paixão calada, originally titled Emoções clandestinas [Clandestine emotions], reenacts in condensed form almost twenty years of the experiences of some of Brazil's most famous theatrical and political figures of the dictatorship (Galvão 1988, 215–16). It was written in 1980, opened in 1984 and was performed again in 1990. The first performance, Assunção's seventh play production, echoed the tone of optimism in the country as elections and the process of abertura (political liberalization) were underway, but by the 1990 performance the nation's dire economic situation and political turmoil were in conflict with its outlook (Guzik 1997, 28).

Boca molhada de paixão calada picks up where À prova de fogo ends and offers an historical replay of the dictatorship through the eyes of a couple who participated in student politics, went into exile, and finally returned to Brazil. In a trip down Assunção's memory lane that Alberto Guzik calls "um exame da trajetória de sua geração" [an examination of the history of her generation] (27), the characters Antônio and Camila employ confession, personal history, and fantasy to recover the lost history of Brazil's leftist community. The meta-theatrical frame of performing the past has as its immediate goal the desire to rekindle the passion from the early years of their marriage. But it also helps the couple discard old semblances and begin creating improved versions of themselves. After time traveling to cities and continents far away, the couple realizes that nothing in that past sparks their emotions. They decide to end their search and their marriage, but then find a point of connection as they think about the future. In the closing moments, they affirm their desire to re-engage politically with their country and emotionally with each other (Assunção 1988, 361).

I will argue that in these two plays the protagonists' egalitarian political and personal praxis clashes with traditional models of masculine institutional and personal power, jeopardizing their homes. These personal and political tensions between the characters are reinforced theatrically with the use of conflicting mimetic and diegetic spaces. Consuelo de Castro's tragedy demonstrates how repressive masculine power operating from outside the university can crush the idealism of rebellious students within. In a parallel to the external action, dominating boyfriends and student leaders inside the university building control the actions of their girlfriends. Leilah Assunção's comedy, on the other hand, suggests that couples can save the integrity of the home by making a cathartic change in their lives when they abandon masculinist models from the past and commit themselves to egalitarian ideals for the future.

Both plays take place in a substitute space for the family home, a site where the political values of autonomy and equality intersect with sexual difference. Although neither of these places resembles the traditional theatrical setting of a drawing room, both of them imitate the home by attempting to offer their inhabitants a safe and comforting refuge. In À prova de fogo the students have transformed a traditional classroom building into a fortress that now serves as their home. The stage directions describe four floors that provide spaces for all the activities of the students—their governance, self-defense, political action, and sustenance. In this temporary and alternative space, the students are united by their common political and educational goals and by their resistance to the outside world. Their vocabulary, manifestos, and music refer to the Marxist ideals of community and class solidarity that they are trying to put into practice. In contrast, the couple in Boca molhada de paixão calada meet in an apartment decorated with pornographic pictures and other accouterments of a bachelor pad. In this masculine space, associated with the erotic and forbidden, they remember, reenact, and reject all their former sexually stimulating moments. Their search for new ways to achieve sexual excitement resuscitates moments from their lives as 1960s political activists, 1970s counter-culture exiles, and 1980s alienated repatriates.

Both plays present the audience with high levels of physical activity and conflict within and beyond the space that is serving as a temporary home. The students in À prova de fogo move around and between rooms throughout the play's three scenes discussing incessantly their political cause, their options for action, and their personal relations. They also leave the university building to participate in a demonstration. Their activity inside the home and away from it is constantly threatened by the unseen authority of parents who call on the phone, the radio announcer who exhorts the students to desist, and the troops who appear at the student demonstration and then later carry out their ultimatum to invade. The play sets up a classic theatrical antithesis between the powerful, those who cannot be seen but are referred to in the original title *Invasão dos bárbaros*, and the powerless (Issacharoff 1981, 215). Thus, its division of space pits the mimetic world of communitarian ideals of rebellious youth against the diegetic world of traditional authoritarian and patriarchal values of the older generation. But the play adds to that model by locating a similar power imbalance between male and female students within the mimetic space of the home.

À prova de fogo also heightens the impact of the conflicts by extending the student world onstage into the audience. The stage directions suggest that the walls of the theater building should be covered with the same political posters as those on stage and that the main aisle through the audience also should serve as an exit and entrance for the characters (1977, 2). Thus, both the decorations and the main aisle push the fictitious world of the students out beyond the stage encompassing and involving the audience. This staging does more than encourage sympathy and support—it makes the audience an accomplice with the students in their resistance.[12] The home on stage is united with "the house" in the theater, reinforcing the unity of both worlds as a place of defiance against the dictatorship. When the students are driven from the classroom building in the final moments of the play, it not only signals the invasion of military forces into their home, but also the occupation of the theater building, an action that actually took place in the late-1960s when vigilante forces known as the *Comando de Caça aos Comunistas* (command force to hunt down communists) invaded theaters and terrorized actors.

In the student-created home, Marxist ideology and vocabulary create a sense of community and solidarity. But often personal views about sex roles are at odds with these espoused political ideals. It is easier for the students to vote to unite against parents, military, and police forces and to confront those same repressive forces on the streets of São Paulo than to apply the lessons of equality to their personal lives and loves. In spite of the professed political goals, life inside the school building divides itself according to traditional sex roles with men assuming both leadership and vigilance over the women.

The love triangle formed by Zé—Júlia—Rosa, exemplifies some of the problems the students exhibit as they attempt to practice their Marxist theory both inside and outside their home.

The student leader Zé compromises his political credibility with his propensity for sexual conquest, a duplicity that his followers both criticize and envy. He abandons Júlia and his obligation to their unborn child with the worn-out claim that he needs his freedom only to turn his attention to Rosa, an industrialist's daughter. In order to seduce Rosa, Zé uses his rhetorical skills and political teachings to condemn her religious and bourgeois values of virginity and her four-year engagement to Fredi. When these persuasive arguments fail, he gives her an ultimatum. While similar in approach to the police ultimatum used against the students, Zé's pressure on Rosa achieves a more traditional form of feminine surrender. Zé is equally dogged at trying to regain power and negotiate a safe exit in order to stop the students' escalating efforts at confrontation. Although he remains loyal to the principles of the movement and the safety of its members, Zé betrays and compromises his relations with Júlia and Rosa, because he does not perceive the conflict between his personal behavior and his political ideals. His behavior in both arenas causes him to lose his power of persuasion over the students, as well as his ability to keep Júlia safe and to reconcile the relationship between Rosa and Fredi that he compromised.

Júlia stages a coup and assumes the leadership of the students from Zé while he is absent. She, too, is caught between her political ambitions and the traditional expectations for her sex. As a student leader she upsets normal gender divisions by sending men to the kitchen to prepare a meal; by recognizing she has a *papel histórico a cumprir* (an historic role to play) [30]; by escalating the student action to a confrontation with the government; and by exercising a more inclusive, less hierarchical leadership style than Zé (52). Nonetheless, the students are not completely convinced by her motives and suspect that her overthrow of Zé's leadership is an act of personal vengeance rather than of political differences (35–37). In fact, Julia's feminism and sense of duty are constantly in conflict with her personal affection for Zé and her indecision regarding her unplanned pregnancy. She receives harsher treatment in the play than Zé when she becomes a victim first of his emotional indifference and later of state violence. After she leaves the building at the end of the second scene to lead the student protest march and to have an abortion, she does not return. Student informers later describe her torture and possible miscarriage at the hands of the police.

Rosa, an entering freshman who is attracted to Zé from the first day of school, joins the student movement as a means of defying her overprotective father as well as exercising a little self-determination with her fiancé Fredi. Her bourgeois values represent a political and sexual challenge to Zé, who both insults her intelligence and clings to her as the events of the play intensify. Rosa eventually rejects the student leader for personal reasons, such as his predatory and manipulative ways and the damage (pregnancy) that he causes women. She wants to marry Fredi, maintain her religious connections, her status, wealth, and privileges (92). For her the events of the student occupation have not expanded her views of politics, although they have compromised her future plans with Fredi. Unlike her fiancé, who claims that the events around them have changed his thinking, Rosa wants to escape from the inevitable destruction the students face. She pays a high personal price for staying with the student protesters. Her father has a heart attack and Fredi breaks their engagement after learning of her night with Zé. Although he claimed to be enlightened by the Marxist ideology of the students, Fredi's own values concerning virginity and marriage remain well-preserved with regard to Rosa and their engagement. While both he and Rosa are spared the inevitable invasion of the military forces as they leave just minutes before the troops arrive, it is also obvious that the events they have witnessed will be remembered more as a nightmare, than as a political lesson for life.

The play repeatedly points out the contradictions between the masculine models of dominance and the ideological models of equality. Fredi and several other boyfriends state that they are guarding their girlfriends' behavior (i.e., sexual purity) while at the same time they are guarding the building (i.e., political loyalty). At the end of scene 2 the students leave the stage to participate in the demonstration carrying hand lettered signs that say Down with the Dictatorship yet that same concept is not applied to relations between couples. Fredi tells Rosa

"Você tem um compromisso com eles" [You have an obligation to them], as he orders her to participate in the student march. She, on the other hand, attempts to assert herself by reminding him

"Você não manda em mim" [You don't boss me around] (57).

The overzealous military forces, that are only heard but never seen, drive the students from their home at the end of À prova de fogo confirming their power to threaten the university's autonomy and the students' lives. Zé observes correctly that the students' "home" with its oppositional space of political liberation and sexual cohabitation is destroyed, because it endangered too many sacred institutions (108). As the play makes evident through the voice of the loudspeaker in the closing moments, neither political or personal action could have saved this idealistic group of young people in their resistance to an enormous military force organized against them. The stage directions indicate that the voice over the loudspeaker orders the students to abandon the building because the military forces are authorized to shoot to kill. Long after Zé has carried the body of the dead student out the theater door leaving the stage empty, the loudspeaker continues: *falando obsessivamente, como um disco quebrado, até que o último espectador se retire da platéia* [speaking obsessively, like a broken record, until the last spectator leaves the building] (120).

Both the mimetic home of the students onstage and the theatrical space of the "house" in the audience are threatened and then occupied by the sounds of the military from diegetic space. With a shocking display of power that guns down one of the students from the top of the school building, the noise continues to hound the spectators in the audience even after the play has ended. Thus, the unity that was created by extending the mimetic space out into the theater and joining the students on stage with the theater audience breaks and then is overwhelmed by an invisible, intimidating power representing the state.

In contrast to the realism and intensity of À prova de fogo, Boca molhada de paixão calada adopts a metatheatrical frame in which its characters role play their past, and that of many Brazilians of their generation, within the mimetic space of an apartment. According to Issacharoff, "Where mimetic space is fixed (where a single set is used), the odds are that the diegetic space will be nonfixed, that is, to say, manifold" (1981, 222). This is what happens in Boca molhada de paixão *calada* where mimetic space is the one room of the apartment and diegetic space is the many worlds created in the words and actions of the characters. The mimetic space provides a stage where the characters can dramatize the diegetic space of the past in order to review and reconsider its applicability to the present. Thus, present and past appear side by side as Antônio and Camila act out and then comment on the emotional potential of their scenes. As the characters perform, they trigger each other's imaginations and respond to each other's cues, much like an improvisation, except that some of the content of the material portrayed has already been experienced, while other features are created spontaneously.

Antônio and Camila summon the past in order to analyze and understand their former selves and times. That past, which in this play exists in imagined or diegetic space, is made real through the power of the words of the characters and is imagined and acted upon by them as if it were real. Therefore, a space that exists only in verbal terms comes to share and sometimes even replace the mimetic space seen on stage (Issacharoff 1981, 218). Rather than functioning as an invasion of mimetic space, these imagined spaces function in a vital way as signs of exhausted models of behavior and values. The worlds of the past are evoked through the descriptions and actions of the characters and made to live on the stage as the major events of the play. At the same time that Antônio and Camila act out their past, they also comment on it and on their former selves. They travel through time, although not in a linear fashion, and through space to the cities where they resided during their exile, and they portray various earlier versions of themselves. But the layering is even more complicated since the fictional lives they recreate are then expanded and reworked into new fictions, because they hold the promise to be more sexually stimulating.

Boca molhada de paixão calada provides a second chance for the characters and the audience to examine the egalitarian values from the 1960s that were lost during the Brazilian dictatorship. Antônio and Camila could be the aging students of Castro's *À prova de fogo*. Antônio shares many of Zé's character traits—he was a politically committed student, a leftist who divided his time between politics and sexual adventures with Camila. Like many leftists, he was forced into exile when the Brazilian military began hunting down student revolutionaries following the coup. Antônio also could be considered a victim of the repression, since he spent a good portion of his life escaping from Brazil through drugs, exile, art, and mental illness. The only job he has been able to keep since his return, that of a state bureaucrat, must be seen as an ironic political sellout. Unlike Júlia of À prova de fogo, Camila was more of a groupie in the student movement than a committed member and leader. She married Antônio and followed him into exile, but upon their return to Brazil she begins to take a more proactive role in her own life by completing her education and making a career as a psychologist. While Antônio seems to struggle to redefine his life, Camila relishes in developing hers for the first time.

What keeps the couple searching as they relive the past is the fact that they have an egalitarian agenda—the emotion they are looking for must be felt equally by both of them. Neither will accept fakery or accommodation as a substitute for the emoção maior (the big thrill) they wish to feel. As they speak critically and truthfully about the past, they deflate many androcentric sexual and political myths. For example, Antônio remembers "taking" Camila's virginity and the birth of their son because for him these were both big emotional moments. For Camila, neither event was big or emotional, because they hurt her physically. On the other hand, she confesses to having multiple orgasms with someone else, and criticizes his maior orgulho (pride and joy) that was not always erect. In one role-playing sequence, she takes the aggressor/ masculine role by mounting him, while he assumes the "passive" feminine role. Through their replaying of scenes Antônio and Camila come to understand that the entrega (surrender) they seek has been blocked by a life in opposition to one another constructed by historical conditions and their own small town upbringing.

As a student, Antônio accepted the philosophy of the student movement not to mix politics and sex (1988, 303–4), yet this was an impossible ideal that neither he nor many others were able to accomplish. The military dictatorship ended his active, engaged political life and caused his inability to speak when he became alienated from the very thing that had given his life meaning. What actually restores him to life is the abandonment of all the substitutes or escapes (drugs, painting, sexual experimentation) and the commitment to a new unity between sex and politics. The same is true for Camila, who followed a different path. Only after completing her education, bearing children, and establishing herself in the work-world does she find pride in herself, her sex, and her goals. She admits to the corrupting use of sex, such as her *transa de poder* (sexual affair with power) with Borges the military man while her husband was in an asylum. But, in the closing moments of the play, she joins with Antônio in a renewed belief in passion for married life and party politics.

The improvisations created by the characters serve an important role as the vehicles for analysis. However, because the "reality" of this diegetic space depends on the words spoken and acted on by the characters, it is forever changing but always subordinated to their will to discover a sexually stimulating memory. While the characters are acting out the past, they also have an intent or a motivation that keeps them focused on their goal. Their two worlds, mimetic and diegetic, exist side by side until the seductive power of the diegetic space loses its appeal to them. After reviewing their pasts Antônio and Camila come to a dead-end in their search and in their marriage. It is at this point that they finally are able to reconnect with one another.

The reconciliation of the characters and their resumption of a life of commitment is reflected in the theatrical setting when Antônio and Camila remove the trappings of the bachelor pad to reveal the furnishings of their own apartment. The earlier setting of masculine conquest served as a backdrop for past stories of sexual experimentation and excess that not only were old-fashioned but no longer stimulate their minds or their bodies and thus no longer meet their needs.

Their improvisations served to empty that past of its meaning so that it no longer can seduce or haunt them in postdictatorship Brazil. The new setting, a rediscovery of the "home," suggests that the couple has created a new association based on mutual surrender and egalitarian values, and therefore they have revitalized their domestic life. For Antônio and Camila this new sense of *entrega* (surrender) that they feel creates a wholeness. Their life begins again in a passionate embrace that welcomes a new understanding of the connection between politics and sex.

For Antônio students politics was a partially successful place, and like Zé, one in which at least he could exercise his passions. But for Camila, like Júlia and Rosa, it was an unfriendly place where the burdens of traditional sex roles limited opportunities. As Camila remembers, the male leaders only took an interest in her when she told them she wanted to study *datilografia*, since typing/secretarial skills would make her useful to them. In the new home that the middle-aged Antônio and Camila revive, sex and politics do mix, because the characters have developed a new consciousness that operates beyond the patterns of patriarchy. In fact, both their sexual desire and their political commitment come full circle, or as critic Elza Cunha de Vincenzo remarks: they reach "o ideal de ser jovens e sábios ao mesmo tempo" [the ideal of being young and wise at the same time] (1992, 140). That is to suggest, that the couple still maintains the vitality to partake of life and to participate in constructing new meanings, but it also is wise enough to realize that the traditional patterns of the past have no place in the egalitarian world under construction.

As students the characters in À prova de fogo and Boca molhada de paixão calada could not reach their dreams of liberty, fraternity, and equality through political action. Rather than provide a meaningful alternative to the dictatorship, both plays point to the fact that the student movement of the 1960s heralded greater sexual experimentation than socialist revolution. For the students in À prova de fogo the action of living together in the university building for one month and the action of taking birth control pills, signal the students' participation in a growing movement for sexual liberation. Júlia is the character who represents that experimentation with both sexual freedom and political leadership. Her progressive views about sex and politics are not rewarded, and she pays a much higher personal toll than that paid by Zé, who typifies the more traditional predatory male. Yet, even Zé fails at his political goals of rescuing the students from a confrontation with the military forces. What the play suggests, and later history confirmed, was that student demonstrations for reform and equality triggered a strong repressive response from the military dictatorship. The Brazilian people lived under that dictatorship for almost twenty years. The university building, where the students reveled in the questioning of the past and the visioning for the future, was unable to provide the necessary protection for its rebellious students who could imagine, although not necessarily put into practice, alternative models for human interaction. While the student movement portrayed in Castro's play failed, the political and sexual values the students believed in were revitalized in the post-abertura years described in Assunção's play.

À prova de fogo plots a course in which idealistic students lose their "home" and their voice of opposition to the authoritarian and patriarchal powers of Brazil in the 1960s. Some twenty years later those same "homeless" students return to occupy a new house in *Boca molhada de paixão calada*. While both optimistic and utopian in its vision, Assunção's play champions the power of individuals to nurture their own transformations from victims of political repression into persons with a capacity and a drive to exercise egalitarian ideals and sexual passion. What Camila and Antônio achieve together is the very ideal that María Luisa was searching for in *El vuelo de la grulla* but could not reach because she was acting alone. In addition, her dreams in diegetic space never became more concrete than the words and imagination she invested in them. Camila and Antônio were able to profit from their past by reliving it and then moving on to find a more meaningful relationship marked by the rediscovery of their home. *Boca molhada de paixão calada* shares with *Cariño malo* a ritual of cleansing that first identifies and then expels the sometimes painful, sometimes useless models of the past in favor of new models. Unlike the three other plays, however, *Cariño malo* envisions a rebirth of the feminine self, the creation of a new identity, as the necessary step that must precede any romantic involvement.

Gender Bending

Casa llena by Estela Leñero, and *Whisky & Cocaína* by Thais Erminy dramatize young women who defy the feminine script of passivity by defending themselves from lovers who attempt to conquer their apartments and their bodies. *Casa llena* [Full house] won a drama contest sponsored by the magazine *Puntos de partida* in 1983. It was first staged at the Centro Universitario de Teatro (UNAM) and published in the collection *La pareja* by the Universidad Autónoma de Puebla in 1986. *Whisky & Cocaína* [Whisky and Cocaine] won honorable mention in the VIII Bienal Literaria of the University of Oriente in 1984. It was first staged in the same year at the El Nuevo Grupo theater and published in a private edition along with another Erminy play, *La tercera mujer*.[13]

The two plays stage the unexpected arrival of a male companion to the small studio apartment of the female protagonist where each couple lived before separating. Even though both of the protagonists live alone in their own apartments, these spaces are not entirely their own, since both were previously shared with lovers. In *Casa llena*, the couple has split up and no longer sees each other while in *Whisky & Cocaína*, the couple no longer lives together but still maintains a romantic relationship, although not a monogamous one. In both plays, the males attempt to lay claim to the apartments by invading them and the psyches of their female owners, as Myrna S. Gann has remarked in reference to *Casa llena* (1998, 236). Rather than falling victim to their lovers because of a loss of self, these protagonists maintain or recover their strong sense of self in order to prevent a reconquest. The women characters reestablish their property rights over the apartments and over themselves by fighting aggressively in their own defense. Each sees through the manipulations of her companion and comes to realize why this individual is not worthy of the emotional investment each woman made. When put to the test, both protagonists assert a life-saving response rather than the traditional passive submission so commonly represented by female characters on Latin American stages. Both plays are surprising for their representation of physical violence between the sexes and of feminine anger and revenge.[14]

I will argue that the protagonists perform role-reversals in order to defend their homes and their independent selves. Carolina of *Whisky & Cocaína* and Sara of *Casa llena* are strong women who defy the traditional socialization of femininity. At first the women characters are blind to the dangerous intentions of their lovers, much like the protagonists of *Cariño malo* and *El vuelo de la grulla*. Even though both men are "invaders," the women fail to recognize their presence as threatening and do not immediately question their intentions. The women do not realize that it is their own behavior that has provoked the men. By asserting their own definitions of womanhood, which include individual and sexual independence, the protagonists have violated the rules of patriarchy that their partners uphold. These rules demand that women be attached to men, that is, sexually faithful even when men are not, and emotionally and financially dependent on them. From the men's perspective, the women are engaged in inappropriate behavior that they can only understand as immoral. The only label they can find to blame the protagonists and justify their own aggressive actions is to accuse the women of promiscuity. This insinuation intends to degrade the women by suggesting that rather than honorable women worthy of respect, they are prostitutes who deserve to be treated roughly.

That the women are acting as if they were men causes their companions alarm and disdain. Miguel Angel of *Whisky & Cocaína* complains to Carolina:

"Tú lo que quieres es hacer abiertamente, lo que los hombres hacemos a escondidas" [What you want is to do openly what we men do secretly] (29).

In their debates about the double standard, the male characters contend that they follow the norm in sexual mores for men while the women defy traditional female mores. In fact, Carolina does claim equality with men and asserts her right to follow the same rules that they demand for themselves alone. She demands the same *libertad sexual* (sexual liberty) for herself that society traditionally considers normal for men (31).

In *Whisky & Cocaína*'s battle between the sexes, Carolina is an even match for Miguel Angel. She is described as *alta, atractiva, imponente* (tall, attractive, imposing) while he is *bien parecido, varonil* (handsome, virile) [5]. Together they make an attractive couple, and each is easily identified with the movie/theater world where he exercises the traditional masculine role of a director and she the traditional seductive role of an actress. However, Carolina refuses to live the role of a traditional woman subordinated to a man and maintains her right to conduct her life as she pleases. She is not intimidated by Miguel Angel and defends herself and her apartment *como una tigre* (like a tigress) [38].

The actress echoes the words of the student activist Zé in *À prova de fogo* in her defense of sexual liberty and its accompanying criticism of the unhealthy bonds of bourgeois marriage. Both Zé and Carolina argue that sexual satisfaction and emotional commitment are different human needs that cannot be answered within the institution of marriage. Zé utilizes this liberating message in a traditional masculine way in order to seduce a succession of attractive female students. For him sexual conquest is disguised as a politically revolutionary act, making it difficult to refuse. Carolina attempts to employ the same message of sexual freedom in self-defense against her traditional lover who, like Zé, defines conquest as an exclusively male activity.

Martín and Sara of *Casa llena* are not described at all in the stage directions or dialogue; however, the text makes references to her physical exercise both outside and inside the apartment and to her decisiveness in separating from Martín. Martín scoffs at exercising, but he is able to turn off the leaking water faucet when she cannot, suggesting he has greater physical strength. He is portrayed as a stubborn and insensitive person who expects Sara to allow him to move back in. Like Miguel Angel what provokes him the most about Sara's actions is her revelation that she has male friends. He concludes that she is promiscuous,

"Eres una cabrona" [You are a bitch] (1986, 88),

and uses this information to justify hurting her. In spite of Martín's words and actions, Sara refuses to be either seduced or forced to allow him to move back into her apartment.

The escalating action of the male antagonists, their manipulations and incursions, causes the protagonists to react in self-defense only when they come to realize that their lives and personal integrity are threatened. There are no limits to the aggression the male characters employ as they demean, torture, and attempt to both frighten and subdue the women. In *Casa llena*, the escalating action culminates when Sara finally turns against Martín and acts to harm him with a box of tools and by appropriating his eyeglasses and breaking them. This short, intense moment leads immediately to the play's climax and conclusion in which Martín walks out the door. In contrast, *Whisky & Cocaína* portrays an extended battle between the characters as they struggle over possession of the revolver, which contains one bullet, and the bag of cocaine. The dramatic tension increases each time one of the characters pulls the gun away from the other, aims it and tries to fire the weapon at the other. Since the gun repeatedly fails to fire, the potential to actually inflict damage is prolonged, and the violence keeps escalating as each character hurls additional insults and demands demeaning actions with each possession of the gun.

Both plays take place in studio apartments, spaces where all belongings and activities are concentrated into one room. The audience has complete visual access to the characters and their intimate world. This space is so compact that even the decorations on the wall take on an important role in both plays. In *Whisky & Cocaína* movie posters of Carolina reinforce her celebrity status by showing her image in various contexts and sizes. They also magnify her presence and dominance in the room. In *Casa llena*, Sara's wall decorations and shelves of books mark the space as her own, so that when Martín attempts to move in he begins by placing his posters on top of hers and removing her books from the shelves so that his will fit there.

In such a small space, women are particularly vulnerable since there are no other rooms or hiding places that they can go to in order to escape, as Myrna S. Gann aptly has noted with regard to *Casa llena* (1998, 235). In *Whisky & Cocaína*, Miguel Angel's invasion, his unannounced and unexpected entrance, carries a threat with it from the beginning since he is holding a gun and has used his own keys to unlock the door. We know he has interrupted Carolina's day because she keeps asking him why he has come (10–11). He still claims ownership of some of her space as can be seen when he begins to search for items he has hidden there. Because he has a romantic and professional relationship with Carolina, the obvious danger of his gun is temporarily obscured and explained as both a necessary defense weapon for him as a drug user and as a prop in the play he is rehearsing with Carolina, but not as a firearm to be used against her. Only after Miguel Angel has become frustrated and angry with Carolina and places a bullet in the gun does its real threat to her become clear. Martín, on the other hand, must co-opt the housekeeper in order to gain entrance into Sara's apartment. He steals Sara's extra set of keys in scene 2 and then in scene 3 he begins moving in. Thus, since he demonstrates his will to stay there by bringing in his own things, Martín's presence in the apartment begins with an aggressive and deceptive move and escalates.

The title of Leñero's play, *Casa llena* [Full house], indicates that the space Sara occupies is already full enough so that when Martín attempts to move in, the house and its resident find it too crowded. Martín tips the balance and harmony within by inserting himself into a space where he doesn't fit. His physical presence pushes Sara out to the edges of the room while he occupies the middle. She goes to the kitchen and to the bathroom while he maintains his dominance in the central space of the apartment either at the dining table or on the bed. At the end of scene 1, he rejects Sara's directions to sleep on the couch and moves into her bed even though she protests

"No entiendes que no cabes en mi cama" [Don't you understand that you don't fit in my bed] (63).

In the confining space of Sara's apartment, most of the properties serve the key function of characterizing her. In scene 1, Martín
associates the unpredictable leaking faucet with Sara's anger, suggesting that as long as she doesn't get mad the faucet won't leak (60). In
fact, Sara's anger does function like the faucet. While Martín manages
to shut off the running water in scene 1, Sara's anger builds up in
response to Martín's increasing aggression until both the faucet and
Sara explode in scene 3. At that point, Sara's resentment and anger
flow out of her like the water gushing out of the faucet.

Other properties communicate how Sara's life has changed now
that she lives alone. For example, there are repeated references to her
exercise bicycle, which she mounts several times, and to the fact that
she goes running every day. This information communicates that Sara
is physically active, strengthening, and enjoying herself. Even so,
Martín makes a reference to her "weakness," and he demonstrates
that he can overpower her by pushing her onto the bed, turning off
the faucet, and pushing her off the exercise bicycle. His "weakness,"
in turn, is myopia, as is apparent in his need for glasses. In defense of
her apartment, Sara takes the eyeglasses and uses them as a weapon
to regain her home and herself. When he cannot see, he is forced to
hear her complaints against him and her anger at his behavior. Her
words finally force him to hear, that is, to understand, why she will
not allow him to invade and recolonize her apartment. During his
blindness, Sara makes Martín "see" her and listen to her unwillingness
to accept his return. While all her earlier implications of why she no
longer wishes to share her life with him were ignored, this final move
helps her gain power over him. It also helps her capture his attention
in an unequivocal manner since he is helpless when he cannot see.

Thais Erminy's title, *Whisky & Cocaína*, suggests the dangerous
substances that lead to the play's violent outcome. The excessive use
of stimulants by individuals confined to a small space proves toxic in
this play, causing both characters to resort to abusive behavior. Miguel
Angel associates himself with cocaine from the minute he enters the
apartment, and he criticizes Carolina for not sharing his interest in
the drug. Although Carolina portrays an alcoholic in the play she is
rehearsing, she scorns Miguel Angel's indulgence and that of the character she portrays as escapes from reality (15).

Similarly to *Casa llena* properties not only serve here to characterize Carolina, but they also assume a dual role in *Whisky & Cocaína's*

construction. These properties—a mirror, a revolver, a bottle of whisky, and bags of cocaine, and a case of theater makeup—constitute the essential elements of two plays that are unfolding and changing on stage. The meaning and use of these properties are altered as they move from the frame play to the play-within-a-play. In the frame play, Miguel Angel invades Carolina's apartment and attempts to punish her for having a one night affair with another man. In the play-within-a-play, Carolina rehearses a more familiar plot of sexual betrayal by the husband Arturo and its impact on his suffering wife, La Chata (pug-nosed woman). The mirror, a key property in most of the plays discussed in this book, assists Carolina in preparing for her rehearsal by helping her see how her makeup must age her from a young woman of thirty to a woman in her fifties. In her role and in her scene as La Chata, Carolina must communicate the familiar story of an aging woman who is betrayed by her husband and his younger lover. She performs this scene in front of the mirror as she both looks into the mirror and recounts her years as wife of the character Arturo. Later the mirror becomes a chalkboard upon which Miguel Angel is forced at gun point, by Carolina, to paint and kiss a face of La Chata with the same theater makeup that she had previously used to portray the betrayed wife. The revolver functions first as a weapon of self-defense for Miguel Angel and is related to the protection of his drug habit. Then the revolver becomes a property in the play about La Chata where it serves to enhance the theatricality of Carolina's performance as a desperate and lonely character who employs the revolver to demonstrate her unfulfilled sexual longing. Finally, it becomes a physical threat to both characters when Miguel Angel puts in one bullet and the characters struggle over who will hold the revolver and use it to intimidate the other. Possession of the revolver gives the power of life and death to the owner and at the same time it forces the other to listen, much as Sara's possession of Martín's glasses make him hear her complaints.

The bottle of whisky and the bag of cocaine, mentioned in the title of the play, suggest both the escape from and the cause for the conflict between the characters. As Carolina prepares to rehearse she places the whisky bottle and a glass in an accessible and visible location to signal her character's alcoholism. She uses the drink to show her deteriorating emotional state as her theatrical scene progresses. Later, the whisky contributes to the conflict between Miguel Angel and Carolina when he forces her to actually drink it and she becomes dizzy and somewhat inebriated (rather than acting drunk as La Chata in the rehearsal). The cocaine powder impacts Miguel Angel's behavior as director of the play and as Carolina's lover. We learn that it is the cause of the break up of the couple and that Miguel Angel has been addicted for at least a year. He spends most of his time either searching for hidden pouches, preparing to inhale it, or inhaling it. In spite of his obvious addiction, he even uses the cocaine as an excuse for his emotional instability (27). Ironically, it is the cocaine and not the revolver that drives Miguel Angel out of Carolina's apartment. When she dumps his last bag on the floor, he attempts to consume all of it and then reacts wildly by stepping out onto the apartment ledge and preparing to jump.

In these two cases of invasion of mimetic space by domineering men, there is an assumption by the men that they own both the women and the space. That is, that their masculinity earns them access to and submission from the women. It is this prerogative that the women refuse to accept, especially since it is being exercised within the privacy of their own apartments. Carolina's posters of herself and Sara's decorations connect each woman to and identify her with the space she inhabits. Moreover, since both women have only recently regained sole ownership of their apartments, they are inspired to defend themselves and their space against the invaders that would deny them ownership. Hanna Scolnicov's equation of woman's theatrical space with her social standing, her body and her sexuality seems particularly relevant here (1994, 7). The protagonists are not just defending their turf, they are defending the integrity of their bodies including their individual rights to exercise their sexuality as they see fit. The only space that they can claim, their apartments, represents their autonomy and sexual freedom. That identification between the two, woman and space, helps to explain the actions of the protagonists and their drive to fight so aggressively.

The mimetic and diegetic spaces of Casa llena are evoked in the words that the couple uses to describe their earlier relationship as compared to the current one. In those words, Martín summons a better past or antes in which he remembers fondly their living together. His insistent repetition of this antes helps to keep his hopes alive for reestablishing this relationship. Sara, on the other hand, both rejects and clarifies these references to the past, rewriting Martín's version of their life together. She speaks and eventually acts in defense of the present, the *ahora* in which she has the freedom to be her own person and make her own decisions as she states here:

> "Desde que no estamos juntos. Desde entonces hago lo que quiero" [Since we broke up. Since then I do what I want] (73).

Sara's increased agitation during the play, which begins as nervous movement around the room, then becomes more focused on riding the exercise bicycle in scene 2, and finally in scene 3 becomes an outburst of yelling, hitting, and finally removing Martín's glasses, represents her building anxiety that she will lose her *ahora* if Martín stays.

The discussion of their past appears innocent enough, at first, as Myrna S. Gann has observed (1998, 235). Sara first enters the apartment carrying groceries and when Martín expresses an interest in what she buys these days she calls out the names of each item. Then she refers to their earlier times together when her shopping included more luxuries. The opposition between *antes* and *ahora* then becomes a topic for further conversation and storytelling by Martín about his experiences grocery shopping. Soon, however Martín begins making references to other shared moments such as their trips to Oxaca. At the end of scene 1, Sara begins distancing herself from the past life she shared with Martín when she refuses to accept his explanations of why he shouldn't leave as she has requested. When he asks:

> "Soy convincente, ¿no?" [Aren't I convincing?], she replies: "Antes, ahora es distinto." [Maybe before, but now things are different] (61).

The phone conversations in which Sara makes social plans for the following evening, and the calls she makes to various friends confirm that Sara's claim to a better "now" in mimetic space is accurate. Martín's references to his lack of housing, lack of ambition, and desire to find refuge with Sara bespeak his decline since their affair ended. Martín is so jealous of Sara's new life apart from him that he not only attempts to invade and occupy her apartment, but he also attempts to cut her off from her new circle of friends, such as when he answers her phone and identifies himself as her husband (81).

In scene 3, Sara finally reveals the turning point in the *antes* that caused their break up. In a long speech, she explains her loneliness caused by his absences and her efforts to create new friendships, even new relationships with other men:

"Comencé a tenerte coraje, una rabia infinita; y jamás te diste cuenta. Nunca supiste qué sentía, qué pensaba, adónde iba" [I began to get mad, it was an infinite anger that you never perceived. You never knew what I was feeling, what I thought, where I was going] (87).

Sara makes the final reference to their earlier life as she holds and crushes Martín's eyeglasses:

"*(con coraje)*: Ahora no te doy nada. Antes si querías te daba mi cuerpo, si querías te daba café, mis besos y todo. Ahora no te doy nada, ni mi cariño, ni mi casa, ni tus lentes." [*(with anger)*: Now, I don't give you anything. Before I gave you my body, if you wanted it I gave you coffee, my kisses, everything. Now I won't give you anything, not my love, or my house, or even your glasses.] (90)

It is possible that Martín's increasingly belligerent behavior and Sara's persistent efforts to get him to leave would have been enough justification for the concluding explosion between them. However, the repeated references to their former relationship, a memory of different proportions depending on who describes it, ultimately warrant Sara's actions. The ever-expanding contrast between the Sara on stage and the Sara of diegetic space emphasizes the impossibility of renewing any bonds of affection. While Sara has created a new person for herself, the Martín on stage, who claims that he will change this time, appears no more attractive now than he was then. Sara's words of pain and disappointment about her past, so long bottled up inside her, slowly construct this unsympathetic version of Martín. When she finally defends herself and forces him to leave, both she and the audience feel relieved that her present self is no longer threatened. Gann has pointed out that Martín's humiliation at being rendered helpless causes him to finally leave (1998, 236), but Sara's determination to hold on to her new self and her apartment under threatening circumstances also contributes to Martín's resignation.

In contrast to *Casa llena*'s conflict between the mimetic space of the present and the diegetic space of the past, *Whisky & Cocaína* developes a frame play and a play-within-a-play in the same mimetic space on the stage. These two plays make manifest through their contrasting situations the incompatibility that *Casa llena* implied in its past and present versions of the relationship between Sara and Martín. Rather than imagine the previous love life of Sara and Martín, Erminy provides two plays and four characters as a reference for comparison. The frame play features Carolina rehearsing the role of La Chata. As an actress, Carolina gives life to La Chata as she simultaneously acts out and criticizes her character's womanhood. She also "creates" La Chata's husband, Arturo, when she addresses him during her scene. This fictional couple, La Chata and Arturo, represent a common occurrence of infidelity in patriarchal marriage in which the husband regularly deceives his wife and then finally abandons her for a younger woman.

The theme of sexual betrayal and its debilitating impact on the character La Chata occupies Carolina as she tries to concentrate on portraying her character in the opening sequence. But with Miguel Angel's arrival, betrayal becomes a point of contact between both plays being represented in mimetic space. Miguel Angel reveals that he chose to direct this play because of its similarity to their romantic situation, and he sets up the scene in which the actions of La Chata include reacting to a photograph of her husband's latest extramarital adventure. Miguel Angel replaces the fictitious newspaper clipping used for rehearsal with a recent exposé of Carolina and another man outside of a local motel. When Carolina finally notices and responds to the photo, the causes of conflict in both the frame play and the play-within-a-play become the same.

In the play-within-a-play, Carolina acts the role of the betrayed La Chata while in the frame play she defends herself from Miguel Angel's accusations of being the betrayer. Miguel Angel employs the excuse of a rehearsal to communicate his jealousy and anger over her public display. While Miguel Angel compares himself to La Chata as the betrayed one, Carolina is challenged to produce the actions and emotions of a character she despises as a woman. In the play-within-a-play, Carolina portrays the conventional victimized wife serving her husband while suffering from a lack of emotional and sexual attention. The frame play with Miguel Angel and

Carolina, on the other hand, displays the unconventional image of a female who claims equality and operates according to rules traditionally granted to men.

Miguel Angel has an agenda to push Carolina to find her deepest sense of anguish and pain at her character's loss, so she will feel his own sense of violation. Carolina is not La Chata, but she is an excellent actress and she responds to his directing. In the repeated efforts to get her scene right, Carolina appears to fuse the play-within-a-play, in which La Chata desires revenge against her husband Arturo, with the frame play, in which she feels angry at Miguel Angel for his need to control and possess her. Her heightened perceptions, generated in the rehearsal process and then exacerbated by the whisky he forces her to drink, produce the real revenge that La Chata the character would have liked to take against her husband Arturo. In a parallel to Miguel Angel's action of placing a real news photo on the set, Carolina directs a scene at gun point in which she commands him to use the theatrical makeup to draw a picture of La Chata, the real woman of his dreams, on the mirror and then to act the appropriate emotions toward that image as he kisses it (40).

The two pictures used on stage, the newspaper photo inserted into the rehearsal and the drawing of La Chata on the mirror from the frame play, reproduce the expected dichotomy of femininity in Latin American culture that pertains to both life and the theater. The photo of Carolina, capturing her romantic escapade, exposes the wanton woman, the temptress who flaunts her sexuality. The image of La Chata drawn on the mirror, suggests the long-suffering woman, the madonna, who sacrifices herself for the love of others. Erminy's use of them in both plays reinforces Carolina's claim to her own version of womanhood that is neither constrained to flat models of representation nor to the existing either-or options.

Erminy's metatheatrical structure not only critiques society's patriarchal values, it also takes aim at the theater that perpetuates those same values in plays. The play-within-the-play, that is directed by Miguel Angel, performs the common and accepted theatrical image of wives agonizing over their unfair treatment in marriage. Rather than focusing on the inequality of the marriage contract, the play-within-the-play overemphasizes the inevitable suffering of wives. Erminy's frame play, in contrast, counters that traditional portrait with a more combative feminine response. Whereas Carolina might accept the role of portraying the dependent, needy wife on stage, she is not willing to live that role offstage. In both words and deeds, Carolina not only adopts a defiant stance in which she claims equal opportunity, but she also backs it up with her own self-protective and angry actions against Miguel Angel. In her efforts to protect her own space and values, Carolina assumes another characteristic of masculine behavior, aggressive action. Thus, her role-reversal not only declares sexual equality, but it also backs it up with self-defensive action. Unlike her character La Chata, Carolina's behavior undermines culture's assumptions of romantic love that socialize women into dependent and defenseless roles in their relationships with men.

Both plays use the mimetic space on stage and its unexpected image of a strong female to counter the traditional portrait of strong males and accommodating females that are respresented in diegetic space (and the world outside the theater) in *Casa llena* and in the play-within-a-play in *Whisky & Cocaína*. In these battles between the sexes, the women win dangerous confrontations with men. The victory of the female protagonist enacts a role-reversal that contradicts the world imagined in diegetic space where women do not own their space or their sense of self and therefore feel obliged to give in to men. By limiting the focus to just one couple, each play highlights not only the resourcefulness and power of women, but also the intensity and magnitude of the threat that their role-reversal poses to traditional masculine power.

It could be claimed that without the influence of drugs, the action in *Whisky & Cocaína* might not have reached its dramatic and destructive end. That is, that the aggressive and vengeful actions of the couple are abnormal and cannot serve as meaningful commentary on Latin American life. But *Casa llena* suggests otherwise since its characters follow a similar path but without the assistance of drugs. Myrna S. Gann has argued that Sara's victory is still subject to the control of the greater *machista* society that governs feminine space and therefore that neither she nor her space are safe (1998, 235–36). Certainly both Martín and Miguel Angel operate as if they were the owners of both the women and their spaces. Yet, the details of decoration and the types of properties in the apartments both emphasize the unique presence of the women there. I would argue that it is the very identification between the female protagonists, their apartments, and their independence that inspires them to defend themselves so aggressively. The imposition of male presence and male dominance defiles the space owned by and identified with the protagonists of *Casa llena* and *Whisky & Cocaína*. Such an invasion attempts to impose masculine order on a feminine space that has declared itself free from such dominance, just as its occupants have demonstrated their liberty to act as they please. The only possible response, other than abandoning the space, consists of opposing the occupation and when given no other option, forcing the men out in order to cleanse the tiny space so it can be made habitable to its owner again. *Casa llena* and *Whisky & Cocaína* demonstrate not only why women must defend themselves and their spaces, but also that they can empower themselves to act for their own safety.

Estela Leñero and Thais Erminy propose that in spite of longstanding models of male dominance and violence against women, a female response to that behavior can be constructed as strong, selfprotective and openly challenging of masculine privilege. Such a stance requires that women cast off double standards or guilt and confront men about their claims to different and separate rules. Such a response is based both on necessity and choice so that while women reclaim their space and their safety within their homes they also reaffirm their feminine selves. These two plays provide new options for women to consider when responding to masculine possessiveness.

In the final section of this chapter, *Roda cor de roda*, and *Uno/ El bigote*, take as their starting point the same situation of betrayal that was under rehearsal in Erminy's *Whisky & Cocaína*. Both plays begin with the same scene of a wife waiting for the return of her husband after his night out with another woman. However, following this rather traditional theatrical set up of a romantic triangle, both plays take unexpected turns. In displays of cross-dressing, androgyny, bisexuality, and homosexuality, these plays by Leilah Assunção and Sabina Berman exploit the theatrical tradition in which "miraculous transformations and shape-shifting take place," according to Laurence Senelick ("The Illusions" 1996, 15). More than any of the plays studied so far, these two utilize the theater's magic to suspend conventions, break taboos, and display otherwise impermissible behavior (Senelick). In their inversions, both plays upset the social conventions and civil laws that govern proper behavior in marriage by proposing the radical ideas of sexual equality and sexual liberation as replacements for the hierarchy and double standard of patriarchal unions. I will argue that both plays challenge patriarchal marriage by playing with the traditional norms of sex roles and gender identity within and beyond the home.

Leilah Assunção's *Roda cor de roda* [The circle game] was first performed in Rio de Janeiro with the title *Amanhã, Amélia, de manhã* [Tomorrow Amelia, in the morning] in 1973.[15] After rewriting the play and battling with censors over its content for two years, Assunção brought it to the São Paulo stage in 1975 where it ran for a year. It won awards for the dramatist, the director, and the actress who played Amélia, and later was published in the trilogy of Assunção's plays *Da fala ao grito* [From speaking to shouting] (1977). An important year for women, 1975 is remembered as the International Year of the Woman in honor of the decree passed by the United Nations. Assunção's play participated in the international conversations about improving the status of women that were generated by the egalitarian message advanced in the UN decree. In doing so the play openly contradicted the repressive Brazilian military dictatorship that promoted traditional patriarchal family values.

Roda cor de roda's language and its unexpected role-reversals make fun of the sexual double standard, the Brazilian Civil Code governing marriage, the stereotypical and suffocating nature of gender roles, and the traditional sanctity of the home and the family. According to Elza Cunha de Vincenzo, Assunção's play created an uproar for its carnivalesque inversions and its attack on the institution of the family and its most sacred values (1992, 107). Almost ten years after its performance, *Roda cor de roda* was acknowledged as one of the major contributors to the efforts to produce the 1984 "Novo Estatuto Civil da Mulher" [New Civil Statute for Women] (108). Vincenzo's observation about the play, that it is probably one of the most shocking comedies ever written in Brazil, remains true even from the distance of more than a quarter of a century.

In *Roda cor de roda*, the saintly housewife Amélia rebels against her cheating husband Orlando by initiating a series of role-reversals between the couple and his mistress Marieta in which each dresses up and/or cross-dresses, exaggerating parodies of the other.[16] Without ever moving from her home, Amélia finds a new career and a new power by exchanging roles with her husband's mistress and with her husband in the five movements of the one-act play. In the first movement she becomes a professional prostitute and bans her husband from the home.

In the second movement, Orlando returns to his home where Amélia, now known as Batalha, demands payment for sex and then, after he repents his wayward ways, takes him back as her wife. Meanwhile in the love nest, Marieta the mistress now plays wife to Orlando, who rarely comes home now that he is obligated to serve Amélia as her wife. In the third movement, Marieta declares her love for Amélia and moves in with her to take over the wifely duties Orlando abandoned when he was taken to the insane asylum. In the fourth movement, Amélia accepts the rehabilitated Orlando as a lover while keeping Marieta as her wife. In the fifth movement, Amélia and Orlando propose that Marieta serve them both as husband and wife while they will become her lovers, a suggestion that she rejects. She claims the right to take her turn as the boss in order to direct the role-reversals for her benefit. The fifth movement ends with Marieta encircling her captives with yarn as they turn around and around in circles, an appropriate final image for the play's treatment of role-reversal as little more than a recycling or exchanging of three existing roles.

Sabina Berman's *Uno/El bigote* [#1/The mustache], published just a few years after *Roda cor de roda*, offers a revised image from the stage that suggests an alternative to Assunção's closed circle. Rather than dressing up to accentuate gender difference, the sophisticated androgynous couple of Berman's play dresses down to minimize their gender identification. Instead of reversing roles to explore new identities, Berman's characters appear to annul gender difference in their physical appearance except for one distinguishing feature, a mustache. The talk about the mustache and its movement between the two individuals contributes a carnivalesque atmosphere to Berman's play, albeit on a smaller scale, that echoes the feel of the Brazilian play. *Uno/El bigote* belongs to a collection of three one-act plays originally called *El jardín de las delicias* [The garden of delights] (c 1977), but later retitled *El suplicio del placer: tres obras de un acto sobre un tema* [The agony of ecstasy: three works in one-act about the same theme] (1984–87). Of the three plays in Berman's collection, the first one has received the most critical attention for its intriguing use of a moveable mustache.[17] *El suplicio del placer* was first performed in Mexico City in 1986 and again in 1991 and 1992. It has also been staged in the United States and has been translated into English.

In both their behavior and their appearance, the two characters in Berman's short one-act piece, referred to simply as He and She, evoke an image of sexual neutrality and sophistication. Described as "thin, beautiful and elegant," Él (He) and Ella (She) not only look alike in their hair cuts and features, but they also dress alike in white silk pants and shirts (*Uno/El bigote* 1994, 161). In contrast to Amélia, who rages against her husband's infidelity, Ella calmly reads the newspaper and drinks her morning tea as her partner walks into their hotel room after staying out all night. Her actions appear to demonstrate that his encounters with other women are of less concern to her than the morning headlines. Later, she relishes helping Él remember his night out by both telling and enacting his moves of seduction. During their conversation, the characters explain their unusual behavior to be the result of *nuestro pacto* (our agreement), that is, their arrangement on sexual freedom and the way each observes it. The enabler for this agreement is a mustache that they share. The mustache is both a theatrical property and a signifier of masculinity, as Amalia Gladhart (2000, 135) and Kati Röttger (1999, 117) have argued. Its magical properties empower the wearer with virility that can both attract women and repel men. When Él wears it, he becomes powerful and irresistible to other women. When Ella wears it, she becomes irresistible to other women as well as protected from aggressive men whose advances she wishes to rebuff.

The neutrality of their appearance and the affirmation of their agreement on *amor libre* (free love) suggest that Él and Ella are neither encumbered by the emotions of jealousy and possessiveness nor the promises of fidelity that characterize traditional male-female relations in *Roda cor de roda*. Rather, this couple has attained the freedom to engage in extramarital affairs without remorse and at the same time maintain each other's affection. In fact, both their androgyny, which Laurence Senelick calls "the fusion of genders" (*Changing* 2000, 2), and their dialogue reinforce the sense that they are unique and superior to others. Thus, the characters in *Uno/El bigote* suggest an alternative to the heterosexual and patriarchal constraints of male-female relations. They are able to put on or take off gender according to their own desires while circulating in a glamorous world of hotels and nightclubs, far removed from the mundane life of married people at home. However, as the short play unfolds, the public version of their neutrality comes into conflict with the private reality of the couple. Instead of demonstrating the advantages of their approach to minimizing gender, the couple's behavior and dialogue mirror those of traditional unions, which in turn undermines their agreement on equality.

The problems in their relationship can be seen best by analyzing the function of the mustache that they share. In public the mustache endows the wearer with virility and the power to either attract women or repel men. The sexual orientation of the character moves from neutral to heterosexual, as Röttger claims, or more specifically from neutral to masculine (1999, 118). But the other partner loses by becoming vulnerable or more feminine and therefore unable to exert any power to protect him/herself or to make advances toward others. Thus, the mustache is a scarce resource and its placement favors its wearer and disadvantages the other. At first Ella appears to be the one who is favored as owner, and it is she who lends the mustache to her partner so he can conquer the *morena* (dark-skinned woman). With the help of the mustache, Él pumps up his masculinity to play the traditional role of a Don Juan with success. By contrast, Ella dons the mustache in order to increase her ability to perform the traditional feminine role of resisting seduction. That feminine social role, however, is disguised behind a masculine façade marked by the mustache. Él also lays partial claim to the mustache when he refers to it as "our" mustache, because it makes both of them irresistible to women. Therefore, in public the couple exerts a confusing and somewhat deviant power over their hapless, but beautiful victims, with the help of the mustache that makes them into sexual magnets that either pull or repel their prey. However, being androgynous in a heterosexual world is not as rewarding as it first appears. The characters must adopt a sex in order to circulate in a world defined by difference, and only one of them can assume that sex at a time. Second, while the powers of the mustache are truly phenomenal, they reduce the game of seduction to one of surrender, since none of their victims can resist. At best, Él and Ella come off as little more than predatory consumers and voyeurs. The real limitations of their unusual life are exposed in the confidences they exchange in their base of operations, a hotel room.

In the private space of their hotel suite, Él, described as *Varón afeminado* (effeminate man), and Ella as, *Mujer masculinoide* (masculine woman) [161], appear to have fused the extremes of gender identity. Él's personality echoes that of Amélia in the opening scene of *Roda cor de roda*—dependent, needy, emotional, and apologetic. The insecurity he shows contrasts sharply with the actions that Ella describes as she tells of his assertiveness the night before. Meanwhile, Ella demonstrates a cool, confident self-assurance commonly attributed to men. She defends her choice to use the mustache to protect herself from aggressors by declaring that hers is the liberated and morally superior version of expressing sexuality. In the hotel room, she is the dominant person who controls her own desires and his as well.

However, Ella is not a modern example of sexual liberation, but rather a traditional model of frigidity dependent on an artificial stimulant to perform. Her strength resides in her command of herself and in her positioning of abstinence as being beyond all need. However, as Amalia Gladhart aptly notes: "Él recognizes action as the only proof—even the only existence—of that freedom" (2000, 138). Él practices his liberation by using the mustache to seduce beautiful young girls, but his ability to perform successfully in that role comes into doubt. As he relishes in recounting the beauty of the young *morena* he took to bed, he also confesses his impotence. For this couple, then, the mustache helps exude animal magnetism, but it doesn't improve their equality in gaining sexual gratification outside their relationship, or within it, for that matter. It could be said they are more democratic in their choices of lovers, since they both admit to desiring both men and women as lovers. Gladhart rightly concludes that "they can blur their gender because of privilege, not because of an inherent instability in the notion of gender" (2000, 139). While on the surface this couple challenges society's need to recognize sexual difference, and in their actions they seem to both exchange and reaffirm traditional gender roles, they are still caught within the social construction of gender binaries. The self-importance that Berman attributes to the characters in her introductory portrait, invites the audience to look for cracks in their façade of sameness and satisfaction. Their version of normality looks like an innovation, but it is more shocking in form than in content.

Leilah Assunção's characters present a bawdier version of gender revolt, but its consequences are much the same—more superficial than real. *Roda cor de roda* shocks the audience with exaggerated costuming and physical movement, and through inversions of gender-marked language. The play employs linguistic puns, jokes, clichés, and repeating gag lines to ridicule traditional conceptions of sex roles and responsibilities in marriage. The characters utter every possible negative term used to demean women for their lack of morality or honor; first in reference to Marieta as the other woman, but also with regard to Amélia as a professional prostitute and to Orlando as wife. In

Assunção's play, these weighty terms lose their ability to defame when each character takes pride in their meaning rather than recoiling from them. For example, Amélia, the wife turned prostitute, brags about the number of clients she has served and the extent of her sexual skills in sharp contrast to the monogamy and sexual frigidity she demonstrated as wife. Orlando, the husband turned wife to Amélia, is absorbed with his physical appearance and his countless efforts to keep his mate interested in him, in contrast to his role as husband when he expected these feminine wiles to be used to benefit him.

In the rotation of roles, changing the gender of the individual requires changing not only the gender of the adjectives used to describe that individual, but oftentimes the entire vocabulary. Thus, Orlando as wife refers to himself as *matrono bem gordo*, and *rameiro*, *vagabundo* and *vulgar*, terms commonly used to criticize women for being overweight and complacent in their marriages, or for having lost their respected marital status and thus becoming targets for sexual advances (236–37). Amélia, as the working person, assumes the vocabulary commonly used by businessmen when she complains about the traffic and the pollution, the demands and status of her clients, and her physical exhaustion and stress from the hectic pace of life.

The play also repeats popular expressions used to indoctrinate men and women, civil laws that govern marriage, and humorous gag lines about affairs. For example, Amélia insults Marieta calling her a

> "caixa registradora que tilinta o dia inteiro tirando o pão da boca dos meus queridos filhinhos" [a cash register that rings all day stealing the bread from my beloved children] (191).

This insult cycles through the play and comes out of the mouths of Orlando and Marieta as each adopts the role of wife and condemns the role of the mistress. In these ways, the script is a replay of society's values regarding the traditional role behavior for husbands and wives, and even the vocabulary of affairs. The terms in the proverbs and laws that previously seemed normal and natural suddenly betray their prejudices and masculinist values when spoken by other characters. That is to say that as the words move from one gender to another they begin to sound strange, ridiculous, and finally unfair. Their power can be questioned, laughed at, and deflated of its traditional hold over women and men. Senelick's observation with regard to the theatrical performance of gender applies to *Roda cor de roda*—"if the stage is a mirror, it is a funhouse mirror, magnifying, distorting, and ultimately sending out an image in which the shock of recognition is promoted by an alienation effect" (*Changing*, 7).

The inversions and manipulations of language are reinforced by the cross-dressing and parodying of sex roles as the characters assume each others' postures and personae. In contrast to the societal acceptance of the dichotomy of the sexes, the script and photographs of the performances demonstrate the ease with which the actors/characters change costumes and adopt behaviors considered both unnatural and abnormal. Thus, they perform as transvestites putting on the stereotypical behavior of either aggressive breadwinner, passive wife, or sexy mistress. Equally unexpected are the direct displays or indirect references to homosexuality in *Roda cor de roda*. For example, Marieta, as the wife, declares her love for Amélia, as the husband, in front of Orlando, as the lover, who then mutters in bewilderment one of the play's best lines

"Minha própria mulher está declarando amor para minha própria mulher" [My own wife is declaring love to my own wife] (247).

The humor of the scene derives not only from the sudden revelation that the women prefer each other, but also from the position of dominance exerted by Orlando. He claims both women as his own with the term *minha própria mulher* while at the same time acknowledging that he has lost both of them to each other. Later, the play also suggests that Orlando engaged in homosexual relations while in a mental asylum, although this type of behavior is not openly portrayed on stage.

In *Roda cor de roda*, the characters adopt new roles with conviction, because to them it is freedom, a release from the limitations of their earlier situation. The play sets up a pattern in which first Amélia rebels, declaring her sexual freedom, then Orlando explodes and tries, but fails to return the characters to their original roles, and finally Marieta demands her turn as she calls for a utopia that goes beyond merely exchanging places. As each character assumes a new role, the others move to occupy the remaining roles. But the number of roles is limited, and the manner in which each one must be played is also seemingly predetermined, and therefore resistant to any improvisation. When each of the characters play the housewife role, for example, they suggest to the husband the necessity of increasing the family income by allowing the wife to work outside the home. But none of the husbands will permit such a change and each gives the same excuse—the home is a sacred place where wives and children are protected from the cold, cruel world. (Similar words were used by the husband Esteban in *El vuelo de la grulla*.)

The use of mimetic and diegetic space in these two plays attempts to follow the traditional division between the sacred home represented on stage and the immoral love nest referred to only in diegetic space. However, those divisions quickly break down accompanying and reinforcing the surprising reversals and exchanges that the characters undergo. The mimetic space of *Roda cor de roda* opens with all eyes focused on a sitting room of a middle-class home, its iconic religious and modern decorations, and a wife. This hallowed space of the home represents the honor of the family and it serves to protect wife and children from the dangers of the outside. Yet, within the first movement of the play, the safety of that space is violated by the appearance of the mistress, whose voice is heard from offstage. First, the mistress enters mimetic space and confronts the wife, then when the wife rejects her domestic duties for the world of prostitution, the space of the home becomes a brothel (where the kitchen and domestic appliances are used to service customers), and the brothel becomes a home (where Marieta plays mom to the three unseen children). In a further confusion of the legitimate and illegitmate worlds, both the former home now brothel and the love nest now home are represented on stage side by side. In addition, all three characters in both "homes" speak on the phone to each other, sharing confidences and reactions to the ever-changing events. Thus, these two worlds are connected and in relationship to each other.

Placing both "homes" in mimetic space allows the audience to perceive the advantages husbands maintain with their easy access to the women in both spaces, but they also confuse that traditional separation by placing the women in each others' roles which in turn changes the character of the spaces they occupy. Saintly or sullied spaces are not characterized by their furnishings alone, but by the roles played by the individuals inside. After Orlando returns to Amélia, but in his new role as wife, the brothel turns back into a home again since a "wife" cannot live in immoral space. At this point there are two versions of the home in mimetic space, and each offers some aspect of sacred family life. The mimetic space of the home(s), then, serves to question the notion of separate scenarios defined by the honor or lack of it of the women who occupy it. Finally the two "homes" collapse into one in the closing moments of the play when all three characters are together again. In the fifth movement, Orlando and Amélia suggest that their roles as lovers to Marieta, who will be both husband and wife, provide a new option for family life in a home that appears to shelter these new relations. However, Marieta is prophetic in her demand for a better world beyond the home of mimetic space. For her the real possibilities for marriage and male-female relations lie beyond the stage, somewhere in the utopia of diegetic space.

Such a manipulation of the home in mimetic space makes a strong critique of the dichotomies of male versus female, private versus public, moral versus immoral that for so long have defined patriarchal marriage and separated women into categories defined by their legitimate or illegitimate sexual relationship to men. It is interesting to note that few references in *Roda Cor de Roda* refer to diegetic space, but when they do they are more socially unacceptable or unattainable than the shocking behaviors presented onstage. For example, Marieta's ideas about utopia were partially formed by a childhood sweetheart who, we learn later, becomes a homosexual lover to Orlando in the insane asylum.

In contrast, the mimetic space of two chairs and a table with a tea service in *Uno/El bigote* is unremarkable except it is not a home. The stage directions call it a "suite," and when Él mentions that he rented another suite for his evening adventure, we must conclude that the couple lives in a hotel or at least frequents them on a regular basis. In both plays hotel rooms are identified as immoral spaces destined for illicit sexual encounters. At first, Amélia operates her prostitution business out of the home by transforming it into a brothel. But once Orlando becomes her wife and not her customer, he must occupy an honest home and she moves her business to hotels. The same association between sex and a hotel is communicated in the opening scene with Él and Ella. They do not seem to have any other "home" that exists in opposition to their hotel suite and its connection with the forbidden. They live in a place known for rendezvous, which reflects their main activity, seduction of each other and others. Equally important to *Uno/El bigote*, however, is the fact that the hotel room contains no particular characteristics, no unique features that identify its inhabitants. There are numerous hotel rooms in a building, and all of them look much the same. Hotel rooms erase the individuality of ownership in order to serve all potential inhabitants equally well. In a similar fashion, the clothes and haircuts of Él and Ella erase their association with one gender or the other so the couple can move through a gender-marked society incognito.

The hotel room and its guests, with their pleasing but neutral appearances, exist in contrast to the diegetic space of *Uno/El bigote* that is created by her words as she tells of his conquest the night before. It is also the world both of them create as they discuss where and how they act when not together in their hotel rooms. This diegetic world beyond their hotel room is the monogamous, conventional world of nightclubs and evenings out on the town that is unable to resist them sexually. In terms of mimetic versus diegetic space, the world beyond them is much more varied and interesting than their mimetic world inside the hotel room. Amalia Gladhart has observed that "A certain level of economic privilege and the comforts it affords make possible these games of gender ambiguity" (2000, 139). In fact, the couple seems almost bored by the world they occupy and consider their games of sexual hide and seek a necessity to keep their relationship going. Gladhart points out that Él's knowledge of wines and music reflect his experience in elegant hotels, and that the couple adopts an attitude of superiority over the rest of the world and their foolish conventions (139). That is to say, they circulate in a social milieu of the sophisticated elite, disconnected from the traditional values or mores that impinge on the characters in *Roda Cor de Roda* and driven more by ennui than anything else. Gladhart mentions that "The self-consciousness of their language contributes to a sense of repetition, as if the scene, or one very like it, has been played out many times before" (139).

Although the costuming and the game of wearing the mustache call attention to the difference between social role and gender identity, the couple in *Uno/El bigote* nevertheless remains tied to conventions of traditional male-female behavior. For example, even though Ella appears not to care about her partner's behavior, her response to his morning after hangover and disorientation are as cold as the tea she offers him. Meanwhile, he is defensive and apologetic for his traditional masculine behavior while she is protective of her traditional feminine approach to not engage in sexual freedom in the same way as he does. She treats him like a little boy, and he responds to her as if she were a castrating mother. Where is the sexual freedom or even equality in their relationship if he feels guilty and she feels superior? In fact, this couple ultimately resembles the stereotypical saintly wife and the philandering husband of *Roda cor de roda*. The problem of sexual and social repression of women in *Roda* is not really resolved in *Uno/El bigote*, because Ella negates her desire by stating that she does not need sexual conquest. When Él tries a second time to encourage Ella to have affairs as he does, or as he calls it "to share herself and enact her own sexual democracy," she again refuses by countering that she has a life on an abstract level that does not require such behavior. Unlike Amélia, who rebels in order to gain sexual expression, Ella claims to transcend it, a stereotypical wifely response.

Clearly, *Roda cor de roda* contains a critique of the sexual and social repression of housewives—Amélia was the first of the three characters to protest her suffocating condition and in turn, all the others confess that being a housewife was the worst role they had to play. But the comedy also makes fun of the narrowness of the husband's role, since it too must be performed in a specific way. The only liberating role is that of lover—at least as constructed in Assunção's game—because it does not require work but only the fulfillment of sexual fantasies and pleasures. However, even this role is questioned by Marieta who describes herself as the *válvula de escape* (escape valve) for both husband and wife. Thus, Assunção's play unveils the paradigms of roles assigned by patriarchy and the binary of gender that only accepts one place for each member of the relationship and one set of responsibilities for each. The play suggests that within patriarchal marriage as constructed in Latin American society, the complementary roles of men and women and the traditional sexual conventions of passive wife and aggressive husband require a third necessary role, that of the mistress. The play demonstrates the social and religious lessons that instruct wives not to be sexual beings to their husbands or for themselves. Instead, it shows how they are trapped within the confines of "honor" (read frigidity) and "service" (read reproductive and physical labor).[18] Therefore, sexual relations beyond those for reproduction are available only to men and must be conducted outside the household with mistresses and prostitutes.

At first glance, it appears that Berman's play represents a solution to the problems raised by Assunção. Yet on further analysis, it is possible to discern that both dramatists present critiques of the problem of confinement and sexual repression in married life. Amélia temporarily reclaims and redefines her home as a place for sexual pleasure when she transforms it into a brothel. However, that change is short-lived and soon the characters and the roles they must play have made the brothel into a home again, and the love nest into an escape. Ella and Él abandon the home completely in order to practice their sexual freedom to have affairs with others, but that freedom is not equally exercised. In addition, the couple seems to be stuck in a repeating scenario of conquests and rebuffs that reproduce traditional sexual relations rather than exceed them. Their physical similarity does not guarantee sexual equality, instead it serves as a strategic weapon against others.

How do these two plays contribute to this chapter's discussion of traditional patriarchal marriage, gender roles, and the confinement of the home? First, they create outrageous situations in which it is possible to extend the discussion of marriage and sexuality beyond the traditional frames allowed in theatrical realism. Comedy permits exaggeration, parody, reversals, and unacceptable behavior to be laughed at, enjoyed, and questioned in a less threatening way. It permits the audience to see the impossible and consider why society deems it impossible. The plays also demonstrate that the so-called complementary roles in marriage do not hold true for sexual relations. Following up on the theme of inequality in sexual relations portrayed in *Casa llena* and *Whisky & Cocaína*, these two plays take as their theme the idea or ideal of sexual equality in male-female relations. While they do expose the limitations of the gender roles already in existence, they also expose the connectedness and interdependence of the sexes in those roles. That is to say that the plays show the existing system is closed and cannot be altered by only changing one part of the story. *Roda cor de roda* makes this point as it cycles through the three available roles for its characters. It expands the critique of traditional patriarchal marriage by pointing out that the actual number of participants in that marriage is three not two, and that extramarital lovers participate in the maintenance of patriarchal unions. *Uno/El bigote* tries to annul sexual difference, making it a mere affectation that can be moved from one individual to another and "invoked according to need," as Gladhart has noted (2000, 136). Clearly this is as humorous an idea as honorable wives opening a brothel, and it challenges the entrenched notions of marriage. Yet the mechanisms of sexual conquest are neither altered nor are the emotional reactions to its success or failure. Even though Él and Ella appear to congratulate themselves on the advantages of their superior lifestyle that yields them a seemingly limitless supply of lovers, the play ends with a reconciliation and a sense of simple contentment with each other. Adam Versényi argues that in the closing moments of the play the characters no longer exist as individuals but have effected a symbiosis and become one (2003, xiii). If that is the case, then their efforts at gender democracy produce gender erasure, an imaginative but somehow less than optimum solution to the inequalities of patriarchal matrimony.

The title of this chapter, reclaiming the home, points to the need of the women protagonists to reclaim the domestic space of the home as they redefine their roles within patriarchal relationships. These two plays expand the traditional space of wives to encompass an alternate space, the immoral hotel or love nest. Both plays dramatize the function of that space as a participant in the tightly constructed scenario of gender relations that relies on a separate space for sexual expression, since the home does not cultivate it. Whereas the couples of Assunção and Berman's plays believe they can escape the values of the home when they enter this sexually charged space, they have, in fact, only reaffirmed those values.

Roda cor de roda and *Uno/El bigote* critique gender roles by making their stability into a game of reversals and exchanges, but neither play deconstructs gender roles nor offers meaningful alternatives to the suffocating ways in which those roles limit individual expression. Both plays also expand the notion of the sacred, private space of the home versus the libidinous, public space of the hotel or brothel in order to display the interconnectedness of this social division. Both plays present strong protagonists who dare to challenge, if not alter, the intractable system of patriarchal marriage. With the assistance of outrageous costuming and behavior, these female protagonists confirm Judith Butler's often repeated contention that gender is a performance, an act taught within the confines of particular cultural values and space (1990, 276–77). Assunção and Berman expand on Ibsen's portrait of the home and patriarchal marriage

by revealing both the constructedness of gender roles and its participation in the division of social space.

Reclaiming the home is just the first step in a complicated process of remaking gender roles and relationships between men and
women in marriage in Latin America. Because the home is where the
values of marriage and the performances of gender are first taught, it
figures as the most important place to stage a critique. The eight plays
presented in this chapter assume the responsibility of addressing the
meaning of the home as both a physical place and a symbol for
patriarchal marriage. In the use of mimetic and diegetic space, the
plays call attention to two sets of ideals or alternatives. Diegetic space
often refers to the traditional notions of relations and divisions, those
that characterize past relationships and that continue to hold sway in
society at the expense of the protagonists. Mimetic space, on the
other hand, connects the protagonists to their present situation and
its potential to offer an alternative, a better distribution of power,
sexual satisfaction, or independence.

The critiques of patriarchal marriage and romance made by these
eight plays suggest several possible challenges to the status quo, but
few models for how to remake it. Four of the plays, *El vuelo de la grulla*,
À prova de fogo, *Uno/El bigote*, and *Roda cor de roda* analyze the existing rules governing male-female relations and point out their inequities. The plays expose and parody what has previously been labeled
the "natural" or "traditional" way of life. While the female protagonists contest the existing rules and expectations of their partners,
boyfriends, and spouses, none of them manage to redefine the rules of
the home.[19] As a result, the plays function by raising awareness of the
conditions in the home, but they do not provide models for reclaiming it. Two of the plays, *Casa llena* and *Whisky & Cocaína* show protagonists engaged in aggressive defenses of their homes and of feminine
equality with men, including their rights to sexual expression and
independence. However, the suggestion of domestic abuse by both
men and women in these two plays as a result of the female protagonists' strong actions is problematic. While it is courageous to respond
in defiance to invasive action, such action seems to serve best as a
response to an emergency and not as a strategy for improving male-
female relations. Finally, two plays actually make proposals, albeit
utopian ones, to end the battle between the sexes. *Boca molhada de
paixão calada* proposes new egalitarian guidelines that model methods

for claiming an equal place in male-female relationships and an equal space in which to live life. *Cariño malo* proposes a reconfiguration of the feminine self before any engagement with men. The play counters the cultural message that women must find a man to love with a new message—find and love the female inside first. Rather than emphasize the home as a contested space for women, Inés Margarita Stranger's play points to feminine identity as the key place in which to begin contesting culture's views of romance and marriage. In its call for reshaping the self, *Cariño malo* ties us to the subject of the next chapter, mother-daugther relations, since it is within their relationships with mothers that daughters first learn the rules of the feminine self that will govern their interactions with men.

CHAPTER 2

Questioning Motherhood

"We should take care to remember that what happens to mothers happens to us all."

— Daly and Reddy, *Narrating Mothers*

"The loss of the daughter to the mother, the mother to the daughter, is the essential female tragedy."

— Adrienne Rich, *Of Woman Born*

The mother-daughter bond is the first and most powerful identification between females. According to Liesbeth Woertman, clinicians theorize that every contact between women is influenced by mother symbolism and by experiences in the primary mother-daughter relationship (1993, 57). Mothers provide both the care and the image of femaleness to their young daughters who, in turn, reflect it back to their mothers as they grow up. Mother-daughter relationships can be found at the core of women's writing, especially short stories, autobiographies, and biographies (Nice 1992, 1). Mothers and daughters also have been the focus of extensive psychological attention in the United States since the 1970s as a result of the publication of such feminist works as Adrienne Rich's *Of Woman Born* (1976), Dorothy Dinnerstein's *The Mermaid and the Minotaur* (1976), and Nancy Chodorow's *The Reproduction of Mothering* (1978).

Latin American society parallels that of most patriarchal societies which grant mothers greater reverence than all other adult women. Héctor Bonaparte confirms this view with these words heard from an interviewee: "Al padre se lo escuchaba y a la madre se la respetaba" [You had to listen to your father and respect your mother] (60). Halldis Leira and Madelien Krips have noted that motherhood gives the married woman cultural dignity and respect (1993, 91). Mothers occupy a hallowed place in Latin American society where they are exalted for their role as the center of home life. The task of child-rearing, which has been glorified as women's greatest contribution to society, still is accepted as the most noble occupation for women, as Sara Castro-Klarén confirms: "Even the discourse of recent feminists continues to posit women primordially as the seat of biological and cultural reproduction within the domestic sphere" (1992, 10). As a testimony to their importance, images of great mothers from folklore and Catholicism are displayed in homes, stores, churches, and shrines, and the stories of their lives are told again and again. Yet in spite of the status of mothers and the concomitant importance of the mother-daughter bond, the relationship between mothers and daughters is one of the least explored areas of familial life in Latin America from either on or offstage.

In this chapter, I will argue that women dramatists in Latin America challenge the glorification of motherhood by emphasizing conflicts between mothers and daughters. These conflicts reveal that the cult of motherhood is a form of payment to mothers from the patriarchal family and society who in turn use them to raise their daughters to accept their traditional subordinate roles. The plays also show that motherhood itself limits the subjectivity of women by providing very narrow definitions of acceptable feminine behavior. Lastly, these plays offer the possibility that mother-daughter relations can be reconfigured in adulthood through engagement and negotiation in order to move both women toward a more productive, egalitarian, and reciprocal relationship.

The eight plays studied in this chapter are divided into two groups according to the type of relationship and ages of the mothers and daughters. The first section studies four plays *Marcadas pela culpa* (Brazil, 1989) by Isis Baião; *Madre nuestra que estás en la tierra* (Costa Rica, 1989) by Ana Istarú; *En un desván olvidado* (Venezuela, 1991) by Thais Erminy; and *De compras* (Mexico, 1995) by Rebecca Bowman. In these plays, mothers seem hardened by life's circumstances and they devise all forms of manipulation to encourage their young daughters to behave. The second set of four plays, *La partida* (Mexico, 1989) by Pilar Campesino; *Querida mamãe* (Brazil, 1995) by Maria Adelaide Amaral; *Amantíssima* (Argentina, 1988) by Susana Torres Molina; and *Casa matriz* (Argentina, 1989) by Diana Raznovich, focus on the relationship between an older mother and her adult daughter in which the women revisit and renegotiate their relationship.

My analysis of the plays employs two models from female devel-opmental psychology utilized in clinical and theoretical feminist prac-tice in the United States. In the first section, I work with the patriarchal mother model suggested by Susan Suleiman and others while in the second section I employ the relational model developed by Carol Gilligan and her colleagues. Additional readings from the extensive critical bibliography in psychology and sociology help ground this discussion of motherhood.

The plays in the first section problematize mother-daughter re-lations as difficult and conflictive, because the purpose of the femi-nine relationship is to prepare daughters for a grown woman's life. Instead of supporting and nurturing their daughters, the mothers in these plays badger and manipulate their daughters into conforming to social expectations that the mothers do not question. These relation-ships stage women as the *mal-amada* (poorly loved) in scholar Elódia Xavier's terms because neither mother nor daughter gets the attention she needs (1991, 13). Mothers are not emotionally supported by fa-thers and daughters are not nurtured by mothers. In the second sec-tion, the four plays bring to the stage the negotiations between mother and daughter that can contribute to the formation of an independent self. Rather than presenting daughters as young victims of antagonis-tic mothers, these plays present grown daughters as equals to their mothers. And rather than presenting antagonistic mothers pushing their rebellious daughters to conform, these plays show maturing daugh-ters pushing against their mothers as they attempt to establish them-selves as autonomous individuals. Leaving home to pursue relationships and work opportunities provides the impetus for daughters to attach themselves to something other than their mothers. But, as we will see, relations between mothers and daughters always involve conflict and require ongoing negotiations.

Latin American mothers who leave the safety of the home to enter the theater might be surprised to see their relations with daugh-ters unfolding under the glare of the footlights. These eight Latin American plays make public the fact that women in the home invest emotional energy in each other. Opening up the family's doors to the bedrooms, kitchens, and dining rooms where mothers and daughters confide in each other reveals the complexity of the intimate relation-ships between women that develop within this domestic space. By bringing the subject of mother-daughter relations into the theater, the playwrights acknowledge first, that behind the façade of the tranquil and stable feminine home there are women whose stories can be staged; second, that placing mother and daughter alone on stage draws attention to a relationship common to at least half of the population as daughters, if not as mothers of daughters; third, that staging mother-daughter relations recognizes their significance in the lives of women and the family; and lastly, that the images of mothers and daughters on stage offer an alternative to the traditional story of generational conflict with patriarchal fathers.

The topic of mother-daughter relations has not received extensive scholarly attention in Latin America. A search of *Hispanic American Periodicals Index* (*HAPI*) and *Libros en Venta*, the Spanish-language listing of *Books in Print*, confirms this view. *HAPI* listed twenty titles about motherhood and three about mothers and daughters while *Libros* registered sixty-two titles referring to motherhood. Three of the articles listed in *HAPI* were literary studies, similar to this one, of mothers in works written by women authors. In spite of the greater numbers in *Libros*, only three titles made specific reference to mother-daughter relations. One was a translation of Elizabeth Debold, Marie Wilson, and Idelisse Malave's (1993) *Mother Daughter Revolution: From Betrayal to Power*. A second title, *Entre madres e hijas* [Between mothers and daughters], published in Buenos Aires in 1986 and written by the psychoanalyst Alicia Lombardi, studies the generational conflict the author has seen among her patients and their mothers. The third, also published in Buenos Aires in 1989, *Salirse de madre* [an idiomatic expression meaning to lose self-control], is the creative work of a group of Argentine women writers whose plays, stories, poems, and short commentaries speak about relations between the writers and their mothers. The first two sources will figure in this chapter's arguments, and the third, *Salirse de madre*, contained the first version of Diana Raznovich's play *Casa matriz*, that will be discussed in the final section of this chapter.

Plays about mothers and daughters told from a woman's viewpoint are extremely rare in drama, notes Gayle Austin in her book *Feminist Theories for Dramatic Criticism* (1990, 66). She reasons that the lack is the result of difficulties between the adult female playwright and her mother (67).[1] In Latin America the scarcity of plays might also be attributed to additional factors, such as the protected and enshrined status of mothers. The work of Latinas in the United

States, especially Chicana writer Cherríe Moraga, suggests another possible explanation, that mother-daughter relationships have been overshadowed by cultural values that encourage mothers to show primary allegiance to sons (Jay 1996, 99). Vivien E. Nice indicates that this preference begins with the birth of the first child, a joyful event if a boy but a disappointment if a daughter (1992, 20–21). Thus, mother-son relations, which often encourage the veneration of mothers in gratitude for their preferential treatment, assume greater familial and social importance than mother-daughter relations. In the world of Latin American drama, we can conclude that several layers of social conditioning are at work buffering mothers from any critical scrutiny on stage.

Examining motherhood and the role of mothers as the educators of children and the reproducers of future mothers is a complex and risky task in Latin America. The topic is controversial for both conservative and liberal social forces. Conservative individuals and institutions, such as the Roman Catholic Church, might interpret critique as an effort to dethrone mothers or devalue their important contributions to society. Mothers are key figures in the relationship between the church and the family, shouldering the responsibility for maintaining religious teachings in the home. On the other hand, liberal or feminist forces might wish to obscure any analysis of mothers that implicates them as perpetrators of women's inferior status in society since this would suggest a "blame the victim" mentality. Feminists in Latin America who are familiar with the extensive bibliography on mother-daughter relations in the United States might fear the influence of early studies, such as those by Nancy Chodorow and Adrienne Rich, that adopted an anti-mother perspective, that is, one that blamed all the problems of women on their mothers.[2]

In addition, the topic of mother-daughter relations generates little dramatic potential. The socialization of women, or their "cultural script" encourages them to be invisible and selfless in their service to husbands and children (Willard 1988, 225). In the Western dramatic tradition that values clashes between individual wills, good mothers offer little promise since they are engaged in the giving away of self not in its affirmation. One might wonder, then, if bad mothers might make better subjects. Ann Willard notes that in the field of psychology only bad mothers have been studied because they, at least, have a self to examine (228). If we accept Ann Willard's views that

Western cultural scripts posit only two options for women, the good and selfless mother or the bad and selfish mother, then it becomes easier to see why mothers rarely if ever occupy center stage. Selfless mothers are boring while selfish mothers are bad examples that the public might not accept. Mother-daughter relations are bound by this same cultural script suggesting they have little dramatic appeal either. Daughters are raised to comply with their mothers' wishes and become selfless too, making them as dramatically uninteresting as good mothers. Bad daughters who challenge their mothers with their defiant and sassy attitudes are even less acceptable than bad mothers.

Yet, in spite of the paucity of plays about the mother-daughter relationship, the women dramatists studied in the first section of this chapter delve into the techniques that mothers use to further the cause of patriarchy. Vivien E. Nice describes mothers as serving male interest by passing on the subordinate role from mother to daughter (1992, 12). According to Penelope Dixon: "The patriarchal society in which we live needs women to act as mothers for its survival" (1991, 5). These women playwrights affirm that patriarchy depends on mothers to propagate and legitimize its values. But, since mothering is only an act that mothers perform in accordance with patriarchal rules and that they reproduce in their daughters, then it is an act that can be changed. That is, since it is a social construction rather than an essential female trait, this makes it alterable, although not easily so. These plays not only reveal mothers acting on behalf of patriarchy, but they also suggest different power relationships, different roles, that mothers and daughters might play.

In the second section women dramatists address feminine subjectivity in plays that isolate daughters and mothers on stage giving emphasis to their feminine world. Yet this world resides within the larger context of traditional patriarchal society where women have few opportunities to attain any sense of self, since their most important role is as selfless mother. The plays query how daughters and mothers can become actors in life if culture positions them as domestic servants and handmaidens to patriarchy. The idealization of motherhood rewards mothers for their sacrifices of self but not for their attempts to become their own persons. In these dramatic examples, mothers and daughters who negotiate and unite for one another's benefit come closer to achieving subjectivity than those who argue and separate.

Mother-daughter plays rework the masculinist theatrical conventions that call for action, autonomy, conflict, and resolution. All
the plays I have isolated for study in the present chapter operate on
a small scale within a confining space, feature minimal dramatis
personae, and involve minimal if any overt action. Rather than
explore the political and social issues that have preoccupied Latin
American dramatists for many years, these women dramatists
portray an intimate view of politics from within the home. The
action of the plays exemplifies the restraints placed on feminine
behavior, limiting it to verbal duels, controlled emotions, and very
little physical movement.

None of the plays suggest that either mothers or daughters can
be autonomous within the confines of the traditional familial and
societal structures that privilege men. Mothers are valued for the web
of relationships that they support to hold the family together. But the
real power that keeps mothers connected to the home is exercised in
the privileges and authority of men who reside within the home and
who legislate and enforce the laws beyond it. Even though the stage
features only feminine characters, the dramatists have constructed
their plays in order to demonstrate that women's lives are shaped by
the values of their socialization that educate them to accept the
authority and superiority of men.

In defiance of Latin American social conventions that dictate
that daughters should be the allies and helpers of mothers in the
home rather than their enemies, the majority of these plays present
mother-daughter relations as a battle. In the first section of this chapter, we will see how in this dramatic contest of wills adolescent daughters are positioned as protagonists who attempt to gain a sense of
wholeness against their antagonistic mothers. While it is not uncom-
mon for the closeness of mother and daughter to undergo stress during
adolescence, according to Shelley Phillips (1996, 46), staging mothers
as antagonists not only defies the traditional images of mothers as
nurturers and caregivers whose presence in the home radiates well-
being, but it also suggests that these homes are not the refuges of
harmony that masculinist values glorify. In the second section of this
chapter, in contrast, adult daughters and their mothers display a greater
balance in their relationship so that the roles of protagonist and antagonist are not so clearly divided or easily maintained. In both instances staging the relationship between mothers and daughters as

changing and complex undermines the image of mothers and daughters as constant, essentialized feminine beings.

In these eight plays, women dramatists make public what is hidden behind social taboos that discourage examination of mothers. By manipulating dramatic positions in the plays, the authors show an unwillingness to locate their characters in the same socially sanctioned roles to which they are confined in society and to which they have been assigned in the theater as well. In the same manner, women playwrights resist the temptation to impose a happy or satisfying resolution to the conflict. One play ends tragically, several plays simply suspend the events, suggesting they will resume again, and at least two plays imply movement toward resolution without allowing it to be fully developed. Therefore, of the four classic elements in theater—action, autonomy, conflict, and resolution—women dramatists retain only conflict as the component with greatest relevance for the discussion of mothers and daughters. Conflict, which showcases both the sources and the outcomes of human wills at odds, is the necessary element for playwrights to challenge existing myths about motherhood.

The cult of motherhood has a long history in Latin American society where mothers are glorified and granted power in the domestic sphere while denied true power in either the home or the public sphere (Cypess 1989, 289). The loving respect paid to mothers hides the fact that their power is authorized through men and the Roman Catholic Church. It is a negotiated power that rests on a spark of truth that mothers, in fact, are all powerful when children are totally dependent on them as infants (Debold, Wilson, Malave 1993, 22). Reinforcing the idea of women's importance in the home has required maintaining the notion that women are naturally best suited to raising children and that the domestic sphere is the best environment in which to accomplish this task.

The best and most enduring model of motherhood for girls is the Virgin Mary whose followers are legendary in number and devotion in the predominately Catholic countries of Latin America.[3] As several scholars have noted, the Virgin Mary functions as the myth of the ideal mother, making her a powerful model for all women no matter what their social status (Leira and Krips 1993, 87; and González 1996, 154). The lessons of womanhood taught by the Virgin Mary glorify the spiritual and moral superiority of mothers as well as their sacrifices as nurturers. Bad mothers, such as Mexico's La Malinche and La

Llorona, also provide models from history and folklore that educate by negative example.[4]

The cult of motherhood also has endured because mothers serve and perpetuate patriarchy. Latin American women are socialized to confine their energies and creativity to the domestic tasks of maintaining children and home; thus, their laboring benefits society with future workers at the same time that it supports and nourishes existing workers. Latin American mothers do not challenge the public world outside the home because they are made to believe they are an important shield against its corrupting influences, and a conscience for the family. Reverence in the home can mean that mothers attain a certain level of status within their own domain, which is their payoff, while remaining economically and politically powerless in the public and private worlds of ruling-class men (Sayers 1993, 65). Debold, Wilson, and Malave describe mothers as the middle managers of patriarchy who shoulder enormous responsibility but with no real power even in the domestic sphere (1993, 184). Mothers participate in the maintenance of the status quo by raising their sons to take full advantage of the benefits of their privileged position and their daughters to conform to their secondary role.

In exchange for their elevated status in the home, mothers in Latin American society give preference to husbands and sons, who command the status and power in the home and in society. This means that daughters are not supported adequately because their mothers' nurturing favors the men in the home. In fact, daughters are often asked to play the role of little mothers, providing care and attention to the men in the house, and serving them while going emotionally hungry themselves (Nice 1992, 95). Norma Alarcón describes this situation in the home as "el abandono y la orfandad y el hambre psíquico/emocional de la mujer" [the abandonment, orphanage, and psychological/emotional hunger of women] (238). Daughters are taught to accept this lack of emotional care from mothers because they are convinced that if they defer their needs they will be fulfilled when they become mothers with children of their own (Garner 1991, 83).

Because the ideals of womanhood have been inextricably tied to women's biological role in society as reproducers, the ideals of womanhood and the ideals of motherhood often become conflated. Most women in Latin American society have a single future planned for them, that of marriage and motherhood. As a result, mothers raising daughters are preparing girls for their role as mothers and not as female individuals. For example, Eduardo Pavanetti's book discussed below includes a chapter titled "Madres, formadoras de madres" [Mothers, shapers of mothers]. The idea that mothers are raising future mothers increases the investment made in the task and in society's expectations for how the task is performed. The trap of motherhood, glorified at home and demeaned in public holds mothers to ever escalating standards of altruistic behavior. It is, as Shirley Nelson Garner has pointed out, a masochistic destiny (1991, 76).

The cultural expectations for womanhood are not only limiting, but they also are impossible, as Tey Diana Rebolledo and others have suggested and yet these ideals continue to be promoted and reinforced (1995, 204). A handbook written for mothers by Catholic educator Pavanetti, *La madre educadora en un mundo que cambia* [The mother as educator in a changing world] and published in the International Year of the Woman, 1975, carefully outlines the traditional argument that women are naturally endowed with the perfect talents to raise children. Pavanetti, who describes educating children as *la gran obra* (the great work), develops the following list of expectations for mothers: "un amor realista, una experiencia iluminada, una sabiduría humana, una ciencia muy clara de medios y fines y una voluntad muy firme y perseverante para llegar al fin" [a realistic love, an enlightened experience, a human understanding, a clear science of means and ends, and a firm and persevering will to reach the end] (1975, 22).

Constructing and maintaining motherhood as a privileged and powerful position, albeit circumscribed within the home, furthers the goals of patriarchy in Latin America. But it problematizes motherhood by calling for a complete sacrifice of self. Mothers do their best work, according to Pavanetti, when they give themselves completely to their children and to the task of raising them. "La madre no se pertenece: en ese darse generosamente va madurando su amor oblativo que agiganta su personalidad" [The mother does not belong to herself: in this generous giving to her children she increases her loving gift of self which makes her personality even greater] (24). While on the surface self-sacrifice is promoted as a beneficial model, and certainly the examples of both the Virgin Mary and her crucified son Jesus have been held up as ideals to emulate, the truth about self-sacrifice is that it exacts a high human cost for women. Research conducted by Sue Lanci Villani and Jane E. Ryan in the United States with stay-at-home mothers in the 1970s and again in the 1990s concluded "that motherhood undermines individuality, and that women lacking either knowledge of or commitment to their own wants, needs, and ideals fall quickly into a crisis of self-esteem" (1997, 31).

Yet even considering the high cost to women, motherhood is an institution supported by tradition, family pressure, and societal legitimization. Even when society offers greater opportunities for women, as in the case of Latinas growing up in the United States, the cultural values of the home and the community reinforce the choice for motherhood. Research on attitudes about the homemaker role reported that 83 percent of Latina high school students would not like or enjoy being a homemaker, yet over a third expect that this is the role they will have to assume (qtd. in Debold, Wilson, Malave 1993, 16). Among middle-school Chicano girls in Los Angeles, Ruth Wodak and Muriel Schulz found a surprising 50 percent responded negatively to questions about their desire to marry and have children, even though both girls and boys expressed unequivocal devotion to their mothers. The researchers report that "The role of the mother remains a contradiction in values in the Mexican-American community. Because she is a woman in a male dominated society, the mother role has low value, while the father has social and sexual freedom denied to her. But because the mother is the central figure in the home and because home ties are highly valued, the mother figure is accorded enormous love and gratitude" (1986, 137).[5]

The majority of the playwrights in this chapter were at midlife when they composed their dramas about mothers and daughters in the late 1980s through mid-1990s. In their plays, the characters are mothers who are also at midlife with daughters who are adolescents or adults. Terri Apter's study of midlife women and their relations with their mothers provides insights into why the playwrights might have chosen this particular time of life to write about mother-daughter relations and to create mother characters their own ages. Apter has observed that mature daughters often remain blind to their mother's experiences until they reach midlife. At that point, daughters begin to "open their eyes to their own mothers' feelings." Apter notes that mothers are so important to daughters that even when daughters become mothers themselves, they are unable to apply their own experiences of mothering toward an understanding of their mothers until they reach midlife (1995, 271). In fact, Ramona T. Mercer, Elizabeth

G. Nichols, and Glen Caspers Doyle learned in their study that "women talked more about their own mothers and the mothering that they had received than the mothering they initiated" (1989, 20). Given the very public nature of the theater, Apter's statement that " At forty women begin to note that they no longer care in the same way about what their mothers think" (1995, 279) suggests that these Latin American women playwrights have arrived at a time when staging their insights into mother-daughter relationships are not as risky. Apter discovered that "midlife women want new engagements with mother," and that "Looking back on their childhood, midlife women expressed a new curiosity about what things were like for their mother" (292). Based on Apter's work, we might theorize that these plays represent the opportunity for the dramatists to create and understand their mothers' worlds and by doing so to find new vehicles with which to interact with them.

The eight plays written about mother-daughter relations, dated 1988–1995, stage generational conflicts within the private world of the home, the center of feminine activity. All but two of the plays take place in a realistic domestic setting, and all but one are developed in one act. In most of the plays, the action rises and falls in the conversations exchanged between mothers and daughters. Words serve as the medium that engages mother and daughter in each other and in conflict, or as Graciela Ravetti and Sara Rojo have stated about *Querida mamãe*, "os atos de fala tornam-se performativos" (the acts of speaking become performative) [1996, 46].

The majority of the mothers and daughters dramatized have no male partner. The women are either widowed, abandoned, divorced, or their men are absent during the events of the play. In spite of their physical absence, in six of the eight plays women are dependent on men as the sole supporters of their families and the determining factor in their social status. Thus, the presence of men is constant in the memories, words, and loss that they represent to mothers and daughters. For this reason, while the space and bodies on stage are feminine, the cultural context of male power and value within the family is always present. Speaking about men and thus, keeping them alive on stage, serves as a constant reminder that in Western culture families honor the patriarchal father who gives identity and value to the women in the home, and whose interests are served by the socialization that mothers give to daughters (Nice 1992, 88).

Patriarchal Mothers and Rebellious Daughters

The four plays that make visible the destructive effects mothers can
have on their young children are *Madre nuestra que estás en la tierra*
by Ana Istarú; *Marcadas pela culpa* by Isis Baião; *En un desván olvidado*
by Thais Erminy; and *De compras* by Rebecca Bowman.[6] Three of the
four plays are short, emotional vignettes that illustrate a key moment
in the characters' lives. The fourth play, *Madre nuestra que estás en la
tierra*, adopts the same structure of short, emotional moments, but the
period of time is extended through three acts, representing three different historical points in the women's lives. I will argue that conflict
uncovers the naturalized actions and words mothers use to socialize
girls into women and, at the same time, highlights the voices of
daughters who resist their mothers.

There is nothing lighthearted about the conflict between mothers and daughters in these four plays, which explains a preference for
melodrama or drama, but not comedy. *Marcadas pela culpa* [Marked by
guilt] exaggerates the heavy-handedness of *telenovelas*, or soap operas
in its melodramatic treatment of three generations of women whose
recriminations poison their family life just as the excess salt ruins
their dinner soufflé. *En un desván* [In a forgotten cellar] enacts the
abuse of a daughter by her inaccessible mother that leads to the formation of multiple personalities, including that of her own mother.
De compras [Gone shopping], on the other hand, captures a poignant
moment between mother and daughter immediately preceding a family social obligation while *Madre nuestra que estás en la tierra* [Our
mother who art on earth] portrays three Christmas evenings in a
family of three generations of women whose comfortable life threatens to collapse following the death of the father. All four plays include adolescence as a key moment when daughters resist their mothers
as they attempt to understand what they want to be as women.

In these plays, mothers employ harsh techniques in order to
prevent their daughters from repeating their own mistakes. Unfortunately, each mother's manipulations attempt to confine her daughters'
feminine selfhood. Thus, the mothers' relentless pursuit of "mothering" leads to conflict and rebellion in their daughters who find their
own forms of resistance. In the worst outcomes, the daughters either
conform or die while in the best there is a truce or the beginnings of
a negotiation for better understanding.

In these plays by Ana Istarú, Isis Baião, Thais Erminy, and Rebecca Bowman domineering mothers are opposed by adolescent daughters, who are presented in a sympathetic manner as idealistic persons resisting a monolithic force determined to break their will. The four plays question the cult of motherhood through a negative representation of what those women can do to their offspring. The truth they dramatize is that mothers abuse their power over their young daughters rather than providing them with loving support and nurture. As a result, daughters crave their mothers' attention, and are needy and uncertain about themselves and their futures. Staging mothers as tools of male privilege and daughters as victims helps audiences see how mother-daughter relations can trap women into an inferior status.

The dramatists in this group of plays uncover the dark secret behind the cult of motherhood: that mothers are the promoters and defenders of male privilege who endanger their relationships with their daughters and their daughters' very identity by preparing them to value men more than themselves. In realistic domestic settings designed to echo the homes of the audience, the bonds between mother and daughter are strained by mothers who enforce society's message of subordination and conformity against their daughters' drive to autonomy. In a interview about her dramaturgy, Costa Rican poet and dramatist Ana Istarú describes her task in Madre nuestra que estás en la tierra as "a revisar un poco el papel de la mujer misma como reproductora de la ideología machista, en tanto que madre" [to reexamine the role of the woman herself as a reproducer of machista ideology, in her capacity as mother] (qtd. in Andrade and Cramsie 1991, 226).

The conflicts in the four plays studied in this section are staged by patriarchal mothers and rebellious adolescent daughters. "Patriarchal mothers" as Susan Rubin Suleiman calls them, support and defend the superiority of men to their daughters ("Daughters" 1990, 165–66). The patriarchal mother is compelled to raise her daughter to conform to traditional roles and expectations of motherhood. As represented in these plays, she is single-minded in her efforts but as a woman she is not totally closed-minded to her daughter's needs. Rebellious daughters are torn by the desire to be their own persons and at the same time maintain an attachment to their mothers. These rebellious daughters represent psychologist Carol Gilligan's model of moral development in adolescents. Gilligan has argued that girls follow a different developmental pattern than the one first proposed by Sigmund Freud. The Freudian model posits that adolescents must break their symbiosis with mothers by separating and individuating. Gilligan and others have argued that girls can and should gain autonomy but without emotionally separating from their mothers, because it is connection and not separation that keeps girls strong and whole (1988, 13–14).

The three short plays about adolescence revolve around one single event—in De compras, it is dressing to attend a wedding; in En un desván olvidado, it is celebrating a birthday; and in Marcadas pela culpa, it is the mother's wish to go out for the evening. Yet the desire to accomplish these simple tasks is thwarted by conflict between mothers and daughters. That conflict is communicated in the harsh words and gentle pleas spoken by the women on stage. But it can also be heard in the long pauses in the dialogue as the characters either move nervously around the room or disengage from each other by looking away. Communication is difficult for mothers and daughters, because it never operates as an equal exchange. Mothers are invested in making their daughters obey, and they employ a range of techniques to reach their goal. Although daughters have less power, they attempt to defend themselves by resisting their mothers' words. Their resistance to their mothers' maneuvers not only creates the conflict in the plays, but also it reveals the manipulative intentions behind their mothers' action.

The mother in Baião's Marcadas pela culpa, who plans to go out for the evening, is ruthlessly blamed for family problems involving her own mother and father, her divorce, her young children, and her teenage daughter. At the conclusion of these direct and indirect attacks aimed at her by her own mother and teenage daughter, she is overwhelmed by a sense of guilt at her failures and she abandons her plans for the evening by agreeing to stay home. At the evening meal, the mother becomes the victim of verbal assaults and coercion, but the dialogue at the table points to a pattern of aggression that is often directed at the teenage daughter and her younger siblings as well. By placing three generations at the table, Baião reveals the verbal machinations of feminine victimization from grandmother to mother to daughter.

The mother in Bowman's De compras attempts to force her daughter to prepare to attend a family wedding. Just as grandmother and daughter bombarded the mother in Marcadas with evidence of her faults, so the mother in *De compras* employs a series of arguments to convince her daughter to go to the family event. While the mother repeatedly tells her daughter to forget the past and dress for the wedding, the daughter lingers in her memories of a recent, secret abortion. Here the daughter passively resists her mother's insistent requests by engaging in conversation but refraining from making the necessary moves to bathe and dress. The two women reach a truce when the mother agrees to listen to her daughter's feelings for which the daughter, in turn, agrees to prepare to attend the wedding.

Erminy's *En un desván* relies on only one character, the daughter Tacha, to enact the roles of her mother and other significant persons in her life, real and imagined, while a life-sized doll serves as her alter ego. The play presents two types of actions: first, dramatic moments in the past and present when the daughter portrays family members and friends who engage in short scenes with her while she is represented by the doll Yoyi, and second, the daughter as her present middle-aged self, isolated and confined to her basement prison waiting for her mother to come celebrate her fortieth birthday. There is only a memory of love and care in the portraits of her childhood with her father, mother, and aunt. The one individual who appears to care for her, Giraluna, is a personality Tacha has watched on television. Here the dependent, and mentally unstable daughter, who is not an adolescent but still acts like one, waits to receive the affection her mother has never given her.

Istarú's *Madre nuestra que estás en la tierra*, a title that parodies the opening lines of the Lord's Prayer "Our Father who art in heaven" (Luke 11.2), demonstrates three key moments in a young daughter's life. While the daughter dreams of the future, her mother worries about the family's loss of social standing and schemes to use her daughter's marriageability as the vehicle for recovering it. As an adolescent of fifteen, a young woman of twenty, and an adult of twenty-five, the daughter's desires to learn and live life fully are either denied or deflected into less ambitious goals. In the final scene, the adult daughter confronts her mother and questions her suffocating child-rearing techniques. In the resulting showdown, the daughter claims the right to learn about life on her own terms without her mother's interference. In this surprising exchange, the mother acknowledges her errors, confesses her love for her daughter, and hints at possible changes that she might make to improve their relationship.

These four plays, that expose damaging child-rearing techniques, emphasize the mother's coercion, that is, her efforts to make her child conform to patriarchy through verbal threats. As Lucy Gilbert and Paula Webster explain, "Femininity is enforced by external threats," since it is an "identity that requires the suppression of autonomous and aggressive desires" (1982, 13). The plays portray mothers who are resourceful and relentless in communicating their message of conformity. The mothers employ a range of verbal tactics including invoking the power of the father, the power of society, and the indebtedness that daughters should feel for their mothers' sacrifices. For example, in her opening lines Karla, the mother in *De compras*, reminds her daughter twice that her father has commanded her to be ready on time for the wedding and that not behaving properly brings with it an unspecified promise for punishment (134). Later Karla mentions the social norms beyond the home, referred to in Spanish as *el qué dirán* (What will others say?), that will cause family members and others to gossip about the family and pass judgment on it if the daughter does not attend the family wedding (135).

Patriarchal mothers' second line of defense in their strategies to shape their daughters into women that society will accept is to remind their daughters of their obligation to pay mothers back for their sacrifices. The plays demonstrate that the idealized martyrdom of mothers, encouraged by the church and society, is corrupting. Mothers bargain with their children over the costs and the payments for child rearing. Yet no matter how much is expected of children in payment, it can never be equal to the amount that mothers sacrifice. Thus, children are always in debt to their mothers and mothers seem unable to forgive the debt. For example, in *De compras*, the mother Karla tells the daughter Mireya:

> "Ninguna otra mamá le dio a su hija la libertad que te di ¿con que me lo pagas?" [No other mother gave her daughter the liberty that I gave you, and this is how you repay me?] (136).

This sense of unpaid debt is a recurring theme in *Madre nuestra* as well. For example, in act 1 the mother, Dora, and her daughter Julia make plans for her *quinceñera* or "coming-out party" to mark her entrance into the dating world. When Dora's suggestions are not met with immediate approval by her daughter, her emotions escalate as she recounts all her sacrifices and her daughter's ungratefulness. Her final threat,

"¡Me tenés hasta aquí con tu desconsideración!" [I am up to here with your lack of consideration] (237)

is followed by a fit of crying and dizziness. Such an exalted response moves conversation and discussion out of the normal range and cuts off communication between mother and daughter. It silences Julia who can only internalize her feelings of worthlessness.

When neither the powers of fathers and gossips nor the sacrifices of mothers bring the necessary conformity, mothers turn to their own lives as evidence of the hardships they hope their daughters will avoid. This approach offers great potential in two ways: it shows daughters that mothers are well-meaning and their actions are altruistic, but at the same time it suggests that mothers have been victims and that their suffering need not be repeated if daughters will heed their advice. Mothers argue that their actions are meant to bring about the best for their daughters, as in these words from Karla—

"Siempre quise lo mejor para tí" [I always wanted the best for you] (*De compras*, 138).

Mothers in several of the plays suggest they want to save their daughters from the hardships they have suffered, as in these words:

Karla: "Lo que uno quiere es que no se repita la misma historia" [What one wants is that the same story isn't repeated];

Dora: "No quiero que te pasen las mías" [I don't want you to go through what I did] (*Madre nuestra* 238);

Rosa: "Dile que se cuide, no le vaya a pasar lo que a su mamá" [Tell her to take care of herself, so that she won't have happen to her what happened to her mother] (*En un desván*, 22–23).

Although the words are meant to communicate that mothers' efforts are well-meaning, they don't reveal enough information to be convincing. Rather than helping daughters know their mothers, these stories sound more like a protective shield that hides the truth about their mothers lives from their daughters. Karla in *De Compras* refuses to speak of her disappointments in life. She seems to protect herself from the pain of remembering as she insists that one must move forward and get things done (139).

On the other hand, Dora in *Madre nuestra* speaks openly and complains regularly of the financial hardships of her life. Her disappointment at having to live on a meager pension from her deceased husband is meant to explain her pain, but it serves as a barrier to or possibly an excuse for not forming a close relationship with her daughter. In either case, Dora is unable to give her daughter either financial or emotional security. Both Dora and Karla want their daughters to respond to the idea of their suffering and victimization without actually knowing the specifics of their plight. As a result, they hide the actual cost of their own conformity in order to convince their daughters to conform.

The plays communicate that mothers push their daughters to conform, because it is an expedient method for dispensing with what they see as their burden. It helps them protect their energies and emotions for more important tasks, such as handling family financial matters, responding to the demands of society, or responding to the needs of husbands or sons. Rosa, the mother in *En un desván*, offers the most direct words of disgust at the burden she has accepted by making the decision to keep her daughter and raise her. She calls her *la cosa* (the thing) and declares that she feels obligation, but not love for her daughter (30). We learn later in the play that Rosa's main concern is going out at night and that her passion for men often keeps her away for long periods of time (25). In another example, the granddaughter in *Marcadas* complains that her mother has no time for her kids because she needs to be with men:

> "Você só vivia agarrada no papai e agora que brigou com ele tem que ir pra rua atrás de outro" [You used to cling to dad and now that you broke up with him you have to go out to find another man] (18).

In the closing moments of the play, *Madre nuestra*, the daughter, Julia, demands that her mother engage in a new kind of mothering that is attentive to her needs rather than one focused on a father, husband, or son (259). Her words reveal the priority her mother and grandmother have given to the men absent from their lives rather than to the daughter who is present. The sad truth for mothers who free themselves from obligations to their daughters in order to serve men is that they lose an important emotional connection that could sustain and enrich their lives while at the same time teaching their daughters to seek a sense of value in men rather than in themselves.

Adolescent daughters also become burdens to their mothers because of their budding sexuality. When daughters gain sexual maturity, it means not only that mothers have lost their daughter's childhood innocence with its simpler relations, but it also indicates that life becomes more dangerous as their daughters become vulnerable to the attentions of men. Female sexuality is not celebrated or even acknowledged by the Latin American mothers in these plays, rather it is perceived as a burden that can be exchanged for a "good" marriage. The message from mothers in Western culture is that "a woman needs a man" but that sex is provided in exchange for marriage and to produce children (Gilbert and Webster 1982, 78). Unfortunately, both Mireya of *De compras* and Julia of *Madre nuestra* become sexually active and are abused by partners who do not play by their mothers' rules. Neither daughter has been educated about her sexuality and worse, neither mother understands that her daughters' sexuality is strongly tied to her sense of self. Dora pushes Julia into what she sees as a good match and encourages a relationship even when Julia hints at sexual abuse(245). Karla in *De Compras* wants her daughter to resume her student life by simply erasing the abusive relationship from her memory just as the abortion removed the fruits of that relationship from her body. But in both cases, the daughters have been badly scarred by their experiences with men who used them, and by their mothers' lack of concern. *En un desván* presents the most extreme approach to regulating a daughter's sexuality since Tacha has been locked up in the basement her entire life as a way to keep her safe from a promiscuous world (21).

As social subordinates, the daughters in these plays resist and submit to their mothers' powerful messages. Their first line of defense is to avoid interaction by ignoring their mothers. They feign deafness, give incomplete or vague answers, listen but remain silent, and refuse to move when their mothers insist that they act. As the conflict escalates, daughters adopt more direct methods, such as leaving the room, turning to other women for comfort, or challenging their mothers' intentions. One challenge they make is to question their mothers' love.

Mireya:	"¿Me quieres, mamá?" [Do you love me, mom?] (*De compras*, 140);
Julia:	"¿Alguna vez me quisiste?" [Did you ever love me mom?] (*Madre nuestra*, 256);
Maria do Socorro:	"Você não pensa em mim, não é?" [You don't think about me, do you?] (*Marcadas*, 18).

By questioning their mothers' love, the daughters call attention to what they are lacking in their emotional lives. The mothers' excess, seen in their elaborate techniques of manipulation, makes a strong contrast to the daughters' simple requests for love and support.

Another method daughters employ for gaining a sense of equality in their relationship is passing judgment on how well their mothers' actions correspond to society's ideals of motherhood. In *Marcadas pela culpa*, all three generations of women bear a version of the name of the long-suffering Virgin Mary and the oldest and youngest blame the middle generation for failing to live up to spoken or unspoken models of behavior for mothers. The grandmother, Maria das Dores, complains that her daughter, Maria dos Aflitos, blames everything on her that is wrong in her life:

"Você me culpa de tudo que dá errado na sua vida! Como é difícil ser mãe!" [You blame me for everything that went wrong in your life. It's so difficult to be a mother!] (15).

The granddaughter, Maria do Socorro, accuses her mother of defying the rules for good mothers by wanting to go out at night:

"De noite, tudo quanto é mãe fica em casa com os filhos e o marido" [At night, all mothers are at home with their kids and husbands] (*Marcadas pela culpa*, 16).

Daughters also complain about the limitations their mothers place on them. In *De compras*, Mireya states that her friends have the freedom to enjoy life while she is under constant supervision from her mother who suffocates her and won't leave her alone (138, 136). Tacha's imaginary friend, Giraluna, protests any defense of her mother, Rosa when she says:

> "Rosa es una vieja tostada (*Escucha a la muñeca y se rebela*). No la defiendas, mira que no tiene perdón de Dios. Para criarte así, mejor te hubiera regalado" [Rosa is an old wretch. *She listens to the doll and protests.* Don't defend her, there is no forgiveness from God. For raising you this way, it would have been better to give you away] (*En un desván*, 27).

Daughters gain power in their relationship by judging and criticizing mothers, repeating their mother's techniques of using higher authorities, such as what others might say, to make demands. In addition, daughters replay society's double messages to mothers that demand altruism on the one hand and then blame them no matter what for their self-sacrificing efforts.

What the daughters in these plays are able to perceive, some more clearly than the others, is that their lives as adolescents have brought about changes in themselves and in their relations with their mothers. The daughters mourn the loss of their childhood with its simplicity and hopefulness at the same time that they resist their socialization into womanhood. The price of socialization is expressed in *En un desván* as the loss of dreams and dramatized in the cutting of hair:

> "La tijera, tijera ven, que tengo que cortarle los sueños a Tacha, se está haciendo una mujer" [Scissors, come here because I need to cut off Tacha's dreams, she's becoming a woman] (22).

But the strongest condemnation that the daughters can make of their mothers' example is to express the realization that their mothers have been successful. That is, the daughters realize with horror that they are on their way to becoming their mothers, or they fear they will become like them some day, a fear that was labeled "matriphobia" by United States feminists. For example, Mireya in *De compras:*

> "Te veo a ti y pienso, así voy a ser" [I see you and I think, that's how I am going to be] (141).

Julia in *Madre nuestra que estás en la tierra* recognizes that indeed she might follow in her mother's footsteps, an idea she abhors:

"¡Y no quiero llegar a ser como vos! (*Solloza*). ¡Ni tener hijas como yo!" [I don't want to be like you. *(She sobs.)* Nor have daughters like me] (255).

Conformity is the lesson that mothers teach their daughters because it is the one they know best. Lucy Gilbert and Paula Webster note: "Reproduction of the pernicious gender system is deeply necessary for the emotional survival of most mothers, which makes it irresistible to most daughters" (29). The grandmother Amelia shares her knowledge with Julia in the opening moments of *Madre nuestra*:

"Ya uno viejo entiende que no vale la pena morirse de ganas por nada. Fue lo primero que aprendí cuando me casé" [When one gets old, it is easier to realize that its not worth it to die trying for anything. That was the first thing I learned when I married] (233).

Karla echoes the thought with almost the same words in the closing moments of *De compras*:

"Uno de viejo se hace de cascarón duro, apenas así se puede vivir" [As you get older you get a tough shell, that's the only way you can live] (140).

In these four plays, mothers prepare daughters for the personal losses that conformity to their subordinate status will bring—loss of self-respect, self-esteem, self-expression, and personal development. Karla warns her daughter about her father's anger when his women don't comply with his demands (*De compras*, 134–36). The empty chair at the head of the table reminds the three generations in *Marcadas* that it is the absent grandfather who still controls the household and its financial resources as the granddaughter Maria do Socorro declares:

"Droga! Tudo é pra ele nessa casa" [Rats! Everything is for him in this house] (14).

Daughters learn that men have sexual access to women but no obligation of fidelity to them, so that women alone pay for sexual activity with their bodies and reputations: Mireya, referring to her abusive boyfriend, states:

"Entonces le hablé, batallé para localizarlo. Me dijo: Sabes qué, es tu bronca, y me colgó" [Then I spoke to him, I finally found him. He told me: You know what, its your problem, and he hung up] (*De compras*, 140).

Julia tells a similar story about her beau:

"Erik nunca pensó en casarse conmigo. Después supe que para eso ya tenía su noviecieta, una niña de bien que sí podría presentarle a mami. (*Con dificultad*) Conmigo se conformó con extenderme cuan larga soy en el asiento trasero de ese carro que tanto te gustaba" [Erik never planned to marry me. Later I found out that for that he had a little fiancée, a good little girl of social standing whom he could introduce to his mother. (*With difficulty*.) With me he resigned himself to laying me out my full length in the back seat of that car you so loved] (*Madre nuestra*, 254).

Finally, daughters hear the message that the power of men to attract their mothers is greater than their daughterly love, a concept the mother Rosa makes clear in this speech from *En un desván*:

"Imagínate un hombre de abolengo, estripe y pedegrí sabiendo que yo tengo a Tacha por hija. ¡No, nunca! Si alguna vez te viera le diría que eres hija de una sirvienta que te dejó aquí, o algo por el estilo" [Just imagine if a man with lineage, class, and pedigree knew that I had Tacha as a daughter. No, never! If he were to see you I would tell him you were the daughter of a servant who left you here, or something like that] (31).

Later Rosa threatens Tacha saying that the best thing that could happen to her would be to die:

"Así podría limpiar este lugar y abrirle ventanas para que circule el aire fresco. Podría tener mi amante en paz, sin tener que justificar tantos ruidos extraños" [That way I could clean up this place and open the windows so the fresh air could circulate. I could have my lover in peace, without having to explain all the funny noises] (31).

Yet, daughters do not abandon their mothers. Shelley Phillips notes correctly that "They quarrel because they don't want to give up

on their mothers" (1996, 51). Instead daughters challenge and confront their mothers demanding to be recognized and heard. In the
most difficult and abusive relationship, that of *En un desván olvidado*,
the daughter Tacha opens the play by announcing that time with her
mother, *un buen pedazo de su tiempo* (a good chunk of her time) would
be the best present for her fortieth birthday (18). She later reaffirms
that desire emphasizing the need to be *sola* (alone) with her mother
on this special day (27). Carol Gilligan has identified "the willingness
to speak and to risk disagreement" as the key element in the process
of adolescent development (1988, 17). The daughters in these plays
do display that willingness to speak and to risk conflict in order to
maintain connection with their mothers. Through connection these
rebellious daughters hope to gain back a sense of their identity and
win their mothers' support.

The climactic confrontation between Julia and her mother Dora
in act 3 of *Madre nuestra* best illustrates how conflict and negotiation
can produce a different script for mothers and daughters to enact. The
situation is as follows: Julia, who is now twenty-five, returns home in
the early hours of Christmas morning to find her mother Dora drink-
ing the last of the cognac while she waits up for her daughter. Dora
provokes an argument with her daughter, however, this time Julia's
age and her contribution to the financial support of the household
provide her with the power to confront her mother and declare her
independence. The argument that follows casts Julia as the inquisitor
and her mother as the accused.

The element that makes this showdown between mother and
daughter a productive rather than destructive endeavor is Julia's drive
to discover who she is. She undertakes this search by demanding that
her mother explain the past—her marriage, her mothering, her widowhood, her perceptions of Julia. Dora not only examines and explains her
past, but she also affirms Julia's importance to her. When Julia accepts
her mother's confessions, she also acknowledges them as cornerstones
for her construction of self. Near the end of the confrontation, Dora
moves her relationship with her daughter toward reconciliation by asking for her daughter's forgiveness. In this cathartic moment, Dora signals she is ready to start their relationship over by offering her daughter
what she needs in terms of support and affirmation, rather than repeating her usual attempts at coercion. At the same time Julia teaches her
mother that she must love and support her daughter:

"Uno no puede pasarse la vida suplicando por el amor de un padre o de un marido. O el de un hijo, como abuela. Más bien, algún día va a pedir mi amor. Y ese día no puedo tener las manos vacías" [One cannot spend a lifetime praying for the love of a father or a husband. Or of a son, like grandmother. Better yet, someday someone will want to ask for my love. And that day, I have to be ready to love back] (259).

In this truth telling and teaching scene the outcome is in question since the daughter could decide to leave her mother or to stay and remake their relationship. At the end of the play, Julia's decision to stay home as she searches for her self is a declaration of her independence, but also of her desire to understand and accept her mother. Her decision also empowers her mother to begin to understand herself as well.

This group of patriarchal mother plays encourages identification between the audience and the characters on stage through the realistic settings and costumes. The plays utilize contrast and opposition in those settings, costumes, and music to accentuate the conflict between the characters. The settings for the plays are dining rooms and bedrooms, places that emphasize femininity in their decoration and in the rituals of serving meals, dressing, and grooming. In these feminine worlds, mothers and daughters convey to the audience their differences. Each mother's physical characteristics, her attention to her appearance, her actions, and her efforts to maintain order tell the audience that she has social status, success, and power. She has accepted that "beauty is the prime survival strategy for women" (Debold, Wilson, Malave 1993, 197) since by trading on her looks she gains the comfortable life she lives (203). In contrast, the rebellious daughters dress, act, and keep rooms that defy and reject their mothers values.

Dressing well is a requirement for married women with social standing, because they present themselves to the world outside the home as representatives of the social status and financial well-being inside the home. That status must be maintained and/or improved or the same forces that pass judgment on their daughters, represented in the expression el qué dirán will turn on mothers. As we learn in Madre nuestra, Dora maintains the façade of her social status in a physical appearance that is more elegant than the deteriorating home where she lives. All the mothers in the plays are described as tastefully dressed, wearing makeup, and their hair is always coifed. As midlife women, the mothers worry about conserving their youth and beauty at a time when their daughters are gaining their womanly figures. Mirrors are common in the stage settings, and they serve to remind mothers and daughters of each other's contrasting appearances, but also that an attractive appearance is an important feminine trait.

Daughters, in direct opposition to their mothers, pay little atten- tion to their physical appearance or the order in their rooms. All four daughters are described as sloppily or childishly dressed, their hair uncombed. Mireya (De compras) and Tacha (En un desván) defy their mothers' concern about appearances by wearing their nightgowns during the daytime. Their rooms are also unkept and contain the signs of their liminality between childhood and adulthood in their posters of movie and rock stars and in their dolls and stuffed animals. On the other hand, the family rooms are more orderly and decorated with adult taste. But when daughters enter these rooms the order appears threatened: Maria do Socorro of Marcadas pela culpa sits in the seat reserved for her grandfather, Julia of Madre nuestra que estás en la tierra smokes cigarettes clandestinely and plays popular music. The daughters' grooming and their environments stand in opposition to the beauty and order of their mothers and therefore reinforce the conflict between them. The stage directions describing Maria do Socorro capture perfectly the resistance and vulnerability of all these daughters: Tem o jeito tímido e rebelde dos adolescentes [She has the timid and rebellious manner of adolescents] (14).

Mothers are powerful within the home and their presence in the dining room or bedroom brings order to disorder. For example, Dora (Madre nuestra) dusts and experiments with the placement of the furniture before guests arrive, keeps a mental notebook of the status of the family's formal china and linens, and directs the many tasks necessary for the preparation of the Christmas Eve meal. Similarly, Karla (De compras) cleans and organizes her daughter's room as she talks to her, rarely stopping or resting. Mothers are physically as well as verbally active in these plays and they dominate the space they are in as well as dominating their daughters. These mothers communicate energy, persistence, and control. In sum, they are formidable oppo- nents whose very presence in the room demands attention.

All the plays employ music to accentuate their contrasting and conflictive atmospheres. In the most benign form music separates mother from daughter, as when Mireya puts on her headphones to tune her mother out. In its more integrated form, music emphasizes the contrast between what is desired by the characters, that is an ideal world, and the world they occupy. For example, after Maria dos Aflitos wails that she won't go out for the evening, the climactic loss of her battle, in the closing moments of *Marcadas*, an announcer signals the end of another chapter and music described as *tristíssima* (terribly sad) brings the play to an end (20). These closing markers contain the depressing news that this highly emotional moment, like that of any good soap opera, is not yet finished and will continue tomorrow. The songs employed in *Madre nuestra* and *En un desván* communicate emotion and add meaning to the plays. Tacha sings one song repeatedly throughout *En un desván* that contains words that offer her an escape from her suffocating life in the basement. "Siempre hay algo más" [There's always something more] by Alberto Cortéz calls attention to opportunities left in life to experience, such as moments of caring and beauty. In the context of the play, the song contrasts with the incomplete and unfinished life of Tacha who, at forty, still has reason to want *algo más* from life (13). *Madre nuestra* begins and ends with songs about loss of love and loss of illusions. These songs echo the theme of financial decline and personal sacrifice that have characterized Dora's life. But, the children's songs at the end of the play also suggest a new beginning for Julia and her mother Dora (258–59), as they invoke words from a simpler time in their relationship.

Although the plays are similar, the emotional struggles between mother and daughter reflect the personalities of the characters and set the tone for each play. *Marcadas pela culpa* utilizes extreme and exaggerated emotions to convey the melodramatic context of this soap opera-like script. The emotional extremes reinforce the tragic nature of the family's relations. Victimization is an inherited disease in this household, as pointed out by the stage directions that describe the mother's voice as similar to her own mother's voice (14). In contrast, the stage directions for *De compras* advise actresses to control their voices using *tonos bajos* (low tones) in the most strident speeches. Even in the parts playwright Bowman describes as *más feas* (ugliest), she suggests whispering (134). Thus, unlike the loud and intense emotions which characterize *Marcadas*, the atmosphere in *De compras* is threatening but contained. Restraint in the face of hardship is not only the message that Karla promotes to her daughter, but it is also the medium through which she conveys it.

The flow of dramatic action in the four plays maintains a high emotional level only to come to a conclusion in less than hopeful circumstances in three of the four plays. *En un desván olvidado* leads its audience to the most distressing conclusion in which Tacha brings about her own death by stabbing herself. *De compras* and *Marcadas pela culpa* end in the suspension of the conflicts, but hinting that tomorrow the entire episode will repeat itself with slight variations. *Madre nuestra* builds up to a major confrontation in the final act by creating smaller confrontations that are never realized in acts 1 and 2 because the grandmother Amelia mediates between Dora and her daughter Julia. After Amelia dies at the end of act 2, the tensions between mother and daughter escalate unhampered. But, unlike the other three plays, the characters use this conflict to begin a new relationship, rather than to continue or end the existing one.

What do these four plays communicate to us about patriarchal mothers and rebellious daughters? They chip away at the saintly image of mothers by showing how mothers prepare their daughters to conform to the masculinist values and behaviors that society expects of them. Patriarchal mothers raise daughters to be mothers and wives but not to be feminine individuals. That is, mothers teach their daughters how to serve husbands and children, how to be selfless "good girls," but they don't know how to help their daughters discover who they are as people since they too were denied this opportunity. At the same time, *Madre nuestra* suggests an alternative—rebellious daughters who are searching for themselves can engage their mothers in that search. Daughters like Julia who invest in their mothers and in their relationship with them serve their own interests by strengthening their chances of discovering themselves. Together mother and daughter can redeem their relationship as they gain new insights into themselves and each other. Building bridges between patriarchal mothers and rebellious daughters is the first step toward breaking down the "exclusionary opposition" offered in cultural scripts that position women as selfless, that is at odds with themselves; or defines them as selfish, at odds with others if they so much as attend to their own needs (Gilligan 1988, 16). The trap of mother-daughter relations in adolescence is that maturing daughters can no longer be controlled by mothers, but mothers are slow to make the adjustment in their tactics. Janet Surrey suggests that "Mother's memories hold the images of their children as infants, and throughout life they continue to 'see' (and therefore evoke) the child in their adolescent or adult children" (1993, 121). Thus, even though daughters are growing, mothers respond to their moves toward independence by escalating their efforts at control. When mothers try to force their daughters to behave as if they were little girls they build an emotional gap in the dyad at the very time when both need supporting. The daughter's maturing may remind the mother of her aging and make her even more sensitive to society's message that she has served her purpose. The daughter's precarious entry into adulthood, with its danger and excitement, requires a safe haven. Yet at this very time when women need each other the most, mothers push their daughters away from them and into relationships with young men where the girls are expected to seek the love and attention that mothers do not provide. Debold, Wilson and Malave have compared adolescent girls to sunflowers in this simile: "Like sunflowers, they turn their faces into the glare of men's dominance of women" (1993, 14). But as the plays make clear young men are not the answer. Instead, the answer lies in redefining and renegotiating the mother-daughter bond so as to improve the subjectivity of both women.

Negotiating Mothers and Independent Daughters

In this second set of plays, I will argue that conflict demonstrates expanding relations between mothers and adult daughters in which the best outcome produces not a severing of bonds but a renegotiation of them, in Vivien E. Nice's terms (1992, 129). The plays are: *La partida* by Pilar Campesino; *Querida mamãe* by Maria Adelaide Amaral; *Amantíssima* by Susana Torres Molina; and *Casa matriz* by Diana Raznovich.[7] *La partida* [The departure] offers a tender moment between a mother and daughter at the time of the daughter's preparation to leave home. It expresses in dramatic form Campesino's sensitivity to the challenges of mothering and motherhood.[8] *Querida mamãe* [Dear Mom] examines the relationship between a traditional mother and her problematic, professional daughter. In Amaral's play both women betray a flaw in their performance of the social expectations for their gender roles: the respectable, old-fashioned mother had a long-term secret affair and the independent, liberated daughter continues to seek her mother's approval (Ravetti and Rojo 1996, 46–

47). *Amantíssima* [Beloved], the most abstract work of the eight stud-ied in this chapter emphasizes both the difficulty of relations and the possibility of healing and redemption. *Casa matriz* [Dial-a-Mom or MaTRIX, Inc.] stages mother-daughter relationships through a series of scenes between a daughter and an actress who is contracted to play "mother" for a fee. Together the dyad relives the conflict between generations according to the client's demands. *Casa matriz*, with its metatheatrical context of acting out motherhood and its portrayal of consumers buying dramatized affections, highlights both the perfor-mance of the most idealized of social roles and the negotiation be-tween mothers and daughters.

La *partida* and *Querida mamãe* are each one act long, however, while the latter follows traditional dramatic conventions and is di-vided into seven untitled scenes, representing a series of encounters between mother and daughter, the former is less conventional. *La partida*'s prologue is a poem that is mentioned later in the play and its dialogue and stage directions are written in poetic blank verses. The two plays share the theme of leaving and loss: *La partida* portrays a daughter's preparations to leave home while *Querida mamãe* drama-tizes a mother's arrangements to go on a trip. Both take place in a realistic setting and both plays study the tensions created by a daughter's efforts to become an independent individual.

The two plays address the theme of separation through emo-tional encounters that contain a few lighthearted moments, but nei-ther of the plays is a comedy. *La partida* takes place on the daughter's nineteenth birthday at the very moment she is packing her bags. The play freezes the passage of time at 3:00 P.M. while mother and daughter make peace and say goodbye. As the daughter Adela collects her belongings, her mother Agata tries to express her sense of excitement and loss. The play is a quiet ceremony marking the maturity of the daughter Adela, a long-awaited goal for her, and the aging of the mother Agata, an undesired but inevitable occurrence for her. *Querida mamãe* portrays a more difficult relationship between Ruth, a tradi-tional Brazilian housewife and widow, and her thirtyish divorced daugh-ter Helô. During a series of visits, mother and daughter discuss women's lives in the past and the present. Helô's dissatisfaction with life and her continued dependence on her mother are exacerbated by Ruth's plans to travel to the United States to visit her older daughter Beth whom Helô considers to be her mother's favorite. Like *La partida*,

Querida mamãe emphasizes the potential for loss in the mother-daughter relationship although not as a result of the daughter's move, but rather as a result of the possible illness and death of the mother. Both plays highlight the conflict caused by personality differences between mother and daughter and by choices the daughter now makes as an independent person.

Many of the same issues in mother-daughter relations that were examined in the earlier plays, such as how daughters behave, their sexuality, the choices they make, their appearance, and how they will become adults, are touched on in these two plays. But in these plays the most important issue is how daughters will separate from their mothers. In their study of female social development Romona T. Mercer, Elizabeth G. Nichols, and Glen Caspers Doyle found that women often "anchored their emotional attachment on a male partner as a means of separating and individuating from their mothers" (1989, 106). The daughters in *La partida* and *Querida mamãe* follow that pattern of attachment to others and to a career. Attachment to another begins the process of separation that must eventually lead to independence, defined as "individuation (achievement of a clearer boundary between self and environment) and autonomy (ability to function independently as well as interdependently)" according to Mercer, Nichols and Doyle (59). Their research noted that gaining these attributes often takes women a lifetime to achieve. In these two plays by Pilar Campesino and Maria Adelaide Amaral, then, "knowing one's own identity" as Shelley Phillips defines autonomy (1996, 122), means finding others that will help the self move toward independence. This necessary step, when successful, can help daughters strengthen themselves as they sever their dependence on mothers, as Adela does in *La partida*. But when that step fails it can increase tensions and force the process to be ongoing as in the case of Helô in *Querida mamãe*.

As we have seen in the previous section, separation causes conflict, and it begins in earnest when daughters reach adolescence. Mothers in the earlier plays responded to their daughters' desires to grow up by increasing their efforts at control. That is, mothers overpowered their daughters with their arguments and their presence, because daughters had not yet gained the necessary conditions of maturity to stage an effective rebellion. However, the mothers in *La partida* and *Querida mamãe* cannot engage in such obvious tactics with adult daughters, because they are facing young women who have greater knowledge of the world and thus, greater abilities to understand and determine their own paths. In these plays, adult daughters are not afraid to confront their mothers and challenge their opinions. But confrontation does not mean rejection; rather it means that daughters are negotiating with mothers in order to build a new relationship on an adult-to-adult level. As Phillips has pointed out "A daughter needs a good fighting partner in her mother" (1996, 52). Both plays portray the push-pull of fighting between mothers and daughters as a crucial step toward a healthy separation of the dyad.

Campesino and Amaral both dramatize the relationship between mother and daughter as a shift in the balance of power. Daughters recognize their opportunities beyond the home to develop themselves and with the strength that they gain from the world outside, daughters begin to make decisions about their lives that take them away from their mothers. Adela in *La partida* has plans to make a movie that will take her away from home. Her project gives her strength and a sense of purpose so she can resist her mother's need to cling to her. She advises her mother not to try to stop her from leaving and not to come visit her. Helô in *Querida mamãe*, on the other hand, has been living independently from her mother for many years, yet she is still emotionally dependent on her mother. Her needs and her blaming of her mother for this dependence keep her in constant conflict with her mother. As Nancy Friday has observed: "Blaming mother is just a negative way of clinging to her still" (qtd. in Hirsch 1990, 189). And, in fact, Helô is at war with everyone including herself. She offends her mother and competes with her sister. Unlike Adela who seizes the opportunity to make a film in order to move beyond her home, none of Helô's successes, her medical degree, her employment, nor her own adolescent daughter, affirm her sense of self.

As mentioned earlier, *La partida* represents a ceremony of separation conducted by the daughter Adela on her nineteenth birthday in honor of her relationship with her mother Agata who is celebrating her fortieth year. It is the first step that Adela makes in her process of gaining recognition as an independent person. In their dialogue, Adela asks her mother to forget the tensions of the past:

"Hagamos las paces" [Let's make peace] (44) and she requests her mother's reassurance and love: "Amame siempre" [Love me always] (52).

She also acknowledges the love and respect she feels for her mother by kissing her. Whatever the tensions of the past, this moment emphasizes the affection and respect between mother and daughter.

The play structures Adela's separation as a choice between her own dreams and the needs of the women around her. Adela's dream is to make a film, and she had planned to cast her friend Cristi in the leading role. But Cristi, whose voice is first heard on the telephone and then again during the dialogue, decides to withdraw from the project. At the same time, Adela's mother pleads with her daughter not to go. While Agata supports her daughter and wishes her success:

> "Y que vuelvas tú/brillante de luces" [And that you return shining] (48),

it is the loss that Agata feels deeply. With the loss of her daughter's presence in the home, Agata feels a loss of her identity:

> "¡Madre de nadie! ¿Comprendes?" [Mother to no one! Do you understand?] (57),

and of her daughter's vitality that made her feel younger than her forty years. Vivien E. Nice states "Mothers may feel rejected when they see their daughters moving off into lives they can barely understand, let alone enter. It may not be that mothers feel their daughters are rejecting 'their values' but that they feel a keen loss of the daughter whose main concerns are not now ones that the mother can share and discuss as an equal" (1992, 124). Adela recognizes her mother's fears and in her last moments at home she offers her mother a challenge to change the focus of her life from others to herself:

> "Finalmente es tu vida" [Finally its your life] (57).

At the same time, Adela also liberates herself from Cristi. Cristi's voice, which also calls to Adela to stay home, becomes a faint plea (51) and then is left behind as Adela walks out the door (57).

The separation staged in *La partida* gives equal emphasis to the mother's pain of loss and the daughter's excitement at being on her own for the first time. This equality is achieved in the mutual exchange of birthday gifts, the sharing of wine, the singing of songs, and the reciting and discussing of poetry. Mother and daughter make the moment special—a send-off for the daughter who is leaving and for the mother who is staying behind. In this encounter, both women pay tribute to each other and to their relationship, not as an idealized one, but as one in which each has invested. Adela describes her half of the relationship as:

"¡Con todo y mis culpas?" [With everything and my faults?] (53)

while her mother reaffirms her half:

"Aún soy tu madre" [I am still your mother] (51).

It is a moment of reflection and transition that the stage directions describe as *Unidas en un dulce abrazo/procuran cerrar un capítulo más* [United in a sweet embrace / they try to close one more chapter] (53). Debold, Wilson, Malave have used the expression "redefining their connections" to describe the process that mothers and daughters undertake in adulthood (1993, 20). That expression applies to the steps Adela and Agata take during Campesino's play. The emotions of the moment produce only a few tears from Agata in the closing words with her daughter. But the playwright's stage instructions imply an expectation that the audience will be moved by this intimate moment suspended in time. The directions state *Salen. / La luz se apaga tan lentamente que nadie se atreverá a aplaudir* [They leave. The lights go down so slowly that no one will dare to applaud] (57).

Unlike the patriarchal mothers discussed earlier, Agata has moved beyond the pedagogical mission of mothers to teach dependent daughters how to get along in the world. The tools of coercion have given way to tools of support but also expressions of regret. Adela's attachment is not only to her plans as a filmmaker but also to another person, when Agata asks:

"¿Que tanto le amas?" [You love him that much?]

Adela responds:

"(medida) Le amo" [With measure . . . I love him]

and Agata:

"Debo creerte" [I should believe you] (44).

Mother love, the selfless and sexless feminine love, here is being replaced by romantic and sexualized love described in the stage directions as: *dos cuerpos adolescentes reconociéndose de pies a cabeza* [two adolescent bodies discovering each other from head to toes] (55). Agata is hurt by but resigned to the loss of her daughter to future lovers and projects. Along the lines of definitions of individuation and autonomy proposed by Mercer, Nichols and Dole (1989, 59), Adela's efforts in *La partida* demonstrate attempts to begin to build boundaries between herself and others, in this case her mother and her friend Cristi, and to function independently from the same people with whom it is necessary to act interdependently.

Helô, the daughter in *Querida mamãe*, struggles with both individuation and autonomy in spite of the many years she has lived away from her mother. She sees her mother frequently, as indicated by the continuity between the scenes which reveal successive visits. Familiarity breeds contempt in this relationship in which the daughter's emotional security is unstable and her sense of self is still undefined. Each meeting is a series of duels, according to Alberto Guzik, instigated by Helô to help her define herself against her mother (1994, 9).

Time is suspended in *La partida* while Agata and Adela mark a positive transition in their lives as women, and it is suspended in a more negative way in *Querida mamãe* because Helô and Ruth are caught in a trap. Helô needs to engage with her mother, to discuss, argue, analyze, but she seems unable to improve or change their relationship. Even an extraordinary effort on the part of the mother Ruth, who reveals a long ago love affair in order to move the women closer to understanding, does not change the status of the relationship. Helô's ability and willingness to take responsibility for herself and her life are set in motion more by the threat of losing her mother than by any other revelation or negotiation.

Querida mamãe stages a debilitating routine of engagement and misunderstanding in which the characters suffer from a lack of equality and respect. Ruth, like Agata in *La partida*, contributes to her daughter's growth toward adulthood with support and expressions of regret. But Helô, unlike Adela, does not feel confidence or comfort with any aspect of her life. She is waiting for a sense of completeness, an attachment that will make her feel whole and separate. Ruth and Helô cannot realize a successful rite of separation like the one achieved by Adela and Agata because there is no common ground between them, no mutuality. The women stand at opposite poles in feminine identity: Ruth is connected to the traditional concerns of selfless mothers—maintaining relationships with children and spouse at the expense of self, while Helô is self-centered—her life revolves around her needs and those of others are relegated to secondary status. In her desperate search to know herself, Helô offends and hurts her mother's feelings, physically and verbally abuses her own adolescent daughter, competes with her sister, and searches for a romantic union. She is drawn to the compassion and care that her mother extends to others and receives from them in turn. At the same time, she is repelled by the limitations that such a definition of femininity implies in Brazilian society. She contrasts herself to the women who men adore, like her mother:

"Mulheres femininas, mulheres que não questionam, que não competem, que não os ameaçam, mulheres que se comprazem com as alegrias do lar e da prole." [Feminine women, women who don't ask, don't compete, don't threaten, women who rejoice with the pleasures of home and children] (28).

Helô's search for a meaningful romantic attachment that might give a sense of direction to her life raises the normal tensions and differences with her mother and her daughter to the level of a full blown conflict. When the play begins, Helô is about to break off her affair with a married man. On the rebound, she becomes involved with a costume designer named Leda. As her attachment to Leda grows, so does the conflict with both her mother Ruth and her daughter Priscila. Ruth disapproves of the lesbian relationship because Helô conducts it in her house and in front of her daughter. Priscila also dislikes the affair because she is jealous and protective of her mother's affections. Helô, on the other hand, finds in her lover Leda the affirmation and support missing from her life, and she vows to fight to protect the relationship (42). While she sees the affair as a choice to love and be loved, her mother rejects it as immoral and rejects Helô's identity as that of a lesbian (40–41). When the affair ends, Helô is once again left with a poor sense of self.

It is conceivable that the play could have ended at this point, leaving the audience to imagine a tragic ending for Helô. By mainstream mores a lesbian affair would be the last step before perdition.[9]

From that perspective, Ruth's life and her values would gain credibility as the preferable option for women. But, the conflict does not end with Helô's failed affair. Rather, it is complicated by a concession that Ruth makes in response to her daughter's desolation at the loss of her great love Leda. Ruth offers her confession in order to create a common ground between herself and her daughter and to prove that her own life was not just *uma trivial relação com papai* (a trivial relationship with dad) [66], as Helô describes it. She reveals that she maintained a passionate affair with another man during almost fifteen years of her marriage. Helô welcomes her mother's effort at mutuality, and she even attempts to suggest that she and her mother belong to the same club of outcast lovers. But, from the mother's standpoint, there are numerous differences between her affair and that of her daughter. Ruth presents her romance not as infidelity, but like a fairy tale conducted away from family in a magical land:

"eu vivia uma história extraordinária ... [...] Naquela tarde, eu tinha vivido um sonho e ele tinha a duração de uma fita de cinema" [I lived an extraordinary story. On that afternoon, I had lived a dream and that dream lasted as long as a movie] (72).

Ruth's secret affair suggests that she didn't accept the ruling mores of the time and reveals her own willingness to live dangerously, but not in such contempt as to challenge the heterosexual norm. From Ruth's perspective, Helô's affair is not only immoral but she also suspects that it is the latest effort on Helô's part to rebel and hurt the ones she loves (64).

What brings mother and daughter closer to mutual understanding, in fact, is a concern over Ruth's health. It is ironic and symptomatic of this relationship that Helô, the physician, is the person least involved in her mother's diagnosis and treatment of suspicious tumors and that her own forgetfulness and self-centeredness cause her to lose track of her mother's progress towards surgery. While Ruth's original plans to travel to the United States would have taken her away from Helô for the duration of the trip, the suggestion that her surgery might reveal cancer and thus the possibility of death presents a greater and more permanent loss. But even when faced with such a direct threat, Helô denies support and care for her mother. Instead, when her mother accepts her daughter Beth's offer to come to Brazil to help, Helô becomes jealous of her sister and blames her mother for not involving her in the decision-making process (78–80).

Like many of the plays discussed in this chapter, *Querida mamãe* captures only a segment of the longer story about mothers and daughters. For Ruth and Helô, caught in their "love-hate" knot, there is no simple resolution available (Guzik 1995, 10). On the other hand, the play does make clear that they remain engaged in each other. As the curtain falls the audience is left with the image of mother and daughter connected and cooperating in the task of winding a skein of yarn while saying together that Ruth is not going to die (87). In this moment of temporary mutuality, they invoke their own powers and possibly those beyond them in a plea for yet another chance to resolve their differences and live in peace.

Querida mamãe is similar to *Marcadas pela culpa* and *Madre nuestra que estás en la tierra* in that it presents three generations of women's lives. In its setting, music, and memories, Amaral's play also documents the changing socioeconomic climate from the 1930s to 1990s and the ways in which that climate operated on women's lives. An historical perspective on female development can help us better understand Amaral's play.

Argentine psychologist Alicia Lombardi attributes much of the tension and dissatisfaction between mothers and daughters to the changes in postmodern society that have allowed two competing concepts of motherhood/womanhood to exist side by side. According to Lombardi, a traditional model of mothering reigned supreme between the 1930s and 1950s (1986, 71). The appearance of new options for daughters born since the 1950s has created conflict between mothers and daughters (33–36). Lombardi notes that educated and affluent women of the 1980s and 1990s could choose to work, to be a sexual person, and to be more autonomous (203); all these are opportunities that require new definitions of womanhood. The Argentine clinician calls this situation a "contradictory ideology of double messages" and she asks: "¿Como ser, a la vez luchadora, junto al hombre en un mismo nivel y, por otro, ser la sacerdotisa del hogar?" [How is it possible to be at the same time a fighter along with men and at their same level and the goddess of the home?] (33).

The staging of conflict between old and new definitions of motherhood plays out in *Querida mamãe* as an opposition between the genteel world and values of the mother versus the conflicted and alienated world of the adult daughter. Ruth, like her biblical name-sake, is patient and nurturing, but most importantly, she was raised to think of others, especially children, first. She believes in stability, loyalty, and respect; she likes being a *dona-de-casa* (housewife) [34]; and she invested in and has been rewarded by the efforts she gave to performing that function. She states her accomplishments simply—she was mother to two daughters who had three children of their own (31). Helô, on the other hand, has based her life decisions on follow-ing her own convictions and being truthful to herself. Rather than believing in external signs of respect she believes in frankness. As Lombardi's comment on similar situations suggests, Helô lives in conflicting worlds, and she is a complicated and conflicted person. She is part of the competitive educational and work environment where she has fought to be an equal, but she goes home to the world where domestic skills are valued. Her life can never reflect the dignity and gentility she admires in her mother, because she lives in two separate worlds and she doesn't belong completely in either. It is noteworthy that the daughter living in the United States, Beth, does not appear to have such a difficult, complicated, or painful life. Helô and her mother attribute this difference to Beth's personality—she is a more stable and less dependent person than Helô—but it is equally likely that Beth has lived in a more liberal social setting in which she has been freer to pursue her career and family interests. Nonetheless, the "Superwoman" phenomenon in the United States, like the one described by Lombardi in Argentina, also positioned women in two different worlds where they had to balance conventional femininity at home and male standards in the business world, according to Debold, Wilson, Malave (1993, 59).

In the Maria Adelaide Amaral play the stage setting, music, and Ruth's memories construct a nostalgia for the olden days of the 1950s and the "feminine mystique," or Lombardi's reference to the book by Betty Friedan (1986, 29). Even though this time has long passed (*Querida mamãe*, 72), it lives on as a refuge from the 1990s. It was a time that is easy to idealize when seen through Ruth's eyes and com-municated in her stories of childhood, courtship, and marriage. The histories of Helô's grandmother and mother are brought to life through the clothing that she pulls out of her mother's trunk in several scenes in the play. That past is preserved in the set, a living room of an apartment built and decorated in the style of the 1950s. A modern television set and stereo system contrast with the large mirror, stacks of old records, and a large trunk of hats, gloves, shoes, dresses, and evening gowns from the 1930s–1950s. Music from old records plays throughout and contributes to the impression that Ruth is living in the past. Both the clothing and the music hearken back to an earlier time when social and family events alone gave meaning to women's lives. It is Ruth's world that Helô enters during each of the seven scenes. She can borrow that world of parties and social gatherings when she wears clothes from the trunk to attend a wedding (19) and to decorate her mother's apartment for a special dinner (55). But it is not Helô's world, as she admits to her mother:

"A gente não tem quase nada em comum, não é?" [We don't have hardly anything in common, do we?] (34).

Clothing and appearance are mentioned in *Querida mamãe* as reminders of Ruth's past and in opposition to Helô's modern attitude about "dressing up." The contrast between mother and daughter echoes that of the plays discussed previously in the first section of this chapter. The elegant clothes in the trunk reflect Ruth's views that women must care for their physical appearance. Thus, Ruth's clothes communicate her concerns regarding dressing within the confines of her class and her status, always tastefully and stylishly. Helô's clothing is both a form of defiance and an assertion of self, as it was for the adolescents in the earlier plays. Helô sees her way of dressing as a truthful reflection of her feelings, rather than a cover-up designed to please others, as when she says:

"Quando eu estou mal, estou mal. A coerência é absoluta por dentro e por fora."[When I'm bad, I'm bad. The agreement is absolute inside and out] (29).

Ruth's favorite song "As praias desertas" [The deserted beaches] by Antonio Carlos Jobim, which refers to a romantic encounter waiting to happen on a deserted beach, contains references that apply not only to Ruth's affair, but also metaphorically represents the fact that mother and daughter do not share the same world or viewpoint. Ruth likes this song because it reminds her of that secret romance of years past, but the idea of meetings waiting to take place also refers to Helô and her mother, who like lovers, are drawn together from worlds far away by their love for each other. And like lovers, each is in search of a relationship that will allow her to be true to herself. Jobim's lyrics emphasize the act of waiting and build up an expectation of the lovers' arrival. So, too, Amaral's seven scenes create the expectation that Helô and her mother will reach a point of understanding somewhere in between their two worlds.

There is, however, no in between to span the distance between the worlds of Helô and her mother. Having a professional life as a physician, being divorced, and having her own adolescent daughter to raise are new functions that Helô's grandmother and mother never knew. The difficulties and frustrations that pull Helô in many directions don't just constitute a personal problem that she has yet to resolve, but a symptom of a social disequilibrium that opened up opportunities for women without any concomitant changes in the existing patriarchal structure of work and family life. Women like Helô, who have chosen to pursue those opportunities, have suffered because the workplace and home demand two different kinds of women, yet most of society only knows how to respond to women in the context of the traditional model. Women like Helô struggle to find a place for themselves where there are few if any places and little, if any, understanding afforded them. When Ruth asks her daughter:

> "Você não lamenta que as coisas entre a gente sejam tão difíceis, que a nossa relação seja tão magoada?" [Don't you regret that things have been so difficult for us, that our relationship has been so unhappy?] (61),

she is appealing to the personal level of mother-daughter interaction. But the societal acceptance that Ruth received in the 1950s is not yet available to her daughter, and while Ruth tries to support her daughter, she does not understand how their worlds are different. As a result, mother and daughter remain at the opposite ends of the feminine cultural script waiting for the granddaughters of the future to negotiate the distance.

Querida mamãe stages the efforts that a mother and daughter make to find common ground and mutual understanding within an historical context that has not yet constructed the necessary bridges. Inside the protective refuge of her apartment, the mother conserves the decor, clothing, music, memories, relations with other family members, and values of the past. But she cannot protect her daughter from the changing society outside the home. Helô's life is a history of failures to make meaningful attachments. Most of the important connections that Helô needs to affirm herself and to separate from her mother collapse around her at the same time that her relationship with her mother is threatened by illness. Helô has initiated her separation but has not been able to complete the process, because her attachments do not last; they bring her pain rather than affirmation. The stability that characterized her mother's life cannot be reproduced for Helô because as a woman adopting a profession and motherhood, she is the one who pays for adaptations that society has yet to make.

Querida mamãe and La partida offer bittersweet moments in the relationship between mother and adult daughter. Adela from La partida does not yet know the price for her choices. She leaves home for the first time not only in confidence, but also in innocence to establish herself as a separate person. Helô, on the other hand, is too familiar with the price of transgression since she has been paying for it since she was a girl. Her difficult personality, the result of both internal and external forces, has made taking steps toward independence and autonomy a slow process. The mothers in both plays provide their daughters with love and support, but neither fully understands the new world into which their daughters have ventured. The gap that separates the women was created by the evolution of women's roles in a society that positions mothers and daughters at even greater odds with each other. Both plays suggest the need for the construction of new cultural scripts that allow more freedom of expression between the two existing possibilities for women, selfless and selfish, and between the two existing models of motherhood, the traditional and the postmodern.

The six plays studied so far emphasize that the world on stage and its characters reflect the lives of the audience. As a whole, the Latin American women dramatists who wrote these plays employ realism in their stories granting only an occasional liberty that might call attention to the theatricality of the play. For example, the clock that stops at 3:00 P.M. in La partida, or the magical appearances of the great-grandmother with her cigarettes and jewelry in Madre nuestra remind the audience that these "slice-of-life" events are fictions and not mirror images of reality. But the last two plays to be discussed in this chapter, *Amantíssima* by Susana Torres Molina, and *Casa matriz* by Diana Raznovich manipulate both the form and the content of relations between mothers and daughters with ritual and parody. *Amantíssima* emphasizes visual and aural elements, instead of dialogue, to portray the relationship as a difficult journey of pain and misunderstanding that ultimately resolves in an image of feminine unity. *Casa matriz*, on the other hand, revisits predictable moments in mother-daughter encounters through the theatrical frame of a woman hiring an actress to play "mother" to her. Diana Raznovich presents a failed effort at connection, that is, a show that pretends to offer emotional engagement but delivers only counterfeit feelings.

Susana Torres Molina and Diana Raznovich belong to a growing feminine presence in Argentine dramaturgy identified by Nora Lía Jabif as *Las hijas de Griselda* [Griselda's daughters] (48–51). In fact, Griselda Gambaro (b. 1928), Argentina's most famous woman playwright, has mentored many of this new generation, helping to foster her legacy of feminist theater in Latin America.[10] Torres Molina and Raznovich are contemporaries who challenge their audiences by staging the unexpected; they invert, transgress, and disrupt commonly held views about society and theatrical representation. Both portray the dehumanizing aspects of consumer culture, examine gender identity and women's lives in a *machista* world, and employ metatheatrical techniques such as role- and game-playing to critique Argentine society. Each has contested the boundaries of social propriety and gender binaries by writing about female eroticism, lesbianism, and transsexualism.

Their plays about this most important feminine relationship— the mother-daughter bond—were written between 1987 and 1988, but followed different paths. Torres Molina's *Amantíssima* [Beloved] was performed in 1988 and is available only in manuscript form while Raznovich's *Casa matriz* [Dial-A-Mom or MaTRIX, Inc.] has been published three times. The play has been performed in Europe, the United States, and in Buenos Aires. Torres Molina's play has had less visibility and in its current form is difficult for the critic to work with since it provides only the barest outline of what should happen on stage.

Both of these plays dispute the Argentine truism, *Madre hay una sola* (There's only one mother) by staging relations between characters who portray many versions of mothers and daughters. The plays present mother-daughter relations as *un viaje catártico*, (a cathartic trip) to use Perla Zayas de Lima's words about *Amantíssima* (1998, 336). By focusing on connections between mother and daughter as an adult need, the plays also dispute the traditional model of development that associates attachment with childhood dependence alone. Instead, the plays affirm Terri Apter's observation that emotional connection is a key component for independent daughters as well who work to cultivate and nurture it (277). In Raznovich's *Casa matriz*, the daughter's efforts to gain that engagement fail, and she is left calling out for mother, but in Torres Molina's *Amantíssima*, mother and daughter unite and thus create the potential for resisting patriarchy and its efforts to manipulate mothers and daughters.

The abstract and minimalist approach adopted in *Amantíssima*'s thirty-five rapidly changing scenes produces "una polisemia casi inasible [an almost inaccessible multiplicity of meaning]," according to Perla Zayas de Lima (337). The play challenges its audience to actively construct meaning from its tableaux of gestures, movement, sound score, and limited verbal communication. Scholars and the dramatist herself have attempted to define this *polisemia* in thematic and descriptive terms. Jacqueline Eyring Bixler sums up the play's topic as a catalog of "key moments of female existence, such as birth, mother-daughter bonding and separation, and death" (1998, 227). Zayas de Lima labels the play one part celebration and one part theater of cruelty (1998, 343) in which "El musical y el verbal tienen que ver con hacer florar el subconsciente que con intento de comunicación" [The musical and the verbal have more to do with a flowering of the subconscious than with the intent to communicate] (337). In Torres Molina's own introductory notes, she calls her play "teatro de la imagen" [theater of images] because "el espectáculo investiga el lenguaje de los cuerpos, al ritmo de un montaje cinematográfico" [the performance examines the language of the bodies, to the rhythm of a cinematographic setting]. The playwright rejects the idea that the scenes recreate everyday life since "Se intenta trascender lo natural hacia un ritual de lo femenino" [the scenes attempt to transcend the natural toward a ritual of the feminine] (1).[11] Despite the schematic and complicated nature of the script, the rich textures of sound, light and movement offer new ways to experience the mother-daughter encounter.

Casa matriz, in contrast to *Amantíssima*, builds an elaborate and outrageous frame in which to examine its version of mother-daughter relations. The title, translated as "Dial-A-Mom" and "MaTRIX, Inc." refers to a fictitious company in Buenos Aires that offers its clients the opportunity to rent an actress to come to their home for the purpose of reenacting mother-child relations. Lucy Gilbert and Paula Webster have argued that our relationships to our parents are based largely on unfulfilled needs (1982, 61), suggesting that Raznovich's *Casa matriz* could be a solid economic venture since its customers are as unlimited as their needs. The play captures the visit of an actress, known as the Substitute Mother, to the apartment of a literature professor and playwright named Bárbara on her thirtieth birthday. The substitute mother has been contracted to perform eight different types of mothers as selected in advance by the protagonist from a list of twelve hundred possibilities. For her part, the client is obligated to play eight different daughters that correspond to the mothers she has requested.

In spite of their differences, both plays require virtuoso performances from the actresses and complicated coordination of provocative music, settings, costumes, and properties. Both plays begin with sacred music from Bach that sets the tone for the actions that follow. *Amantíssima* opens and closes with *The Passion According to St. Matthew*, a piece that tells of the persecution, trial, crucifixion, and burial of Jesus. Its use in Torres Molina's play encourages the comparison of the suffering of Jesus to that of mothers and daughters in their relations with one another. Further, it marks mother-daughter relations as a hardship, or difficulty that must be tolerated and reinforces the idea that mothers and daughters are *un calvario* (a calvary) for each other, as the popular expression would describe it. Yet, even though the music and its story code the mother-daughter encounter as painful and defeating, they also establish its value as a significant and restorative earthly experience. Bach's *Magnificat*, a piece that belongs to the tradition of sacred compositions that glorify Mary as the mother of Jesus (based on Luke 1:46–55), creates the potential for a similar transcendent experience in *Casa matriz*. The stage directions state that Bárbara *Está poseída por la espléndida versión del Magníficat que inunda el espacio escénico* [Is possessed by the splendid version of the *Magníficat* that floods the scenic space] (162).[12] But in *Casa matriz*, the reverent music becomes more than background commentary, since it is directed by the protagonist with a maestro's baton while she is dressed in sensual clothing and standing on her unmade bed. Because Bárbara controls the music, it also becomes a player in the scene, representing both her excitement at the arrival of her mother for hire and her desire as client to get her money's worth out of the emotional climate she is creating with the music. Whereas Bach's music in *Amantíssima* serves as a metaphor for adversity in the relationship, in *Casa matriz*, it represents two versions of motherhood, the exalted Mary and her consumable substitute.

The power struggle between mothers and daughters in *Amantíssima* and *Casa matriz* is limited and shaped by the unusual theatrical framework employed by each dramatist. Torres Molina's striking images that repeat and accumulate, evoking more than they explain, guide the audience through a solemn world akin to ritual. In contrast, Raznovich's humorous but nonetheless biting critique simulates game playing, with its rules, expectations for outcomes, and completion. Both works emphasize spectacle, magnifying the setting, costumes, and properties to a position of greater or equal importance than that of the characters and their dialogue.

Amantíssima's abstract world, which Jacqueline Eyring Bixler and the dramatist herself have labeled expressionist (1998, 227; 1988, 1) employs its setting, costumes, properties, and sound effects to highlight the tensions and ironies in mother-daughter relations. The setting divides the stage into two separate regions that are joined by a bridge, a sign and site of potential contact and union. A tunnel connects both sides of the stage area allowing rapid entrances and exits and serving as another representation of passageways between the women. Candles, torches, and spotlights illuminate key areas of the stage or the characters themselves not only signaling attempts to gain insight and understanding, but also indicating profound isolation. During the performance, the events staged change location, moving from one side of the stage to the other, but always placing the characters at a distance from one another. Thus, the physical boundaries that separate the characters in stage space echo the emotional boundaries that often keep mother and daughter from understanding each other.

The characters, along with their costuming and properties, communicate the timeless, ritualistic ambiance of the play through analogy and symbolism. The three characters in *Amantíssima*, Madre (Mother), Hija (Daughter), La maga (Magician or Sorceress), and a

double for each, maintain the pace of scenes that rapidly alter location and content, as the playwright explains in her introductory notes
(1). Although for Bixler, the doubles "imply the presence or at least
the possibility of an Other" (1998, 228), it seems more likely that the
doubled characters are actually part of a larger design to mirror the
feminine condition. Not only do the three characters have doubles,
but all six women look alike, costumed identically in their white
petticoats, short red hair, makeup that accentuates their eyes and
mouths, and bare feet. As a result, the characters appear on stage as
abstractions or archetypes of womanhood first, and only later do they
become mothers, daughters, or sorceresses through their actions and
relationships with one another.

Symbolism from Christian, pagan, and modern sources imbues
the relationships with a sense of continuity and permanency. The
women wear the signs of physical pain and suffering in the blood
stains on their fingers and in the genital area of their petticoats. But
these stains suggest both the ancient prohibitions associated with
menstruation and women's sexuality and at the same time their fertility and capacity to bear children. The petticoat that covers each
woman's body is thematically repeated in color and purpose by bandages on the arms and legs of the performers. Like the stained gar-
ment, the bandages symbolize the emotional wounds and suffering
that mothers and daughters cause each other and the possibility for
healing that they promote by covering and protecting the injury. Bandages and sunglasses over the eyes, ears, and mouths serve to block
out communication and perception, as Bixler has noted (1998, 229),
indicating that mothers and daughters have difficulty seeing or understanding each other. In two scenes, a clump of bandages represents
both the newborn daughter and the baby Jesus in swaddling clothes.
Additional Christian images of a cross and crown of thorns are associated with the mother, in a scene in which she gives birth to the
crown of thorns, and to the daughter who wears the crown of thorns
and carries the cross in several scenes. Thus, the daughter is portrayed
as a burden to her mother, and at the same time as someone who also
suffers while growing up. But the references to Christ contain at least
two messages, for he was both martyr and savior, making the cross and
crown of thorns imply both suffering and salvation.

The music, sound, and theatrical effects for *Amantíssima* not
only contribute to the magical ambiance of the play and heighten its

sensory impact, but they also serve to reinforce the idea of distance and tension in the mother-daughter relationship. Special music that was composed for the performance accompanies at least nine scenes where it calls attention to the slowly changing nature of the relationship. In the first of the nine scenes, "Presentación " [Introduction], the music introduces the characters and their isolation marked by separate but parallel worlds where each represents her own needs. When the music returns in the middle of the play, scene 15, Madre and Hija have changed their relationship by moving into the same stage space; they are now connected to each other by an elastic rope. Madre pulls Hija back toward her each time she attempts to move away, pointing to the daughter's effort to become more independent while her mother still exercises control over her. In three of the closing scenes, from scene 29 until the end, the music focuses attention on the growing reciprocity and nurture in the actions of the dyad.

Sound effects such as heartbeats, gongs, hand cymbals, percussion, and a children's lullaby offer conflicting acoustic qualities to the scenes. In some cases, the sound effects actually instigate action within the scenes as well as serving in the more traditional mode of creating an emotional atmosphere. A gong, an instrument often used to announce important events, functions in a harsh, disruptive fashion in "Despertar" [Wake up] and "Despertar II" [Wake up II] as an alarm clock that interrupts the sleep of the Hija and Maga. In scene 6, "Des-encuentro" [Mis-encounter], the gong signals disruption when mother and daughter reach out but fail to physically touch each other. This same motif is repeated in scene 8, "Negativo y positivo" [Negative and positive], where the gong again calls attention to missed connections. Unlike the gong that loudly breaks the action or conveys failure, heartbeats suggest a more hopeful sound, especially when employed during scenes that occur on the bridge, a site for mother-daughter interaction. In scenes 4, 16, and 23, the sound of the heartbeat intensifies the efforts of Madre and Hija to find one another as they cross the bridge calling out to each other:

"¿Mamá . . . mamá . . . mamá?"

and later in a more direct confrontation on the bridge as they speak to each other. In these scenes, the heartbeats suggest a longing and desperation to connect with the mother that is shared by both mother and daughter.

Special effects present abstract images of the mother-daughter relationship and enhance the representation of barriers between the characters. For example, in scene 24 fragments of body parts extend out like a bas-relief from behind a white sheet that is lit with black light. These images are accompanied by the sound of recorded fragments of speech belonging to the Mother, Hija, and Maga. The scene, titled "Fragmentos"[Fragments] creates three simultaneous references—to women as dehumanized and sexualized body parts, to the play as fragmented pieces of scenes and dialogue, and to the mother-daughter relationship as disconnected. Scene 26, "Pared de sangre" [Wall of blood] reinforces another recurring image of wounds and healing with its white, lighted surface upon which red drops fall and splatter. The play also employs smoke in at least two scenes—one to highlight the unreality of the Hija's dream and the other to surround, obscure, and protect the naked Madre and Hija as they engage in their first face-to-face effort to discover each other.

Amantíssima's plot does not develop in the traditional rise and fall of dramatic action, nor move according to cause and effect, although it does reach a climactic end. Neither do the markers in life, events such as birth (scenes 27, 28, 30), separation (scenes 11, 15), aging (scene 18), or death (scene 25), occur in narrative order, although all of them appear. Instead, images of repetition open and close the play and figure prominently throughout. In the opening scene, two bodies or dolls covered in gauze bandages rotate side by side, signaling the dominant features in mother-daughter relations as injury, separation, and duplication. When the wrapped bodies reappear at the end of the play *chorros de luz* (streams of light) shine from within each body, indicating mutual enlightenment, or understanding (37). Repetition takes place within the scenes, when mothers and daughters replay their movements three times, and it occurs from one scene to the next, when entire scenes are repeated later in the play. This repetition communicates the idea of a feminine legacy that mothers receive and hand down to their daughters who then repeat it and pass it on. The idea of legacy is reinforced in scenes where mother and daughter move toward each other by rotating their bodies separately or by rotating together with their backs touching. Repetition also lends a ritualistic feel to the play by disassociating its events from narrative or logical time. It implies that relations between mothers and daughters are not bound by physical and emotional development and as a result do not progress smoothly, but stop, repeat, stand still, and then move again. This disjointed but repeating presentation focuses attention on each individual scene at the same time that it builds a picture of the effort and energy that mothers and daughters expend in their growing relationship. In addition, it dismantles the traditional psychological developmental model that plots human growth as linear movement from dependency and inequality toward separation and equality. The play attempts to free emotional attachment from its usual link to childhood in order to prepare for reestablishing emotional connections between mother and adult daughter, a step that Carol Gilligan has outlined as fundamental to healthy mother-daughter relations (1988, 14).

Through body movement and facial expressions, the characters convey the emotional and physical tensions between mothers and daughters. The short scenes and intense phrases create the sense of struggle and eventually the move toward understanding. The prevailing characterization of the daughter is communicated in jerky, awkward, and tentative movements that reveal her immaturity and dependence. During most of the scenes she communicates her weakness, suffering, and need. Like the *mal-amada* (the poorly loved) mentioned earlier in the chapter with regard to young daughters, this daughter also does not get the attention she needs (Xavier 1991, 13). The mother's actions communicate her power and vanity, frustration and love, demonstrating that she is torn between the desires to nurture and control her child, on the one hand, and attend to herself, on the other. This situation appeared in plays discussed earlier in this chapter in which patriarchal mothers were caught in an "exclusionary opposition" where their choices were either to be selfless, serving others but at odds with themselves, or selfish, attending to themselves but at odds with others.

Molina's third character, La maga, functions in many roles, "facilitator, spectator, and mirror image" in Bixler's words (1998, 228). She first appears in scene 3 as someone who brings light to the mother and daughter in the form of torches, helping to guide them toward each other. In her multiple roles La maga occupies the same stage locations as both mother and daughter, at times in actions that support the daughter, such as when she claps approvingly or waves her cape; at times reenacting key moments in the mother's or daughter's lives, as if to explain mother and daughter to each other.

Amantíssima portrays the life span of mother-daughter relationships as a push-pull of feelings defined by Nora Glickman as *la pasión* y *el narcisismo* (the passion and the narcissism) in her reference to *Casa matriz* ("Parodia" 1994, 95). Mothers ignore and worry about their daughters. They are blinded and deafened to their daughters' needs by their own images in the mirror that consume their attention and seduce them. This narcissism becomes an obstacle to the daughters' well-being as demonstrated in two key scenes, "Presentación" [Introduction] and "Presentación II" [Introduction II], that show the mother looking at and touching her image in the mirror while her daughter stumbles toward her with her arms outstretched and then falls. These movements are repeated by mother and daughter three times in each of the two scenes. The daughter's actions also are echoed in scene 9 by La maga who imitates and repeats six times the jerky step, arms reaching out, and the fall. However, rather than showing these needy daughters turning to men in the hopes of fulfilling their emotional needs, as was the case in most of the plays in this chapter, Torres Molina provides an alternative model in which mother and daughter nurture each other.

Mothers are not completely insensitive to their daughters' needs since they express frustration with their own abilities as caregivers. These doubts are revealed most clearly in the questions repeated in scenes 3 and 16:

"¿Qué querés? ¿Qué necesitás?" [What do you want? What do you need?]

spoken as the mother moves toward her child, and in her words in scenes 5 and 10:

"No es tu locura en si, lo terrible . . . es mi terminante sensación de fracaso" [It isn't your insanity in itself that is terrible, . . . it is my decisive sensation of failure]

as she moves toward her daughter. In the later scene, she wakes suddenly from a nightmare at the same time as these same phrases are played from a recording.

Daughters not only gravitate toward mothers, but they also attempt to free themselves from their influence. The most powerful images of the need to be with mother are those scenes, such as the introductory ones and others when the daughter walks, rotates, or searches for her mother in her awkward, infantile step or calls out to her repeatedly "¿Mamá? ¿Mamá?" But the images of daughters wanting to control their own futures are equally dynamic. For example, in one scene the daughter stands up and spreads her arms as if to fly away, but the mother covers her with a cloth, almost suffocating her before she can calm her down. This effort to become more independent also is expressed in the lines spoken by the daughter in which she rebels against her mother:

"Para que finalmente me veas, voy a tener que desaparecer de tu vida, de mi vida, . . . de la vida" [In order for you to finally see me, I am going to have to disappear from your life, from my life . . . from life] (17),

and

"Tu ausencia es tan fuerte como tu presencia" [Your absence is as strong as your presence] (22).

The most elaborate portrayal of revolt is scene 21, "El sueño de la hija" [The daughter's dream], in which the daughter plays out a show of power when she places her mother and the magician on stage as if they were dolls and then controls their movements by stamping her feet (22).

Taped commentary and monologues provide clues as to how the conflictive relationship might be changed, reinforcing the idea that mothers and daughters have the power to heal their relationship. One repeating motif, staged from the tunnel, by candlelight, and spoken by La maga, asks:

"¿Qué tenés ahí? . . . Un secreto . . . (Pausa) ¿Qué tenés ahí? . . . Un secreto . . ." [What do you have there? . . . A secret?] (8, 20).

This question seems to refer to both mother and daughter and it introduces the idea that both family members withhold insights, emotions, or gestures that could help the relationship gain greater comprehension. The phrase,

La cordura es una ilusión (Common sense is an illusion),

played from offstage is heard twice in the play, once in response to the daughter's efforts to break away from her mother (scene 11) and again in response to the tentative efforts made by mother and daughter to seek out and connect with each other (scene 23). This phrase seems to say that intellectual understanding is not enough to create engagement. That is, it advises mother and daughter to find a range of methods to build their relationship.

The evidence that the characters don't give up in their efforts to connect takes place in the final scenes of the play in which the push-pull evolves into cathartic actions and images of understanding, caring, and reciprocity. Scene 29 marks the beginning of negotiations toward achieving a common ground that culminates in the concluding scene, scene 35, with the rotating figures exuding light. This movement confirms Bixler's description of the play as a journey toward understanding (1998, 227). Earlier motifs begin to take on transformative power, while efforts to see and understand seem to bring mutual comprehension to the characters. Scene 29 "Almas" [Souls] contains the first step toward understanding when the mother and daughter rise up leaving their clothed bodies on the floor and stand before each other naked and vulnerable. With light from candles they explore each other's bodies in a dance of mutual discovery (30). The next step occurs in scene 31 "Espejo roto" [Broken mirror] when the mother, who appears hypnotized by her hand mirror, a scene presented earlier, suddenly throws it on the floor breaking it into pieces. If we accept that the mirror previously stood for vanity, self-absorption, or even as Jenijoy LaBelle suggests, the effort to see the daughter in the future (1988, 81), then breaking the mirror frees the mother from a seductive trap, liberating her from worries about her own external beauty in order to attend to her daughter. In scene 32, "Curación" [Healing] the mother not only appears to lick her daughters wounds, symbolizing their healing, but she also places her daughter's arm over her own heart and lies down on her daughter's legs in an inversion of the Pietá. The earlier reference to keeping secrets, spoken by La maga:

"¿Qué tenés ahí? . . . Un secreto . . . (Pausa) ¿Qué tenés ahí? . . . Un secreto . . ." [What do you have there? A secret?] (8, 20),

takes on new meaning when the daughter repeats the same lines while placing her hands on her heart in scene 33, since she suggests that her secret is contained in her heart or affections. The mother reveals her secret in an offstage recording while a candle burns inside the tunnel in scene 34:

> "El secreto es . . . poder llegar a decir, en el último minuto antes de desencarnar . . . estoy en paz con mi conciencia . . . soy feliz" [The secret is . . . being able to say, in the last minute before losing life . . . I am at peace with my conscience . . . I am happy] (35).

The secrets portrayed by mother and daughter in these two scenes, then, are as simple as love, given to others and self, and happiness.

The culminating scene 35, "Ofrendas" [Offerings] demonstrates the resolution of conflict through the act of loving others and self. It involves all six characters in the three stage spaces: on one side Madre and Hija meet and exchange gifts, on the bridge the two Magas intertwine their bodies in what the script describes as *una perfecta simbiosis* (a perfect symbiosis) [36]; on the opposite side of the stage the double Madre and double Hija appear to begin a relationship by enacting the events that appeared in scene 2 "Presentación." Madre and Hija reach out to each other, put their gifts down, touch hands, and hold them firmly. Their dialogue implies a willingness to finally come together as each admits that she will take this first step for the other (36). The scene ends as they walk away from the audience and toward a door of bright light, pulling off their bandages as they go. A tape recording plays a final speech in which a voice speaks of the generation upon generation of daughters who will come and go and wonders if the wounds, scars, and thorns will be remembered (37).

In this final scene, *Amantíssima* shows mothers and daughters offering each other love and care as equals in two images of unity and emotional connection, affirming Nice's argument that women can have a strong sense of self and also be concerned with connection to and care for others (1992, 63). But it also reminds its audience that even as these women overcome their tensions and bridge their differences, others are just beginning that journey. The final image of the play, a repetition of the opening one with the addition of light emanating from the figures, leads to the notion of a cyclical process in mother-daughter relations. But what kind of cycle does Torres Molina appear to favor—one of conflict and separation or one of unity?

Torres Molina's *Amantíssima* attempts to build feminine solidarity between mothers and daughters. It privileges the sense of continuity in the female condition and refrains from assigning responsibility or culpability to any generation. In fact, the play's costumes, settings, and properties constantly reinforce the physical similarity between mothers and daughters, a similarity that derives from their common biology and emotionally symbiotic relationship. Torres Molina contrasts that similarity and uniformity of her characters with the strange, alienating, and hurtful actions they perform towards each other. Her play highlights the irony of the mother-daughter conflict, because it is conducted by individuals who appear to be identical in appearance, and yet nonetheless fail to understand or support each other.

From its closed feminine space, *Amantíssima* reaches out to mothers and daughters in the audience and encourages them to understand that old models of pain and suffering can be negotiated in order to reconfigure mother-daughter relations. The concluding scenes demonstrate that as adults the women have the power to initiate healing and overcome the tension that separates them in order to rebuild their emotional attachment. The bridge and tunnel on stage reinforce the idea of union by representing a common ground which spans the two worlds, in order to facilitate the search for understanding and love. The same cannot be said for Diana Raznovich's *Casa matriz* whose setting and characters perform in opposition to each other from the beginning and whose efforts to bridge their differences fail.

Casa matriz's setting, with its decor that evokes a combination bordello and unkempt bedroom, is designed to offend the sensibilities of a traditional Hispanic mother. The room flaunts sexual excess in its decorations of reds and pinks, its unkempt bed, its stacks of books with covers and pages painted violet, and in the color coordinated clothing of the protagonist herself. Yet, at the same time the empty armoire, the unmade bed, and the clothes draped about the room suggest the messiness that provokes a mother's admonition to clean up your room. These preparations are designed to present a challenge to the traditional notions of sexual purity, taste, respectability, and neatness that mothers attempt to instill in their daughters. Together the details of the room reveal an individual who has prepared for her encounter with "mother." Bárbara takes the offensive in setting up her room in a way that will be vulgar to the motherly roles she has preselected.

Casa matriz shares *Amantíssima*'s portrait of mother-daughter relations not only as a conflict that displays itself in the push-pull of feelings, and in the repetition of images and words that convey suffering,
but also in the potential for salvation that is the legacy of mothers and
daughters. The plays are similar in their treatment of mother-daughter
relations as an accumulation of key markers or moments in feminine
development. *Casa matriz* involves different scenes with eight mothers,
including scenes with a dead mother, a nursing mother, and several
mothers of adult daughters, in no specific chronological order. In
Amantíssima, the dramatic movement is minimal until the rise at the
end, whereas in *Casa matriz*, it becomes an obsessive process repeated
each time a scene and mother change. Lastly, the costumes, properties,
and sound effects that reinforce images of conflict, pain and barriers,
and produce the ritualistic and sensorial effects in *Amantíssima* gain a
more specific theatrical purpose in *Casa matriz* where they are used by
both characters to dramatize each of the specific moods and relationships for the scenes to be performed with "mother."

Scholars have observed that renting mothers, which Diana
Raznovich has called "la compra y venta de afectos" [the buying and
selling of love] (1996, 12), provides a provocative angle from which
to examine motherhood. For example, David William Foster points
out that purchasing a substitute mother replicates prostitution in its
sale of fantasies that conventional relationships don't allow (1999,
50), while Nora Glickman calls it the "non plus ultra del consumo"
[the pinnacle of consumption] (1994, 97). Laurietz Seda notes that
the play "presenta la combinación más explosiva para una sociedad
patriarcal: maternidad, trabajo y sexualidad" [presents the most explo-
sive combination for a patriarchal society: maternity, work and sexu-
ality] (1996, 26).[13] But Raznovich's parody of motherhood also presents
the opportunity to investigate the tension in mother-daughter relations contained in its two levels of actions. On one level, the Substitute Mother and Bárbara attempt to fulfill their contract by performing
preselected mothers and their corresponding daughters, while on another level they step away from their scenes in order to discuss how
those roles should best be performed. Thus, the play simultaneously
serves as a rehearsal and a performance.

The play's metatheatrical frame of enacting different types of
mothers makes manifest that motherhood is not a natural, instinctive

feminine characteristic but rather a social role, or performance, that women are required to play by patriarchy (Taylor 1998, 114; Seda 1996, 234; Foster 1999, 51). In addition, the play's complicated layering of metatheatrical techniques, social and commercial expectations, and different mother-daughter relations serves to question the nature of relationships between women (Glickman "Parodia" 1994, 98; "El teatro" 1997, 192); the seduction of materialism, especially the loss of values and sentiments in a society of consumption (Seda, 23); and the maternal as a mythic and degraded state (Foster, 49).

Equally importantly, the existing studies of *Casa matriz* make two key observations about the staging of mother-daughter relations that are significant for this discussion. First, Nora Glickman states that not only are the play's parodies of mothers recognizable stereotypes, such as the typical Jewish or Hispanic mothers, but also when the Substitute Mother adopts different stereotypical roles, she instigates a change in the daughter ("El teatro," 192). Glickman describes the discoveries Raznovich made while participating in a support group of women writers discussing mother-daughter relations. From that experience Raznovich learned that, in Glickman's words, "Cambiada la madre, la hija por fuerza cambia" [When the mother changes so too must the daughter] (1994, 95). Second, the reason that clients contract actress-mothers in *Casa matriz*, asserts David William Foster, is to gain a fleeting but real "sense of solid biological, psychological, emotional, and affective link that real life does not provide" (1999, 50). In fact, in spite of the ever-changing nature of the roles the participants play in *Casa matriz*, their ultimate goal, as in *Amantíssima*, is to build emotional connection or attachment, however temporary.

Whereas *Amantíssima* guides its spectators from conflict to feminine solidarity and attachment, *Casa matriz* structures conflict as virtually the only common ground that mother and daughter share. That is, in this play where the characters constantly adopt new personalities, costumes, and situations, conflict becomes the only constant in their relationship. Performing conflict well drives the encounter between Bárbara and her substitute mother, challenging each to engage with the other in an effort to reach theatrical perfection, or catharsis. Bárbara is striving for the realism of a strong emotional response to the situations she and the Substitute Mother create. But excess, not realism, marks their performances. The play's intense encounters generate only theatrical illusions for Bárbara who is not healed by the role-playing but actually still craving real connection, as she indicates when the final curtain begins to fall and she calls out *"¡Mamaaaaaaaaaaaá!"* (187).

The spectacle of *Casa matriz*, with its gaudy setting and its characters changing costumes in an adult version of dress up, helps emphasize its metatheatrical frame. As mentioned earlier, the room is designed to challenge the sensibilities of a traditional Latin American mother. Its decoration, *creado teatralmente para recibir a la madre sustituta* [theatrically created to receive the substitute mother] (160), calls attention to itself and becomes a topic for comments from several of the mothers performed by the actress. Its disorder also provides the opportunity for Bárbara to request a mother's cleaning. But its garish colors and closed, womb-like unchanging space lead Glickman to describe it as an "asfixia que produce el absurdo" [asphyxiation that produces the absurd] (1994, 96). In essence, the room is an artificial and exaggerated backdrop against which Bárbara and the Substitute Mother perform their theatrical versions of mother-daughter relations.

The environments that the characters create through their costumes, acting, and limited use of properties are surprisingly evocative. In spite of arriving prepared for the wrong client, the Substitute Mother demonstrates advanced acting skills when in a matter of seconds she convincingly adopts the body attitude, social class, speech patterns, and costumes of different, if stereotypical, mothers. She dramatizes difficult emotions, such as crying real tears, but also engages Bárbara in the dramatic moment of the scene by controlling the unfolding events. For her part, Bárbara responds quickly to the Substitute Mother with her own adaptations in costuming and reactions. The two women meet for each scene in a minimalist setting that they create with a piece of furniture, lighting, and sound to suggest a train station, a funeral parlor, or Bárbara's apartment.

Like the patriarchal mothers studied earlier in the chapter, the Substitute Mother dominates the stage space, occupying the room and controlling the scenes with her powerful presence. Everything about her is fascinating to watch because, unlike real patriarchal mothers, she is far superior to the standard issue biological mother. She fulfills perfectly what Jane Flax has described as "fantasies about maternal possibilities," that is, the recurring desire in daughters for a "benign force or agent out there in the world looking out for us, attending to our needs, and ensuring their satisfaction" (1993, 153–54). The Substitute Mother quickly demonstrates that her skill and training surpass that received by normal moms. She is the ultimate fantasy, a ready-made mother complete with all the costumes, properties, special effects, and even magical powers to disappear and reappear. Her abilities include physical strength and agility demonstrated in her self-defense judo moves against Bárbara in the opening minutes of the play, in her speed and adeptness at putting on complicated costuming such as a body cast, and in her efficiency in cleaning up Bárbara's room at twice the normal speed. Her expertise as both professional working woman and domestic goddess are reminders of the title Super Mom often used in the United States during the 1980s. But unlike the exhausted women who actually aspired to that dubious honor, the Substitute Mother handles her responsibilities with aplomb.

The Substitute Mother's skills surpass the imaginations of most of her customers who insist on hiring her to perform the same worn-out roles. Her complaints about the limitations of her career suggest that she is underemployed in jobs that demean and squander her talents. Such an uninspiring job scene reflects the narrow-mindedness of her customers, as she tells Bárbara:

> "Repetir cansa. Y hay tanta repetición en todo esto" [It's tiring to repeat. And there is so much repetition in this] (166).

She demonstrates her dissatisfaction with the roles she must play by chiding Bárbara for selecting both mothers and situations that are clichés. Ultimately she breaks her contract and her boredom when she challenges Bárbara to play the daughter of a mother not listed in the contract. In this role, which Diana Taylor describes as "the transgressive one" (114), the Substitute Mother engages Bárbara in an acting duel. Rather than rebel against the stereotypical Hispanic mother, *la gran madre sufriente* (the great suffering mother), the actress dares Bárbara to rebel against a beautiful, talented, and sexually liberated mother. Bárbara finally wins the duel, after repeated prodding, satisfying both herself and her employer, who attributes her success to her purchasing power:

"Para salir ganadora en algunos juegos" [In order to be the winner in some of the games] (185).

Beyond debunking the myths of motherhood as boring clichés, Raznovich's play makes fun of the predictability of the mother-daughter relationship. As observed previously, each mother produces a corresponding type of daughter, but more importantly those corresponding daughters are the opposites of their mothers. This means that the play posits a mother-daughter version of Sir Isaac Newton's third law of thermodynamics (for every action there is an equal but opposite reaction) in which a mother's energy and action in birthing and raising her daughter produces an equal but opposite daughter. The play offers these examples: a weak, long-suffering mother has a rebellious, defiant daughter; but a distant, cold mother produces a dependent, needy daughter; and an overworked, self-effacing mother must live with a distant, but guilty daughter. In these versions of mother-daughter relationships, opposition is the common characteristic that guarantees mutual incomprehension and conflict.

In addition to the opposing personality traits played by Bárbara and the actress, the client-professor prefers scenes which communicate suffering. Her choices favor either mothers who make her feel inferior for being an unsuccessful daughter, or daughters who are cruel to their mothers. In five of the eight scenes she asks to suffer by feeling guilt, anxiety, dependency, lack of worthiness, and failure. In contrast, in two other scenes she plays the unrepentant despotic daughter who rebels against a suffering mother. Only one scene features a mutually complementary relationship of a triumphant daughter, competent and self-satisfied, and an equally enchanting mother. Bárbara's choices show that she is vulnerable to a mother's judgments and therefore needs to ask for forgiveness, something that the Substitute Mother identifies as a cliché for all of her female clients:

"¡Todas las hijas piensan que le arruinaron la vida a la madre!!!" [All daughters think that they ruined their mothers' lives] (178).

Bárbara is a client who has overinvested in the relationship with the Substitute Mother. She is never totally satisfied with the emotional results she expects from her scenes and as a result she both breaks the illusion of the scene and her part of the contract, according to Laurietz Seda (1996, 23). Her actions mark her as a more difficult and demanding client than those the actress will visit during her long day. After conducting their financial transaction, the Madre Sustituta identifies her as an exception when she states in her leave-taking:

> "Bárbara . . . preferiría . . . no verte por un tiempo. Sos una hija muy . . . ¿demandante es la palabra?" [Barbara, I would prefer not to see for a while. You are a very. . . demanding, isn't it, . . . daughter] (186).

In her effort to make a *viaje catártico* (Zayas de Lima 1998, 336) out of the encounter with "mother," Raznovich's protagonist buys into a simulation that cannot deliver results equal to her longing no matter how well it is played.

The push-pull of relations between mother and daughter can be appreciated best in the negotiations that Bárbara and the Substitute Mother conduct while attempting to play their eight scenes. The characters debate the terms of the contract, or the means under which they are meeting, and the art of theatrical realism, or the end they hope to achieve. The tenor of their negotiations contributes to the humor in the play, since the characters analyze in a rational fashion the irrational emotions associated with mothers and daughters. As a demanding and paying customer, Bárbara expects the Substitute Mother to achieve the perfect level of theatrical realism to evoke her emotions; she believes her requests should be met because of the high price she is paying and the guarantees that the company offers in order to satisfy its customers.

The demands that Bárbara makes as client/daughter begin when the Substitute Mother rings the doorbell and they continue throughout the play. They revolve around three desires that Bárbara hopes to fulfill during the visit: first, she wants a sense of exclusivity and ownership of the Substitute Mother; second, she wants to create realistic scenes that evoke the strong emotions she has contracted to feel; and third, she wants to enjoy a sense of attachment to this "mother." Bárbara and the Substitute Mother begin their time together in conflict, because the employee has forgotten the details of the contract and arrives at the wrong moment portraying the wrong mother. Bárbara is incensed not only that her hard earned money is being wasted on the wrong entrance, but also that she is just one of many clients the mother will meet this day. Thus, she engages in a verbal battle with the Substitute Mother to assert her rights of exclusive ownership (163).

The egotism of the client/child is captured in this encounter that reveals Bárbara's desire to fulfill her fantasy of complete service and attention from "mother." Bárbara demonstrates a patriarchal definition of motherhood, as proposed by Marianne Hirsch, which promotes children's sense of possession of their mothers, that is, permitting no boundaries between women and their children (1990, 14). During the remainder of the scene, the tension rises as the actress mentions details of her other "children," (some of whom Bárbara knows) and as Bárbara attempts to resist her growing jealousy. In an almost slip of the tongue Bárbara accuses the Substitute Mother of being no better than a prostitute, whose sexual services are also available to customers with money:

"... Y para colmo pretende que me apiade de que usted sea una. ... (*Está a punto de decir prostituta*) una ... una ..." [And to top it off, you want me to feel sorry for you because you are a ... (*She's at the point of saying prostitute*) a ... a ...] (164).

The link between substitute and prostitute points out the similarity between the two most common professions for women, one degraded and the other revered. It also suggests that as employee the Substitute Mother must portray similar gender-based roles as those of a prostitute in accordance with patriarchy and as required by the customers. The Substitute Mother acknowledges the popularity of this patriarchal ideal of motherhood when she performs several versions of the totally subservient and self-sacrificing mother, especially the stereotypical model for Latin America known as the "Gran Madre Sufriente" [Great Suffering Mother]:

"Soy la Mater sufriente por excelencia. Vestida de negro, limpiando, llorando, con una hija descarriada y alcohólica y embarazada. Soy la Gran Madre Sufriente. Soy la Madre consagrada por el tango. La literatura se ha ocupado vastamente de mí. Soy una madre bíbilica, "parirás con dolor." Soy la santa madrecita. ¡Mira qué lagrimones!!!" [I am the Great Suffering Mother. The Mother deified in the tango. Literature has treated me in great depth. I am the biblical mother "you will give birth in pain." I am the saintly little mother. See my huge tears!] (182).

But unlike real mothers, who find it difficult to establish boundaries between themselves and the needs of their children, the Substitute Mother is a professional actress who only plays the roles, she does
not live them. In addition, in her performance with Bárbara she
improvises a role not listed in the contract that allows her to portray
a more liberated model than those traditionally requested by her clients. For Laurietz Seda this aspect of performing against the contract,
and therefore against the confining definitions of motherhood, is an
act of resistance which provides the "fisura necesaria para eliminar
esos mismos discursos que generalmente se han utilizado para controlar
a la mujer" [necessary break to eliminate these same arguments that
have generally been utilized to control women] (26).

Bárbara and the Substitute Mother also come into conflict over
the performance of their scenes because each strives for different goals.
As a businesswoman, the Substitute Mother is driven by the goal of
efficiency which encourages her to produce the biggest dramatic effect
in the shortest amount of time. Therefore, her particular style of performance leans toward exaggeration and her justification is that it keeps
her roles separate from those of the client's real mother (179–80). As
an actress, the Substitute Mother is trained to be excessive, to put on
her emotions and stay in control of each scene, as she explains:

"Sabemos cómo comenzar, cómo alcanzar el clímax y cómo cortar a tiempo.
Ese es nuestro arte mayor" [We know how to begin, how to reach the
climax and how to cut off in time. This is our greatest art] (170).

However, it is not theatrical realism, but real life emotions that Bárbara
wants to feel in her scenes. She regularly interrupts and requests that
the scenes be replayed because she isn't feeling the expected emotions. Unfortunately, Bárbara cannot remain in control of the very
emotions she wants to feel and she too often responds excessively. In
addition to her efforts to strangle the actress on one occasion (165),
she also shakes and slaps her so excessively that the Substitute Mother,
playing a corpse, unexpectedly sits up, ruining the ambiance of the
death scene (176).

Whereas the Substitute Mother praises the benefits of this artificial
construction of relationships and emotions, which she calls *Gimnasia
afectiva* (emotional gymnastics) and *Una buena ensalada de afectos* (a
good emotional salad) [176], for Bárbara the qualities of a good per-

formance do not replace the real emotional connection with mother. Ironically, the literature professor, who does quite well in her performances as daughter, is not a good consumer, because she wants more than a "play," more than a theatrical substitute for mother. Although the Substitute Mother rarely allows her own personal feelings or situations to enter into the scenes, even when debating or clarifying what Bárbara wants in order to play the scene again, Bárbara repeatedly interrupts the climate of the scene in order to evaluate its effects on her. This constant effort to get the scene just right, that occurs at least once with each mother performed, presents a professional challenge to the actress. More importantly, it indicates Bárbara's need to obsessively engage in more than just the theatrical details of the scene. Bárbara is searching for real emotions that will establish a connection between herself and another.

Not surprisingly, Bárbara's search and her need for human connection appear to be shared by the Substitute Mother who forgets her professional distance on two occasions, suggesting that she too might have similar feelings. In the scene in which mother and daughter both represent talented, attractive, and accomplished individuals, Bárbara requires several replays in order to get the most from the praise offered by her "mother." As the actress works to refashion her lines describing Bárbara as irreplaceable, she appears caught off guard by the words she speaks:

> "*Soy absolutamente sustituible!* (*Pausa extraña, la madre sustituta se recupera. Vuelve a abrazar a Bárbara*). Perdón. (*Retorna*)." [*I am absolutely replaceable.* (*Strange pause, the substitute mother recovers. She hugs Barbara again.*) Pardon me. (*Returns to the scene*)] (179).

Her words imply that merely performing mothers for her clients fails to provide her with a needed emotional link. A second moment occurs at the end of the play when the two women discuss the cost of the visit and Bárbara's wish to have the Substitute Mother return. As the actress recommends another employee, she reveals a curiosity to know which of the mothers she performed most closely represents Bárbara's real mother (187). In the exchange, the actress appears to struggle with the divisions she has established between her client and herself. These divisions were never so clearly outlined for Bárbara, who also makes strange declarations and inquiries into the real life of the

Substitute Mother. She appears to express more than just a client's preference when she tells the actress that her suggestion for a replacement is not appealing:

"Yo . . . la quiero a usted, es decir, no la quiero" [I . . . want you, that is, I don't mean to say that I love you] (187).

Beyond her inadvertent declaration, Bárbara also inquires if the actress has children and attempts to offer the Substitute Mother a tip as she prepares to leave.

By scheduling her encounter with mother(s) on her thirtieth birthday, Bárbara demonstrates that she wants to feel like she is something special, something extraordinary. The Substitute Mother tries to meet that requirement with her performances even as she tells her client that most of her requests, including the decision to treat herself on her birthday, are not unique. Rather, Bárbara is as common and predictable in her needs as daughter as are the other clients. Yet at the same time, the Substitute Mother also lets slip that she too craves the same feeling of being unique and irreplaceable. Nonetheless, the contract that both have signed brings an end to any potential relationship between them, just as the demands of other clients require that the Substitute Mother leave for her next job. No matter what the longing expressed by "mother" and daughter, the time for mutual support and appreciation ends with only a fleeting reference to the possibility of connection.

While *Casa matriz* may question the social roles performed by mothers within the confines of patriarchy, it does not challenge the fact that mothers are important as emotional anchors to their daughters, or for that matter that daughters play an important role in a mothers' life. The play's ending reaffirms that not having a meaningful connection to mother is traumatic: *Bárbara se queda sola en el espacio. Grita ¡Mamaaaaaaaaaá! [Barbara is alone in the room. She yells . . . Motheeeeeeeeeeer!]* (187).

Casa matriz is the only play to parade the stereotypes of motherhood across the stage and even so it performs this critique in a parodic manner. Nonetheless, the over the top performance that the Substitute Mother gives of these formerly sacred roles destabilizes their idealized status. Rather than exalt the greatness of mothers, she complains of the role's routines and its predictability. A mother's obligations are unmasked as the drudgery and burden of "woman's work." At the same time, the supposed loyalty and emotional payment that children devote to their mothers looks false when performed by Bárbara, who is never satisfied with her scene. As a concluding piece in this chapter, *Casa matriz* replays many of the conflicts witnessed in the earlier pieces. Like most of the models for mother that Bárbara has chosen, the plays in this chapter do not offer good role models for mothers and daughters in the audience. However, the power of parody may cause those witnessing this work to reconsider their versions of mother-daughter relations.

By giving voice to the strong feelings that mothers and daughters harbor inside themselves, these plays may help foster a greater attention to this primary feminine relationship. The plays analyzed here address the need of mothers and daughters for more truth in their relationship, not only to help them see who controls and benefits from the cult of motherhood and who is sacrificed in order to keep the myth alive, but also to encourage them to find new ways of negotiating their relationship to better serve their own needs.

The eight plays discussed here are an inventory of the causes and effects on women of patriarchal family values. The divide and conquer techniques employed by patriarchy in the hands of mothers are unveiled as provocations to daughters who respond with familiar defenses that also have been supplied by patriarchy. It is through feminine conflict that the bodies on stage can expose the truths about this socialization of women within the family framework. In the first set of plays, *Marcadas pela culpa*, *Madre nuestra que estás en la tierra*, *En un desván olvidado*, and *De compras* mothers and adolescent daughters turn their energies on each other, consuming rather than developing each other's potential as they struggle over the meaning of womanhood. Struggles lead to conflict, but that conflict is often misplaced since it directs itself toward mothers as the guardians of patriarchy rather than at the young men and fathers who most benefit from it. The second set of plays, *La partida*, *Querida mamãe*, *Amantíssima*, and *Casa matriz*, offer the promise of a better solution for the self-consuming battles of adolescence and early adulthood. Although conflict remains a possibility in the relations between adult daughters and their mothers, the women in these plays appear more aware of their need for each other and the importance of negotiating toward an understanding.

While the plays are significant for having revealed what has been hidden behind bedroom doors, they propose few successful alternatives. The most positive plays imply movement toward a better relationship. For example, in *Madre nuestra que estás en la tierra* and *Amantíssima*, the characters gain a growing sense of unity that points to greater subjectivity in the closing moments. These plays give testimony to the possibility that women can turn to each other for nurture and care, for a sense of value, and to form alliances as a method of resistance to their manipulation. The plays acknowledge the importance of the mother-daughter bond through a lifetime, and not just during the formative years. What both sets of plays do demonstrate more by negative example than positive ones, is that healthy and mutually engaged mother-daughter relationships are the single strongest investment in feminine well-being. From that solid base, mothers and daughters can move toward new versions of themselves as women.[14] The search for new versions of the mother-daughter bond would be particularly helpful in preparing women to face the last stage of their lives, old age, which will be addressed in the next chapter.

CHAPTER 3

Staging Age and Sexuality

"In fiction, whether by men or women, middle-aged women are virtually invisible. All our heroines are young. Even women writers who are
themselves fifty or over write about young women."

—Germaine Greer, *The Change*.

M iddle-aged and older women are missing from Latin American stages just as they are missing from the creative writing
of most Western industrialized and industrializing nations.
This invisibility on stage reflects a similar invisibility in life as Ruth
B. Web has pointed out "with age we suddenly become invisible as
women—neuters" (1975, 8). Until recently the theater repertoire of
the English speaking world offered one image for aging within one
context: the aging father in generational conflict, as presented in
classics such as *King Lear* and *Death of a Salesman*.[1] Regrettably, the
actual number of plays about aging falls short for a human condition
that has come to represent as much as half of adulthood. Youthfulness
is both a cultural and a literary model for the stories that we want to
see and read about ourselves, because it exalts attractiveness, desirability, strength, fertility, and power. Critic Anne Davis Basting notes
that "Theater is an art form *of* and *by* the young" (1998, 2).

Given this context, it is truly remarkable that Latin American
women dramatists have written and staged plays about aging women.
Their plays shine bright lights on the lives of elder women making
them visible and asserting their worth as human beings. Placing aging
women on center stage in dramatic roles disavows the commonly held
notion that "people in their later years are merely distillations of their
former selves, incapable of change or growth," according to Basting in
her study of United States theater (167). The plays in this chapter
investigate how older women resist society's view of them as unattractive, unacceptable, and useless. In short, Latin American women

153

dramatists are, in Basting's words, "using the transformative power of theater to disrupt stereotypes about aging" (8). The eight plays studied in this chapter are divided into three sections based on the themes and ages of the characters. The first section presents the plays, *Soliloquio de la gorda* by Lidia Rebrij (Venezuela, 1992), and *Espelho, espelho meu* by Isis Baião (Brazil, 1989). These two short works about midlife women portray how they simultaneously resist and accept the messages that society has taught them about maintaining their physical appearance. The largest group of plays, *Esperando al italiano* by Mariela Romero (Venezuela, 1992); *Adorável desgraçada* by Leilah Assunção (Brazil, 1994); *Cuesta abajo* by Gabriela Fiore (Argentina, 1990); and *Parque para dos* by Teresa Marichal (Puerto Rico, 1979), treats aging and sexuality as a series of performances. In three of these four plays, the dramatists employ memories to facilitate their characters' efforts to find new roles for themselves. The final section, composed of two plays, *Que Dios la tenga en la gloria* by Carlota Martínez (Venezuela, 1994) and *A Assaltada* also by Isis Baião, portrays the oldest protagonists, in the range of late sixties to early eighties, engaged in a final act of affirmation or reconciliation.

In this chapter, I will argue that dramatists make aging women visible by placing them at the center of the events on stage, beyond the family and its control, and in nontraditional plots that focus on the range of defenses they mount to resist their culture's myths about aging. Many of the plays employ metatheatrical frameworks such as role-playing, ceremony, the play-within-a-play or literary references, as well as game playing, to heighten the public's awareness of the negative stereotypes about aging. From the perspective of middle age and beyond, the characters take the opportunity to refer back in time and to enact previous versions of themselves in order to use those past images to shape present and future selves. Most of the plays are neither depressing nor nihilistic in their representation of aging. Rather, their characters communicate energy, purpose, creativity, and even humor that upend and undermine existing views about aging women.

Feminist criticism is just beginning to develop a critical framework for and praxis on aging. Although the women's movement of the 1970s promoted the personal as a political issue, aging has remained in the realm of the private (Basting 1998, 118). Margaret Morganroth Gullette points out that deep cultural messages about aging have kept identity politics at arm's length from a topic that normally would seem to qualify for cultural analysis (1997, 201). Kathleen Woodward, in her introduction to the collection *Figuring Age*, agrees with Gullette and suggests a second reason why feminists have overlooked aging and ageism. She argues that the women's movement of the 1970s emphasized issues of interest to younger women, such as reproductive rights, child care, and job access. In a similar fashion the academic world reflected intellectual concerns associated with youth, such as, reproductive technology (1999, xi). As a result, feminist theory on aging cannot play a role in this chapter. However, the social sciences and health professions have studied aging since the 1960s and thus, critical insights from research in gerontology will be applied when appropriate to complement the analysis of dramatic and performance elements.

Old age is the end to which most individuals are destined, but that few will announce as their life goal, as Robert Kastenbaum has noted: "While reaching a good old age has become a common hope, being old has rarely been anyone's ambition" ("Exit" 1979, 77). Youthfulness is equated with productivity and reproduction, making it highly valuable. Aging, on the other hand, is devalued since once labor and youth have been spent the individual loses his/her usefulness, status, and prestige. Latin America shares with Western industrialized nations a system of values based on the capacity to produce, consume, and achieve social position as can be observed in this citation from a recent study on aging, *El liderazgo del anciano en América Latina* [The leadership of elders in Latin America]:

> A la persona se le valora básicamente por su capacidad productiva y por la vigencia de los roles que muestre en el desarrollo de sus actividades vitales. Sin embargo, nuestra sociedad promueve intensamente el proceso de sustitución, con el agravante que para los más viejos no existen alternativas concretas que les ayude a reemplazar lo que les es arrebatado en su sociedad. [Each person earns value in society according to his/her productive capacity and his/her status in the currency of the roles performed in life's activities. Nevertheless, our society promotes the process of substitution, with the aggravating factor that for the elderly there are no concrete alternatives that can help them replace what has been snatched from them in their society] (Bahamón Vargas 1994, 108).

This rigid assignment of human potential, a product of the Industrial Age, has not changed even at the beginning of the new millennium and even though technological advances have increased longevity and productivity. Rather, the extension of life has simply caused the negative sanctions on aging to be delayed to even later years, as observed by both Carmen Lucia Tindó Secco and Anne Davis Basting (1994, 22; 1998, 10). In addition, Western attitudes toward aging tend to dismiss it in one broad sweep compressing differences and emphasizing similarities so that "all of life-after-youth (shrinks) into a foreshortened space," according to Gullette (1997, 212). Therefore, our elders not only are rejected by a youth-oriented society that refuses to envision its own future, but also are denied their own specificity.

Both younger and older writers are impacted adversely by society's cult of youth. For example, two Brazilian dramatists studied in this book, Leilah Assunção (b. 1943) and Consuelo de Castro (b.1946), composed television scripts about menopause ("O remate" and "Almerinda") in the 1970s while they were in their late twenties. Neither of the scripts were produced because the directors argued there was little interest in the topic. In this case, young women dramatists looked ahead to treat issues of feminine aging but received no reinforcement for their efforts. In contrast, Ann M. Wyatt-Brown and Janice Rossen have noted in their study *Aging and Gender in Literature: Studies in Creativity* that as writers age the "fear of losing one's audience has inhibited artistic creativity" (1991, 9). These examples suggest that aging as both artistic topic and bodily process has a powerful impact on creativity, causing younger writers not to speak about it and older writers to fear it to the extent that they lose their ability to write.

Another constraint on writing about aging for the theater is the unusual challenge it presents for performers. If, as Basting claims, theater is of and by the young, then directors casting the roles of older characters must confront head on the reigning images of youth and beauty that dominate most stages. Given these restrictions, the director's choices highlight the problematic nature of staging age: if the director chooses young actors then aging is a mask of makeup and posture assumed and projected out toward the audience in the form of a disguise that can call attention to itself as an uncomfortable costume if not performed correctly. On the other hand, if directors choose older actors who are closer in age to those of the play's characters, then the stage makeup and posture must be subtle in order to not over accent their age and become what Germaine Greer has described as "an unsubtle display" (1992, 294). It is no wonder that younger characters populate the traditional realistic theater, not only because directors can draw on a larger pool of actors without needing to worry about how to present aging to the theater public, but also because the theater public is kept from confronting aging as a warped mirror, reflecting faces and bodies either too young or too garish to be recognized.

If aging devalues the individual, it is particularly hard on women, as Kastenbaum has observed ("Exit," 70). Traditionally, women gain value in society on the basis of their physical attractiveness and their reproductive ability, as we have seen in chapter 2. Graying hair and wrinkles do not add up to respectability for women, as they can for men, but rather as signs of loss. What is particularly damaging to aging women is the notion that an aging body past reproduction has no use, no sexual identity nor sexual desire. Freedom from reproductive abilities has been read as loss of usefulness rather than as entry into a different era of sexual expression. Joanna Freuh speaks of "the prevailing erotophobia regarding older women" (1999, 213) and presents the commonly held prejudice that "The matron, a model of sedate inactivity, is the embodiment of the sedation of eros, having given in to the natural death trap of an aging body" (222).

Not all societies erase aging women as Greer points out in her book *The Change*, in which she describes cultures that grant seniority in order to reward aging women for the contributions that they have made to furthering their race. She provides the example of women in Mediterranean societies who wear black not only as a literal marker of mourning (*lutto*), but also as a symbolic marker of their status in society (1992, 56, 38). Another example can be seen in the contrasting terms used to refer to aging women. In English the word "matron" carries negative connotations related to appearance, such as "lumpy, dumpy and frumpy" (Greer 1992, 295) or "spread-and-shrivel" (Freuh 1999, 213), but the word "matrona" in Portuguese and Spanish refers to social status, and implies respect due to age, estate or conduct, or to motherhood. Latin American women share the Mediterranean tradition of wearing black to signify both the loss of family members and the achievement of a respected status in the community.

The status of research and scholarship on aging in Latin America provides some insight into which aspects are receiving the greatest attention. According to titles found in *Libros en Venta* and *Hispanic*

American Periodicals Index, there were significant numbers of investigations into aging. Over two hundred titles of articles and monographs from both sources appeared on the subject *la vejez* (aging). Women's sexuality is not taboo as a subject of research in Latin America either as evidenced by the more than ninety entries addressing adolescent sexuality, dating and sexuality, marital relations, sexuality and AIDS, and the sexuality of lesbians. However, feminine sexuality was most commonly linked to either physical development or reproduction, not to menopause or aging. Fewer titles, around fifty, were listed under the combined keywords women and aging and only two articles listed under the *edad madura* search. The most revealing results came from the combination of the key words aging and sexuality which produced *cero resultados obtenidos* (no results). Thus, while aging as a human condition attracts the attention of researchers and writers in Latin America, sexuality in aging women and men remains an unexplored and possibly unrecognized topic.

Although Latin America has adopted many of the values of the industrialized nations, it continues to place great importance on the extended family unit. Even while under attack from the effects of migration, urbanization, and the rising cost of living, among other modern phenomena, the family struggles to survive as a supportive and tightly knit unit that serves to buffer the aging from culture's message of uselessness. From the perspective of the Roman Catholic Church, the family provides the best place for the aging: "Dado que la familia es el *espacio natural* para nacer, crecer, envejecer y morir dignamente, nos proponemos pues centrarnos en ese envejecer digno cuyo ámbito natural es el hogar" [Given that the family is the *natural place* to be born, grow up, age, and die with dignity, we propose to focus on aging with dignity whose natural place is the home] (Bahamón Vargas, 49). In contrast to society's emphasis on productivity, a different value system operates within the family unit, as noted in this citation from the same source: "En esta comunidad se mira más a la persona por lo que es que por lo que hace" [In this community one is seen more for what one is than for what one does] (1994, 62). Aging parents, or aunts and uncles, for example, seek and receive shelter with younger members of the family. In this context, where their leadership and experiences are revered, the aging can contribute to the educating and caring for family members until they themselves must receive care. The aforementioned study on aging in Latin America noted that "Hay ancianos insertos a la familia ejerciendo el papel de líderes activos, de maestros en el arte de vivir que siguen siendo un verdadero testimonio de plenitud humana para sus hijos y sus parientes más allegados" [There are elders within the family who exercise their roles as active leaders, masters in the art of living who continue to be a true testimony of human fullness for their children and closest family members] (53).

Within the extended family in Latin America, aging men and women are accorded status for performing the same gendered tasks they fulfilled in their youth. Older men maintain their respectability as patriarchs and often assume leadership roles within the family, while older women are assigned to roles that utilize their skills as mothers and thus are appreciated primarily for their nurturing abilities. Families protect grandmothers, but they also benefit from their free services. Moreover, extended families may attempt to limit a grandmothers' individuality to this role of service, as Baba Copper has written about her own experience (1988, 25). In addition, grandmothers by definition must be asexual, unable or unwilling to evoke sensuality or to demonstrate passionate responses, as literary critic Maria José Barbosa has argued (1997, 35). Research in Canada suggests that some family members go so far as to intervene in potential relationships between widowed older women and a new partner, arguing that elderly women are too old and unattractive for relationships (Neugebauer-Visano 1995, 28).

The attention to staging old age in the mainstream theaters of the Spanish- and Portuguese-speaking Americas has been as invisible as that in the rest of the Western world. Generational conflict between a father and his family is a more common theme in Latin America as elsewhere appearing in dramas of rural life such as the classic play *Barranca abajo* (1905) by the Argentine Florencio Sánchez (1875–1910). The subject of old age reappears in both urban and historical plays by the canonical Mexican dramatist Rodolfo Usigli (1905–1979), most notably in *Los viejos* of 1971. The earliest play about aging women by a Latin American dramatist of this generation, *Fala baixo senão Eu grito*, (1969), was staged by Leilah Assunção. A second play on that topic by Assunção along with seven others from the late twentieth century are addressed in this chapter.

The women dramatists who composed the following eight plays about midlife and old age were in their forties at the time they wrote their plays, although one was slightly older (Assunção, age 51) and one much younger (Marichal, age 23). The performance and publication dates span the years 1979–1994, with seven of the eight plays falling in the late 1980s to early 1990s. Not surprisingly, the plays do not follow the traditional pattern of conflict between a patriarchal father and his children, but propose their own dramatic contexts and their own agendas for aging. Half of the plays address generational conflict through the eyes of female characters. These plays tell of discord between elders and their adult children. All of the plays portray protagonists reacting to society's expectations for them and their own expectations for themselves. In most of the plays, the elders are either alone on stage, or in small groups. That is, they are out of the context of their expected places within marriage and within the extended family. Being alone on stage means that the audience can focus on the characters while they are focusing on themselves. A traditional view of an aging woman alone on stage might connote vulnerability, however, these plays use that situation to explore and experiment with new versions of female aging.

The plays challenge the existing stereotypical notions about aging as loss and decline and recognize feminine sexuality and desire in midlife women as potential elements contributing to personal wholeness. Rather than simply conceding to the narrative of decrepitude that characterizes Western society's image of aging, as developed by Margaret Morganroth Gullette in her book *Declining to Decline*, Latin American women dramatists adopt a more nuanced view of aging that acknowledges the specificity of aging women. Although, according to Anne Davis Basting, "old age is commonly described as a mask that shrouds, disguises and burdens one's ageless sense of self, " she believes that these masks are actually with us all across the life course, we just don't see them in our youth (1998, 184–85). Nancy K. Miller agrees that in our lives we wear "many masks that we put on or peel off in the layering of our selves, the layering of our identity" (1999, 13). Gullette has coined the phrase "age identity" to describe the "substantial sense of self-over-time" (1997, 2) and she encourages her readers to recognize "that we can voluntarily discard identities that have come to seem false" (214). Finally, Jenijoy La Belle identifies the "self" not as "an *entity* but as an *activity*, a continual process" (1988, 3). The mask and the layering of identity throughout life together with the idea of self as activity in process, provide a critical framework for rethinking aging in these plays by Latin American women dramatists.

In my analysis of these eight plays, I will look at the strategies women protagonists employ to understand their own apprehensions about aging and defend themselves against their culture's self-defeating expectations. The protagonists struggle against the limitations placed on them, especially the gaps and restrictions in the roles available to aging women. The largest gap occurs for midlife women after menopause particularly if the stable, predefined role of grandmother does not fit comfortably nor affirm them and their sexuality. Kathleen Woodward acknowledges that "few models exist to guide us" in our own aging, but these theatrical examples dramatize a range of imagined life events that turn women into visible, real persons seeking recognition for their experiences (1999, 155). As the female characters in these plays fight to gain their authenticity they reveal the socialization and cultural messages that devalue them. Gullette calls these messages "age lore" and she insists that they begin early in life to shape each individual's sense of self (207). The power of "age lore" acts on individuals in society because, as Gullette argues, "whatever happens to the body, human beings are aged by culture first of all" (3). In their efforts to become visible and to establish their subjectivity, the women characters in these plays add more layers to feminine identity in Latin America. In addition, they serve as possible role models for women in search of better ways to imagine aging. These eight plays begin to fill in the details of the stages of age, giving specificity to the concerns, challenges, and needs of women as they move through the last cycle of life.

Midlife and Menopause

Menopause marks a normal process of aging in women that could be taken as a time of reassessment and growth if it were not for culture's message that menopause equals loss—loss of fertility, loss of youthful appearance and loss of desirability. These losses at midlife lead to an invisibility that Baba Copper has called "sexual erasure" (1988, 28). Along with the loss of sexual identity come further losses of status. In Germaine Greer's words: "We can only wonder how much less women might suffer at menopause if they were to acquire power, prestige and responsibility instead of losing all three" (1992, 68).

Arriving at menopause, then, marks itself as the point in women's lives when their social assets, most importantly their physical appearance, all have been spent. Midlife and menopausal women, in the crudest terms of exchange that culture can construct, are bankrupt.

"The menopausal woman is the prisoner of a stereotype and will not be rescued from it until she has begun to tell her own story" states Greer (1992, 17). Here, then, are two short sketches of midlife stories. The characters of these one-woman plays are presented only in terms of gender, Mulher [the woman] in *Espelho, espelho meu* by Isis Baião, and La gorda [the fat woman] in *Soliloquio de la gorda* by Lidia Rebrij.[2] Both titles refer to the physical appearance of the characters although not with positive connotations. Rebrij's play focuses on body size while Baião's reveals a common feminine preoccupation with the image in the mirror. Baião's title reproduces the oft repeated lines of the vain fairy tale queen in Snow White who consults her mirror to verify that she is the fairest of them all. In subject matter and theatrical techniques, both plays disrupt the notion that menopausal women should accept their inferior status, quietly retire and disappear from the world.

Rather than portraying the women as resigned to their fate, I will argue that the two plays dramatize protagonists who reassert their midlife vitality and individuality through their sexual desire. *Soliloquio de la gorda* [Soliloquy of the Fat Woman] and *Espelho, espelho meu* [Mirror, mirror, on the wall] employ the domestic space of the home as a protected environment for the women where they can examine themselves and their experiences. In these two plays, the characters communicate their vulnerability to the hurtful messages aimed at them and identify the disparaging remarks of "age lore" that work to dehumanize them. *Espelho, espelho meu* stages a theatrical parody of the Grimm's fairy tale *Snow White* that takes place at the beginning of the day as Mulher awakes and prepares for work. She dusts off her mirror to examine her body and to reaffirm that she is still attractive, but her reflection, represented by a similarly dressed actress wearing a large framed mirror, only notices the signs of deterioration. *Soliloquio de la gorda*, in turn, is a monologue that takes place at the end of the day as La gorda returns from a social event where she has been upbraided for letting herself go. She analyzes for the audience her doubly demeaning status as an older and larger woman. Both plays demonstrate the same dramatic movement which begins with a strong emotional response from the protagonists to the denigrating opinions about appearance and age, then moves into a list of commonly held prejudices about older women and finally ends on a defiant note.

Mulher and La gorda represent each side of the menopausal line, as the former seeks confirmation that she has not yet arrived at it while the latter has passed beyond it. Both characters speak of menopause as a time of transition. In Gullette's words menopause is "a critical moment, an event . . . that divides all women's lives into two parts, the better Before and the worse After" (98). Thus, for Mulher the bleeding of menstruation still links her to youthfulness and keeps the inevitable "worse After" at bay:

> "Eu não estou na menopausa. (*Mete a mão entre as pernas, mostra o sangue*). Olha aqui, menstruação! Ainda menstruo!" [I am not in menopause. (*Puts her hands between her legs, shows the blood.*) See here, menstruation! I am still menstruating!] (Baião, 134).

On the other hand, for La gorda, it is the last event in a series of insults that confirm the low status of aging women:

> "Se supone además que después de los treinta y cinco, la buena presencia disminuye y nuestros accidentes de carácter aumentan cada vez más, y . . . luego . . . luego, la menopausia" [It is assumed that after thirty-five, our good looks diminish and our character faults increase even more, and then . . . then . . . menopause] (Rebrij, 103).

Defending the self against the "worse After" is difficult since menopause involves the cessation of biological reproduction, but it is not the cessation of life, as Greer argues: "Menopause is a change but it is not a change from life to death, or death-in-life" (1992, 41). Nonetheless, menopause and the physical signs of aging erase the midlife woman as a meaningful participant in the flow of life. Baba Copper remembers ironically that "Through the absence of harassment, I discovered the invisibility of age" (1988, 29). La gorda takes note of this disappearance of midlife women like herself from all public life:

> "Ni en los trabajos, ni en ninguna otra parte, ni siquiera nos pueden ver en televisión para recordarles nuestra existencia. . . . Es como si no hubiéramos nacido" [Not at work, nor anywhere, not even on television can we be seen so as to remind others of our existence. It's as if we had not been born] (102–03).

Isis Baião and Lidia Rebrij's protagonists communicate that society treats the normal aging process of midlife and menopause as a crime and/or a sin that they are guilty of committing and that they should work to prevent, as La gorda states:

"Y entonces todos nos hacen a un lado. Nos tratan como a culpables. Cometimos lo peor, aquello que no se nombra, lo que solamente se piensa. ¡Hemos llegado a gordos y a viejos: no nos perdonan haber arribado a la cuarenta (*bajando la voz*), a la cincuenta" [And then they push us aside. They treat us as the guilty. We have committed the worst sin, that which cannot be named, that which is only thought. We have arrived at obesity and old age: they won't forgive us for having arrived at forty (*she lowers her voice*) at fifty] (103).

The proof of the crime of aging can be seen in the body of the criminal. Thus, in *Espelho, espelho meu*, the mirror evaluates Mulher and comments on each feature that provides evidence of her declining state: the tinted hair that reveals its gray roots (132), the tiny wrinkles appearing on her face, the sagging muscles in her arms (133), the cellulite, the less than firm breasts, the varicose veins, and so forth (134). Each physical attribute mentioned undermines Mulher's statement that

"Tô ótima, não estou?" [I'm in great shape, aren't I?] (131)

causing her to engage in an emotional battle to assert her own sense of self:

"Pensa que me derruba, é? Não me derruba não. Não preciso de você pra conservar minha auto-estima. Eu sei que estou bem. Estou ótima, ótima, ótima . . ." [You think you can bring me down, eh? You can't defeat me. I don't need you to help me keep my self esteem. I know I am in good shape. I am doing great, . . . great . . . great] (132).

Midlife and menopause situate women on the negative side of the binaries that are applied to women as appealing sexual objects, putting them in an inferior position to men of all ages as well as to younger women. But comparisons such as young/old, desirable/undesirable, fertile/sterile, growth/loss, also place women at odds with their own younger selves as Margaret Morganroth Gullette has noted: "it makes a woman less than *herself*; inferior to her (apparently biological) self at an earlier phase" (1997, 114). This sensation of not only losing to others but also losing one's self is voiced by La gorda:

> "Nos tratan como si fuéramos animales depredadores. Todo el mundo nos quiere echar el guante para humillarnos . . . como si nunca hubiéramos sido igual que ellos. Porque yo también lo fui." [We are treated as if we were marauding animals. The whole world wants to arrest us to humiliate us . . . as if we were never like them. But I too was like them] (102).

In the beauty market, aging women cannot compete because they cannot turn back the clock nor prevent younger women from taking their places. La gorda complains:

> "¿Cómo podemos competir con esas carnes femeninas, nacaradas, con esos traseros firmes y lustrosos, esas cabelleras leonidas . . . de esas mujeres tan bellas y tan jóvenes que andan por ahí? No, nosotras no podemos rivalizar con ellas" [How can we compete with this feminine flesh, like mother-of-pearl, with these firm and shining bottoms, this tawny-colored hair . . . of these beautiful and young women who walk around here? No, we cannot be rivals to them] (103).

Aging cannot be a private event even though both of these plays take place inside the home. For these characters, aging is a constant reaction against the comments and evaluations of others that requires observation of the self in order to evaluate if the judgments of others are true. In these two plays mirrors offer one means to examine the body for the signs of aging. Mirrors reflect back the values of beauty, youthfulness, and vigor that determine women's indirect power in society as long as they remain young. *Espelho, espelho meu* demonstrates that when Mulher looks into the mirror, her own evaluations are as harsh or harsher than those of the world around her. Mulher begins her day by looking into the mirror and calling to it to tell her how she looks (Baião, 131). When the mirror points out faults rather than confirming beauty, Mulher examines herself even more carefully for the seriousness of each fault and then protests the mirror's opinion. On the other hand, La gorda defends herself from the "truth" of the mirror by limiting the self-destructive analysis that absorbs Mulher's energies in front of her full length mirror. La gorda declares:

"Por eso es que quise quedarme solamente con este espejito. (*Agarra un espejo que tiene un mango*). Así no me veo. Así no me entero" [This is why I only wanted to keep this little mirror. (*She picks up a hand mirror.*) That way I can't see myself. That way I can't find out] (Rebrij 1992, 104).

What is the defense that La gorda and Mulher employ to contest the destructive narrative of midlife loss and decline? It is the energy of their own sexual desire that has not succumbed to the numbing and homogenizing story of aging. "What women in the climacteric are afraid of losing is not femininity, which can always be faked and probably is always fake, but femaleness. After centuries of conditioning of the female into the condition of perpetual girlishness called "femininity," we cannot remember what femaleness is" (Greer 1992, 52). Perhaps La gorda and Mulher do not proffer a new definition of femaleness, as Germaine Greer suggests is necessary, but each asserts the existence of her own sexual desire as a form of resistance. In the closing moments of *Espelho, espelho meu,* Mulher attacks and bites the mirror with her newly grown vampire fangs, rather than sending an apple to be bitten by her competitor Snow White. As she declares her sexual desire, she asks the mirror one last time:

"Espelho, espelho meu, existe alguma outra mais jovem e bela do que eu?"[Mirror, mirror of mine, is there anyone else as young and beautiful as me?] to which the mirror answers in a sensual voice "Não, gostosa, Branca de Neve já é tetravó . . ." [No you tasty little thing, Snow White is a great-great grandmother compared to you] (135).

This humorous twist to the Snow White fairy tale that casts Snow White as the aged one not only turns the tables on the generational competition for beauty, it also reaffirms the sexual vitality of midlife women. That is, the external signs of aging, presented as a relentless list of losses, cannot overpower Mulher's internal expression of desire that serves as the last image and event of the play.

La gorda's sexual desire is expressed through the action of eating chocolates which substitute for the sensual pleasure of having a man:

"Mientras los como es a él al que estoy comiendo, al que estoy chupando, al que estoy desmenuzando con mis dientes . . ." [While I eat the chocolates it is he that I am eating, that I am sucking, that I am tearing into bits with my teeth] (104).

The concluding moments of *Soliloquio de la gorda* emphasize that La gorda has not given up hope that she will encounter *un milagro* (a miracle) of a man, her *Mesías* (Messiah) to meet her emotional and sexual desire, but also that her self-image as a fat woman represents a desirable woman, like the models of Rubens (104). She ends her soliloquy in a state of ecstasy as she compares the opulent and sensual features of Rubens' models, especially their hips, thighs, and breasts, to her own and then calls out to her longed-for lover:

"¡Al Mesías!" [To the Messiah!] (104).

Here La gorda's words proclaim sexual desire and desirability in a model of body roundness that contests the reigning youthful model of thinness. It also is a call for sexual gratification, an affirmation of desire for midlife women cloaked in religious fervor and the imagery of salvation.

The theatrical techniques employed in the two plays, solitary speech and parody, disrupt the normal expectations for drama that are based on dialogue and exchange. Ken Frieden asserts that monologue "signals the active break from norms of ordinary language and is thus allied with innovation, deviant discourse, and creativity" (1985, 20). Rebrij's use of soliloquy in the title connects her protagonist to the tradition of speaking alone on stage, and specifically to the most famous of Western drama's lonely speakers, Hamlet. As Frieden notes: "Hamlet soliloquizes in reaction to a hostile world" (130). Clearly, La gorda's strong words betray the anger and pain that she feels after her evening with friends at a social event that was neither friendly nor sociable. In the solitude and safety of her home she can respond wholeheartedly to the crass observations presumably made by her circle of acquaintances, rather than contain herself and her words as polite decorum requires. Deborah R. Geis has observed that the deviant quality of discourse in monologue has drawn women playwrights to it in order to dramatize the struggle for female subjectivity through its conquest of narrative space (1996, 170). This observation pertains to Rebrij's efforts in *Soliloquio de la gorda* in which the voice of indignation of one character draws attention to the conditions of the many not represented on stage.

Espelho, espelho meu creates a parodic frame that reminds the audience of its intertextuality with the Snow White fairy tale. In

Baião's reconsideration of competition between youthful beauty and a fading queen, it is the queen who becomes the center of attention. In a sympathetic manner, the dramatist gives human contours to a character that previously stood for evil, fitting the definition of parody as outlined by Richard Hornby. The use of this literary reference is a metadramatic technique that "produces a special heightened, acute perception" (1986, 100). By first making the reference obvious, Baião then manages to add a new insight to the traditional fairy tale. Just as La gorda speaks up about her treatment as older and wider, so, too, Mulher exposes the truth behind the competition for beauty. In both cases, the techniques of monologue and parody create individuals whose words and presence on stage challenge accepted values and delineate a clearer image of menopausal women.

The simple setting for *Soliloquio de la gorda*, a recital by a lone female character with accompaniment by a cellist, enhances the emotional level of the presentation as it accentuates the dramatic content of the protagonist's words. La gorda enters from outside wearing a hat and *un abrigo que ayuda a aparentar su gordura* (a coat that helps cover up her obesity) [101]. Before she speaks La gorda hangs up the hat but she keeps the overcoat on. The text does not specify, but the raincoat probably would be black, both for its cultural message of age and for its ability to dissemble. The image of a large woman dressed in a black overcoat directing herself toward the audience would be both powerful, for its unusualness, and shocking, both aesthetically and culturally. Women of La gorda's age and size do not lay claim to visibility either in the theater or beyond it. The box of chocolates that shares the stage with the protagonist and represents her hidden passions, perpetuates a cultural cliché but its use as an enhancement to La gorda's descriptions of passionate encounters with a lover reveals additional meanings not commonly displayed on stage. While the box of chocolates can be seen as an escape from a cruel world or a substitute for romance, the chocolates also become a means of practicing sensuality, a spectacle that La gorda demonstrates by selecting and eating chocolates as she speaks (102).

Whereas La gorda's soliloquy repeats the traditional model with the audience as intended listener to her accusations of poor treatment, *Espelho, espelho meu* stages a version of monologue in which the character converses with herself, only in this case the self has two real bodies. According to the stage directions, the mirror's "responses" actually are voice-overs spoken by the actress playing Mulher that serve to represent her superego (131). Thus, we could say that Mulher is engaged in a duel between her own need for recognition, her "auto-estima," and the mirror's reflection of her acceptance of cultural values that demean aging women like her. This verbal duel must be conducted by a woman in her nightgown, a revealing piece of clothing usually assigned in theater, as in life, to seduce men. However, Mulher's seduc-tion is of her own image and her defense in the battle of youthful physical ideals against loss, is self-love, even self-stimulation. That is, in the closing moments of the play Mulher bites the mirror, her own image held up by a mute individual also dressed like her, and her own voice-over responds to her with *gostosa* (tasty) [135], an erotic term of approval. This surprise ending suggests masturbation, a shocking spec-tacle designed to challenge preconceived notions about midlife women's sexuality and the dominant practice of heterosexual relations.

These two short sketches are surprising for the frank manner in which they document how culture's emphasis on physical appearance destroys a woman's sense of self as she ages. Youthful beauty and power offer false security against cultural values that interpret normal biological processes in women as degradation. The words of the pro-tagonists convey the attitudes and voices of their peers who sit in judgment of their aging bodies. *Espelho, espelho meu* provides a long, detailed inventory of the weak points in an aging woman's body that totals up to a sum that is less than the whole. No other message of human worth surfaces to counteract the importance of physical ap-pearance until the final moments of the play. *Soliloquio de la gorda*, on the other hand, openly critiques the superficiality of those who accept beauty and status as keys to their own worth:

> "todos aparentando, aparentando lo que no son, pareciendo lo que quisieran ser: más importantes, más ricos, más poderosos, ¡y hasta más flacos!" [all of them pretending, pretending to be what they are not, trying to appear what they wish to be: more important, more wealthy, more powerful, and even more thin!] (101).

La gorda claims the right to be herself inside a body that is not approved of by her acquaintances:

> "Y por eso en el fondo no me inquieta ser gorda. Nada tiene demasiada importancia. Porque si los demás me rechazan, yo los distancio a ellos

con mi cuerpo, con esta barricada" [And for this reason in my heart I'm not bothered about being fat. Nothing is that important. Because if others reject me, I will distance them with my body, with this barricade] (104).

Further, both protagonists engage a source of personal energy, their sexuality, as a form of defense against the messages of superficiality. It is the power of sexual desire and the possibility that it might be exercised that appear to offer redemption to these two characters, saving them, if only temporarily, from further degradation. Thus, the two protagonists contest Greer's view that "The right of the middle-aged woman to sexual self-expression is not one that she can exercise in the absence of an interested partner" (1992, 304). For Mulher and La gorda sexual self-expression constitutes a meaningful manifestation and defense from inside the self that does not depend solely on an interested partner. Whereas La gorda calls out to a hoped-for lover in the closing moments of *Soliloquio*, both she and Mulher continue to practice their own self-stimulation and sensuality. Both characters reinforce the drive within them that identifies their femaleness, with or without a man.

Postmenopausal Women and Sexuality

The postmenopausal characters in the four plays discussed below are even more actively engaged in responding to the demeaning messages of their culture than are the menopausal women discussed earlier. Their actions involve using memories, reenactments of the past, and game playing to help them understand themselves and find new identities. The characters are not reminiscing about the good old days, rather they are performing their memories to justify and explain their lives, as Gullette has noted elsewhere (1997, 86). I will argue that the protagonists in these plays are searching for meaningful new versions of themselves that accompany their older status but do not limit them to narrow, sexless categories like grandmother or old maid (*solteirona* or *solterona*). Their actions demonstrate a phenomenon observed by anthropologist David Gutmann in postparental women in Western societies, "that they seek out, take advantage of and even create powerful roles that fit expanding energies and new appetites" (206).

All four plays place their characters in settings that link aging to waiting. Such a setting appears to reinforce the traditional dramatic presentation of women as passive beings who do not act, but wait on or for others (Kintz 1992, 55; Cixous 1984, 546). Waiting for someone to arrive occupies the attentions of the protagonists in all four plays. The women in *Esperando al italiano* wait for an Italian lover to arrive; Guta from *Adorável desgraçada* waits for her childhood friend Maribel; Rita and Carlos in *Cuesta abajo* waits for their true loves to return; and the elderly audience in *Parque para dos* waits for young lovers to come sit on the park bench. Romero's title *Esperando al italiano* [Waiting for the Italian] openly mimics the classic absurdist play *Waiting for Godot* by Samuel Beckett. Beckett's play and the four studied in this section share traits common to the absurdist theatrical tradition: they begin with the dramatic frame of waiting for someone to arrive; they proceed with all manner of game playing; then they end without much having happened. But while *Waiting for Godot* is a vehicle for communicating man's existential angst at the loss of meaning of life, these four plays explore how older women search for a means to understand themselves and express their sexual desire. Rather than using waiting as a sign of hopelessness and stagnation, these plays employ waiting as an activity that serves to prepare the women for action. Thus, the four dramatists rework the traditional dramatic portrayal of women as passive objects by moving them out of the "waiting-room," to use Hélène Cixous's expression, and placing them at center stage. They also rework the absurdist futility of waiting, game-playing, and human miscommunication into a more positive message of cooperation, understanding, and rehearsal for change.

During the waiting that occupies the duration of the plays, the dramatists introduce their characters, establish the relationships between them, and stage the review and reenactment of their past lives. The obvious enigma that first engages the audience and the characters of the plays centers on the person(s) who is to arrive—who is this person, when will she arrive? But that enigma shifts its focus back to the characters themselves, not only with regard to how they will respond to the newcomer once she/he arrives, but more importantly how they are responding to each other as they wait. In three of the plays, none of the individuals so anxiously awaited actually appears on stage, a signal that the waiting is more important than the arrival.

Esperando al italiano and *Adorável desgraçada* [Disgraced darling], similarly to the first plays studied in this chapter, locate their characters within the protected privacy of women's apartments, feminine spaces hidden from the judgmental eyes of family and society. Within the confines of the living and dining rooms, the characters in both plays entertain themselves while waiting. *Cuesta abajo* [Downhill] and *Parque para dos* [A Park for Two] situate their characters on benches in public parks. In these open and anonymous spaces that are available to all citizens, the characters entertain themselves by performing romantic roles.

Esperando al italiano written by Venezuelan Mariela Romero, is a lighthearted, two-act comedy with a bawdy atmosphere and openly suggestive sexual language that defies the traditional image of propriety required of postmenopausal women by Hispanic society.[3] Mariela Romero's play takes place in the realistic setting of a middle-class apartment in downtown Caracas. It portrays the relationships between four friends in their fifties, María Antonia, Rosalba, Teresa, and Juan José, who have been meeting every Saturday at María Antonia's apartment under the attentions of the sixty year old maid, Jacinta. *Esperando al italiano* presents one particular Saturday that breaks the usual routine of gathering to drink and gossip, because the friends are awaiting the arrival of their fifth member, Margarita, who should appear at any moment with an Italian. The audience soon learns that prior to the events staged the women protagonists had formed a cooperative to contract the services of an Italian lover for sixty days. It is the lover and his broker that the friends expect to arrive this Saturday on a plane from Rome. The one male friend, Juan José (nicknamed J.J. or "Jota Jota" by the women) does not participate in the cooperative, but nevertheless joins the women this Saturday as is customary and because he too is curious about the Italian. As the friends wait they listen to music, drink, remember their youthful escapades, dress up, play cards, and reenact scenes from movies and soap operas.[4]

The play is divided into two segments: act 1, in which each member of the group enters María Antonia's apartment and participates in the speculation and excitement about the arrival of their lover, and act 2, some hours later when the women finally decide that no one is going to show up. The friends maintain their optimism about the Italian throughout the play, spending their time joking and teasing each other about embarrassing moments, romantic liaisons, and the uncertain economic and political conditions of Venezuela. In act 2 the characters engage in games of dress up and enact scenes from old movies. In these more playful activities, they speak more directly and truthfully about each other as a result of lowered inhibitions from consuming more alcohol than food.

Adorável desgraçada by Brazilian Leilah Assunção is a monologue of tragic proportions that traces the mental breakdown of a *solteirona* (old maid) on a rainy afternoon before Christmas.[5] Its minimalist setting suggests an apartment of modest furnishings in the metropolis of São Paulo. An undecorated Christmas tree, a stack of wrapped Christmas presents, and a broken television set are its distinguishing features. The play takes place during one evening in which the pro-tagonist, Guta Mello Santos, whose age is described as between forty and fifty, sits alone in her apartment unable to watch the final episode of her soap opera because her television is broken. To entertain her-self, Guta makes telephone calls to her friends, attempts to listen to the neighbor's television through the wall, and remembers her small town childhood adventures through the characters she creates. The events of the play make clear that Guta will not be celebrating a happy holiday this season. In a series of debilitating circumstances, criticized by one reviewer as *improvável e abusadas coincidências* (im-probable and tiresome coincidences) [Coan, n.p.], Guta loses her job and her only circle of friends but gains the return of her long lost best friend, Maribel. However, the Maribel who is returning to Brazil is not the woman Guta hoped to greet. Rather she is the success story that overshadows Guta and her mediocrity and contributes further to Guta's sense of isolation and disappointment.

These two plays offer similar images of female characters question-ing the reigning models for aging women and their sexuality. Both employ a range of theatrical frameworks, such as role-playing, game-playing, ceremonies, and monologues to help the protagonists process their memories and to question the many social roles they learned to play in the past. In both plays, reenacting the past leads to transforma-tion in the present. *Esperando al italiano* uses memories as the catalyst for abandoning past female roles as mother, wife, or lover in order to find a new identity as a desiring older single woman. For those in the audience, these performances replay society's accepted roles for women with the added measure that the roles and the women that play them are no longer in agreement with each other. The audience is "seeing double" as Richard Hornby notes, when it perceives the distances between the past roles the women relive and their current ages and situations in life (1986, 32). This distance between past and present makes it easier for the audience to accompany the women in their journey and to accept the need to find a new identity as older women.

In Romero's play, the women friends meet to reinforce each other against the pressure from family and society to conform to the sexless, servile model of aging defined by grandmotherhood. The women take the initiative to acknowledge their needs and although the Italian never arrives, in the closing moments of the play they reaffirm their desire to keep looking for a lover. *Adorável desgraçada*, on the other hand, uses memories to reconstruct the friendship between Guta and the absent Maribel and to outline the differences between the two women. Unlike *Esperando al italiano* in which the Italian lover never appears, a call from the doorman and the ring of the doorbell announce that Maribel has arrived in the closing moments of *Adorável desgraçada*. However, rather than welcoming her rival with open arms, Guta stages her revenge against Maribel for what she believes are her undeserved successes and her immoral sexual behavior.

Mariela Romero's dramaturgy has been characterized by its use of game-playing, rituals, and role-playing since the performance and publication of her award-winning play *El juego* in 1976. Scholars have associated the techniques in her plays with both the Theater of the Absurd and the Theater of Cruelty. The differences in the readings given to Romero's plays, especially *El juego*, can be understood by dividing them into two groups based on a preference for either one or the other of these influential European theatrical traditions. Critics identify in Romero's plays such absurdist characteristics as closed spaces, inhumanity and anguish, life without meaning, and stasis which serve as metaphors for political and social conditions that critique dictatorships, social injustice, and the inferior status of women. Game-playing is the most frequently used technique in Romero's work that protests the harsh realities of life in Latin America.[6] Those who see connections to Artaud's theories demonstrate how Romero's plays utilize these theatrical devices as a means to liberation. That liberation from political or sexual subordination is performed first in a collective where it serves as a form of resistance that then becomes a strategy of preparation for release from those conditions.[7] My reading of Romero's use of memory and metatheatrical frames in *Esperando al italiano* adheres to the latter interpretation, because it understands performing the past as a productive method for finding new models for being in the future.

Within the confines of María Antonia's Caracas apartment, the women characters of *Esperando al italiano* review and reenact their past lives by performing roles. Their memories are often triggered by the romantic songs they have selected to create the appropriate atmosphere for welcoming the Italian. The women also dramatize the past by staging scenes from old movies, retelling soap operas, and by dressing up in old carnival costumes. Critics Teresa Cajiao Salas and Margarita Vargas suggest that these popular sources re-create the climate of the 1940s (1997, 243). In addition, the idealized and romanticized past of the 1940s provides a vehicle by means of which the women can compare themselves to their own pasts. Through this process they attempt to come to terms with how they have discharged their lives as women. Both Rosalba and Teresa are free from the immediate responsibilities of mothering and all three women are free from romantic relationships with men. Thus, the women are at a perfect moment and a critical distance to examine any unfinished personal business from their past lives. Their performances help them understand their pasts and each other as the character Rosalba confirms:

"El pasado es para comprenderlo" [The past is to be understood] (Romero 1988, 77).

In metatheatrical terms *Esperando al italiano* combines the stability of ceremony, exemplified in the regular Saturday parties at María Antonia's, with the questioning of identity as demonstrated in the role-playing, dress up, and remembering of the past. Applying Hornby's terms, the weekly parties can be understood as a ceremony, because they follow a similar pattern of events that do not vary and their fulfillment engenders feelings of harmony, happiness, and peace among the women (1986, 55). The parties give a stability to the women's lives that contrasts with the confusion and insecurity of the political and social systems governing their lives during the remaining days of the week. Within the framework of this ceremony, the women reinforce the necessary intimacy to experiment with their identities through role-playing. While the voluntary role-playing entertains the audience, it also displays the many social roles that the women learned to portray in their younger years.

During both acts of Romero's play, all the main characters have the opportunity to unburden themselves of the past. Toward the end of act 1, María Antonia becomes the first character to reconcile her longing for her ex-lover, the General. She tells how she finally ran into him at the PX ten years after he had abandoned her (75). The bitterness in her comments and her reluctance to tell her friends what happened during the reencounter confirm that their relationship is still important to María Antonia. As she slowly tells the story María Antonia contrasts her imagined revenge staged among the aisles of domestic household products with her eventual decision to say nothing to her ex-lover (81). She expresses her resignation by singing along with a recording of Lucho Gatica:

"No vale la pena . . . sufrir en la vida . . . si todo acaba . . . si todo se va" [It's not worth it . . . to suffer in life . . . if everything ends . . . if everything goes away] (77).

María Antonia's retelling allows her the opportunity to relish the details of her imagined revenge and her embarrassment at not taking it (82). But at the same time it helps her psychologically to put that past to rest by talking about it and working through her feelings. María Antonia recognizes that she no longer cares to know why her ex-lover abandoned her and by extension it becomes clear that she now realizes she no longer cares for him.

In act 2 the remembering and reenacting of the past occupies most of the characters' attentions. Following in the steps of María Antonia, each woman examines a key relationship as it is evoked through memories or in reenactments. The two images of womanhood that are resuscitated from the past in the movie scenes and carnival costumes represent the traditional dichotomy for young women: either the good self-sacrificing mother or the evil temptress. For Teresa and Rosalba the idealized role of self-sacrificing mother is remembered and replayed when the friends reenact a scene from a Libertad Lamarque movie (87–88). The melodramatic scene of vengeance and victimization is performed by the women and Juan José in honor of Rosalba's dedication as a mother. But unlike the mother played by Libertad Lamarque, both Rosalba and Teresa have placed limits on the sacrifices they are willing to make and the pain they are willing to suffer for their children. Teresa grieves the loss of her only son who committed suicide, but refuses to accept responsibility for his actions:

"Yo era buena madre, ¿verdad María Antonia?, pero también tenía una vida y tenía que vivirla . . ." [I was a good mother, right María Antonia, but I also had a life and I had to live it] (94).

Similarly, Rosalba acknowledges her image as a dedicated mother, but she also protects it by hiding from her family the knowledge of her Saturday party with her friends. When her demanding daughter telephones for her to come home to baby-sit, Rosalba deceives her by having her friends say she is not there (86). For both Teresa and Rosalba, replaying the movie inspires the women to act upon their regrets and guilt and to begin to free themselves from past and present obligations. According to Susana Castillo "Ellas intentan romper los modelos de sacrificio, resignación y pasividad que en otrora hubieran funcionado con convicción y éxito" [They attempt to break the models of sacrifice, resignation and passivity that at another time they would have performed with conviction and success] ("Fantasías," 43).

The female archetype of the evil temptress is also remembered in the play by Rosalba and Teresa: the former by parading around in a carnival costume and recounting her appearances at nightclubs as a flasher, and the later in the retelling of her escapades at nightclubs dressed as a black cat. While physical appearance is a constant concern in the conversations in both acts 1 and 2, it is the explicit reference to sexuality and attractiveness that is significant in these memories from the past. Here the women remember their beauty and their seductive power over men. Rosalba calls Teresa *la torturadora de hombres* (the torturer of men) [92]. Remembering these moments helps the women mediate between their past as desirable young women and their present as desiring older women. In the images of the past, they celebrate when they were desirable to men. Castillo describes these memories as revealing "una sexualidad exuberante y satisfecha" [an exuberant and satisfying sexuality] (1992, 40). As a midlife mother Rosalba can assume the sexless status of a grandmother, but there is no model for middle-aged temptresses that the three women can follow. Castillo notes that they are women without models to imitate who must "imaginarse la vida cada día" [make up life each day] (40). By performing the past the women gain a distance between it and their current lives. They are able to begin the search for the model that represents them as older, sexual women. Their first test for the new model they are creating will take place when the Italian arrives.

The women take two steps toward redefining themselves: they maintain their friendships and their regular meetings as a kind of support group, and they form the cooperative to purchase the Italian's favors. As friends the women offer each other their confidence, their care, and their comfort. They refer to each other affectionately as *manita* (little sister). They also catch each other repeating society's message that they are *viejas* (old women), and they challenge those assumptions with phrases like *no estamos viejas* (we are not getting old), *no somos viejas* (we are not old), and *Estamos en* [. . .] *nuestra hermosa y plena madurez* (We are in our beautiful and full maturity) [76]. Their social gatherings reinforce relationships and help strengthen each woman's self-perception. But forming the co-op is their first big step toward turning desire into action. Rosalba, the originator of the idea, calls on her companions to remember the importance of honoring their feelings:

> "qué hace uno con los sentimientos si no los puede soltar . . . liberar . . . extemporizar" [what can one do with feelings if they cannot be let go . . . liberated . . . improvised] (83).

As independent postmenopausal women, María Antonia, Rosalba, and Teresa have the financial security to search for a lover with all the benefits and none of the limitations of their previous attachments, that is, a lover who can please them and be attentive and intimate but who does not require or pretend to deliver romantic commitment. What's more, since the women are engaged in a commercial transaction, they have the power to determine the rules. Susan Rice has stated that sexuality for the aging is pleasure oriented not performance oriented and it is based on the idea that sex is an expression of self (1995, 64). When the women in Romero's play decide to buy a lover, they turn the tables on the traditional model of men trafficking in women, but as Rice's observation on aging suggests, they go further to define sexual relations as an expression of their own needs, of their own selves. In their new roles as desiring women, the protagonists focus sexuality on pleasure to self, rather than fulfilling the pleasure of others. But it is a difficult concept to absorb, even for the characters themselves. Witness, for example, that at least María Antonia cannot understand why Teresa would spend all her savings on plastic surgery for a new bust since she has no one to please. But, Teresa believes in her right to please herself

> "Me dio la gana. Me quería dar ese gusto" [I felt like doing it. I wanted to give myself that pleasure] (73).

The meetings at María Antonia's apartment are a means for recognizing and supporting basic human needs. Canadian researcher Robynne Neugebauer-Visano has noted that women overcome loneliness after divorce or widowhood by "reaching out to other women for support and intimacy" (1995, 26). Coming together as women, then, signals that although the women are lonely they have found a method for overcoming it. Further, Neugebauer-Visano has found that one way women relieve their sexual urges is to talk about sex with other women and to fantasize about having sex with a famous Hollywood actor (27). In *Esperando al italiano*, the women fantasize about having sex with the Italian and make constant references to each other's former sex lives. Thus, in contrast to Anita Stoll's argument that the Italian is a mere frame for the events in María Antonia's apartment (1998, 45), he becomes the trope for the sexual fulfillment and intimacy that the women seek. He represents an important need that the women's friendship cannot meet and that society refuses to recognize. By seeking sexual gratification with the Italian, the women are hoping to define who they are as older sexual persons. In her discussion of midlife women, Terri Apter has stated: "What will allow a woman to grow stronger in midlife is not release from sexuality, but new ability to read her own sexuality and to act on it, rather than fear rejection or loneliness or disapproval" (1995, 265). In fact, the co-op represents one reading of their sexuality that the women have acted upon even though they were not successful in bringing back the Italian. And, in order to affirm that the quest has only begun, the play ends on a positive note with Rosalba reading a personal advertisement from

> "Español . . . comerciante . . . de edad madura, pero aún de muy buen ver . . . cariñoso . . . inteligente . . . serio . . . desea establecer amistad . . . " [Spaniard, businessman, of a mature age but still good-looking, loving, intelligent, serious, wishes to establish friendship . . .] (99).

As the women come to terms with past definitions of self and begin to find new ones they affirm their value as sexual beings and engage their energies (and income) in their own futures. Game-playing reinforces bonds of friendship that, in turn, support the expression of sexual desire. The quest to find a lover, described by Juan José as *un juego* (a game) [85], is transformed into the expression of a real need that the women propose to fulfill, if not with the Italian, then with someone else. Through games the protagonists divest themselves of the roles that they were required to play in their youth. Rather than presenting a static world in which games give the unhappy and lonely women something to do, as Stoll contends (1998, 51), Romero's play presents the women as empowered and empowering to each other. Anthropologist David Gutmann's description for postparental women includes the idea of being "proactive in creating new leadership possibilities" (1985, 206). Romero's play creates a space for community building and solidarity away from the political arena where competition and domination is valued. The characters take the lead in creating new definitions of self, definitions that defy the debilitating model of aging for women.

As mentioned earlier, Leilah Assunção has demonstrated an interest in the themes of aging and the repression of feminine and sexual identity since the 1960s. At the beginning of her career she created portraits of marginal characters such as the spinster or *solteirona* and the prostitute, as Judith Bissett and Elza Cunha de Vincenzo have observed (1999, 206; 1992, 90). For Assunção the socially stigmatized character of the *solteirona* is an extreme case of the conflict between social education and sexual desire. *Adorável desgraçada* reworks many of these elements that appeared in Assunção's 1969 award-winning first play, *Fala baixo senão Eu grito* [Speak softly or I will scream](Guzik, Guimarães, Lima). Guta, of *Adorável desgraçada*, represents the person that none of the characters in *Esperando al italiano* want to become: the woman with a life of loneliness and loss. Her losses are many—she has friends but they are not loyal; she has lost contact with her family; she doesn't have a husband, lover, or children, she is penniless; and she has no great hope that life will change. Guta embodies the degradation of life that can occur to the aging woman bereft of loving human relations, financial security, and a sense of purpose. However, in contrast to the passive and naive Mariazinha of *Fala baixo* who "não tem absolutamente consciência clara do que lhe falta, nem condições de manifestar nenhuma forma de rebelião [has absolutely no clear conscience of what she is missing, nor the conditions to manifest any form of rebellion] (Vincenzo 1992, 91), Guta finds a method to avenge herself for the losses in her life, although at the expense of another woman.

Assunção highlights the vulnerability of the *solteirona* (old maid) by locating her alone on the stage and by emphasizing her need to be in constant contact with others, such as her colleagues from work and the doorman of her apartment building. Guta considers the television a great companion, because it fills up the empty hours with images and sounds, and it promises to never abandon her. But even the TV lets her down when it breaks, causing her to miss her favorite soap opera and lose her companion at night. Guta fills up the evening hours by role-playing versions of herself and her friend Maribel from the past and by maintaining conversations with God. In her solitary speech with God, Guta imitates the dramatic relationship of medieval and Renaissance monologues according to Ken Frieden (1985, 112). However, it is not prayerful purpose that inspires Guta to call on the divine, but a desire to get even, first outlined to her by the small town priest. In what Mariangela Alves de Lima refers to as "sua personalíssima relação com a divindade" [her overly personal relationship with the divine] (n.p.), Guta asks God to punish others for being evil and console her for goodness (Assunção, 11).

It is not only loneliness and loss that mark Guta's life, but also her loyalty to the traditional social conventions and values of small town life, as Lima has observed. These conventions of sexual and moral behavior have given Guta a rigidity that contrasts with the flexibility and liberty of modern life in the big city and make her a museum relic, a person lost in the values of the past. Guta, like Mariazinha of *Fala baixo*, represents "a excentricidade que a sociedade rejeita" [the eccentricity that society rejects] (Vicenzo, 89). That is, she is strange and incomplete because she has not been successful by the standards of small town life that require marriage and children, and she refuses to live by the self-obsessed rules of the big city which she considers immoral.

Like Mariazinha of *Fala baixo*, Guta's rigidity is the result of repressed sexuality. She is both socially and sexually indeterminate, lacking all the markers that would place her in a recognizable context. She has no past or present sexual identity or images to refer back to for models of how to live as a midlife woman. Unlike the women in *Esperando al italiano*, Guta does not know her own sexual needs nor has she searched for the appropriate outlet for their expression. Guta's rigidity and repressed sexuality contribute to the impression that she is a young girl inside the body of an older woman.

The principal action of *Adorável desgraçada* develops in a series of losses that assault Guta's dignity and lead her to take revenge on her now successful childhood friend Maribel. Memories provide the context of rivalry between the friends and help prepare Guta to take action for the indignities that she has suffered. Just like the characters in *Esperando al italiano*, Guta returns to the past to understand, but she cannot find models that will help her confront her aging. Guta's monologue reconstructs her childhood and that of her friend Maribel in the town of Sertãozinho. The memories are triggered by the objects in the room, the newspaper, the broken television set, and especially the seven Christmas presents purchased each year for the absent Maribel. Guta performs the conflicts between Maribel and herself by role-playing four different versions of herself: Guta Ingênua (Naive Guta), the "good girl"; Gutinha-Fuínha (Gossip Guta), the envious, small town gossip; Guta-Trágica (Tragic Guta), who is trying to control her anger; and Guta-Maribel (Guta/Maribel), the sassy girlfriend and coquette (Assunção, 3).

The memories that Guta enacts from her relationship with Maribel plot the two girls' lives as a study in contrasts. Through the characters of Guta-Ingênua and Guta-Fuínha the protagonist reenacts her past as the "good girl," the good student, the morally correct girl, the religious girl who works hard to maintain her superiority over Maribel although she suffers occasional slips of envy. Guta also creates her own version of her rival Maribel, represented by Guta-Maribel, as the "bad girl," the poor but clever student and libertine whose favorite expression to explain the inequities of life is

"A vida é assim, minha cara" [Life's like that, my dear] (19).

According to her representations, Guta's rivalry with Maribel began during their days in school, at church, and in the community and continued even after they moved to the big city of São Paulo. The rivalry first was encouraged by the neighbors:

" 'Quem vai ser melhor dona-de-casa. A Guta ou Maribel?'—A vinzinhança vivia perguntando isso. Melhor aluna, melhor no esporte" [Who is going to be the best houswife? Guta or Maribel? The neighbors were always asking that. Best student, best athlete.] (13).

But the competition continued because even though Guta was a "good girl," she rarely received the rewards she expected. This deception is remembered best in her description of the school parade that she should have led, but that Maribel was chosen to lead instead (23).

What is striking about the memories and performances that Guta brings to life is that they reveal little difference between the Guta of the past and the Guta of the present. That is, Guta still sees herself as the "good girl" her mother called

"A filha que toda mãe sonha em ter" [The daughter every mother dreams of having] (10).

Unlike the role-playing in *Esperando al italiano* that showed distances between past social roles and present aging bodies, Guta's enacments reinforce her rigidity and lack of maturity in contrast to her aging body. Thus, seeing Guta's performances allows the audience to witness how her life strays from the normal parameters of human development. For example, in her memories of Maribel, Guta remembers only those events in which her friend demonstrated her "badness" through rebellious and openly sexual behavior. In one case, Maribel makes herself available to the attentions of boys at the "footings" in the park and at the debutante ball (20–21). Thus, Guta justifies her life, her "goodness" as a form of defiance of her friend's "badness." This attitude allows Guta to feel superior and at the same time expectant that one day Maribel will be punished for her sins. Guta's theatrical representation of Maribel emphasizes that she is both attractive because of her energy and creativity and repulsive because of her blatant use of her sexuality to get ahead. Guta is trapped by her friendship with Maribel in which she feels conflicting emotions: envy of her successes and righteousness in her belief that her own goodness will pay off someday. The dramatic irony of Guta's superiority, of course, is that her own life, which she performs in both the present and the past, has no appeal at all while that of her friend

Maribel, which she also enacts on stage, sounds adventurous and daring, although morally questionable.

Guta's memories reveal that her submissive and sexually repressed behavior was encouraged by the small town values of family and church which authorized them as normal and good. In this environment Guta learned what therapists Claudia Bepko and Jo-Ann Krestan call the "Code of Goodness" which was reinforced with the concepts of sin and punishment from the church. Together these two sets of rules defined for Guta the "ethical standards of conduct" (1990, 9). The "Code of Goodness" establishes impossible and conflicting standards of behavior that, nevertheless, women use to measure how well they do the work of relating (34). Being skilled at relating to others does not mean just being socially adept, it means taking responsibility for other people's lives (51). Thus, the "Code of Goodness" distorts women's self-perception by defining them according to external sources and depriving them of their own self worth (39). Of the five rules discussed in *Too Good for Her Own Good*, Guta adheres rigidly to two rules: "Be a Lady—A good woman stays in control," and "Be Unselfish and of Service—A good woman loves to give" (29). Guta's religious background accentuates the fervor with which she follows these codes, since failing to follow them is a sin that must be punished.

The rule of staying in control, as outlined by Bepko and Krestan, translates into the efforts women make to mold themselves into submission. The therapists list the following examples of control that women exercise against themselves: control of all impulses such as anger, competitiveness, loudness, aggressiveness or strong emotions, such as sexual desire (19–20). Guta identifies for the audience the many instances when she demonstrated that she is a lady by being in control. She mentions her modesty and her lack of competitiveness in the workplace (Assunção, 17), she refers to her disinterest in sex (18, 27), and her correctness in speaking (37). She even declares to herself and the audience:

"Sou a Guta; meiga e con-tro-la-da" [I am Guta, sweet and in control] (12).

But Guta's efforts to reaffirm her submissiveness and therefore her goodness are undermined by fits of rage and loss of self-control. Bepko and Krestan have noted that staying in control and repressing feelings can cause women to build up a reservoir of anger which can, in turn, cause them to go out of control (105, 62). In *Adorável desgraçada*, Guta loses and then regains control many times. She not only speaks of her *ódio* (hatred) and *raiva* (anger) and labels them as sins (23–24), she also acts out her anger by destroying a delicate fern, hitting the sofa with her fist, tying a knot in a scarf, threatening with the scissors, digging her nails into her wrist, and yelling. After each bout, Guta appears to recover her senses and reestablish her equanimity. Such rage is directed toward the petty inconveniences of her life and toward Maribel's bad behavior which, according to Guta's religious view, must be punished by God. Guta lives in anticipation of that punishment, which will not only serve justice but also will restore balance to her life. She repeatedly wonders when and how Maribel will receive her *Santo Castigo* (Holy Punishment).

As mentioned earlier, the piles of wrapped gifts on the stage represent the circle of associations that Guta believes to be her cohorts. Guta's acceptance of the dictate to be unselfish in tending to relationships can be seen in her ongoing friendship with Maribel and the presents she has purchased for others, but also heard in Guta's concern about her coworkers getting fired in the layoffs (16), of her willingness to invite hometown friends to work where she does (17), and of constant phone calls to her coworkers (25). Her loyalty to those friends extends beyond the memory of their childhood oath, and it survives in spite of the fact that her friends take advantage of her generosity and passivity. Guta repeatedly calls her coworkers not only in order to collect money that she has lent them long ago and that they have not returned, but she also calls them to reassure herself that she maintains a relationship with them.

The debilitating events of the play challenge Guta's "Code of Goodness" by repeatedly demonstrating that her efforts to build and maintain relationships with others and remain in control of herself as a lady have not produced either the rewards for self or the punishment of others that she expected. Her coworkers do not feel the same sense of responsibility toward her that she does to them; they ignore her phone calls. Her childhood friend Teresa, whom Guta worries will be dismissed, actually tells Guta that she is on the list of workers to be fired (41). To Guta's dismay the unanticipated letter from Maribel does not announce her punishment but rather her success. While Guta's coworkers and friends have developed and pursued their own goals, Guta has remained passive and dependent on her "goodness" and God's punishment. Learning of Maribel's success causes her to finally feel that she has been robbed of her self. Worse yet, none of those who sanctioned her goodness as a child—her parents, the school, or the priest at church—are available to reward or support her for this sacrifice.

Thus, *Adorável desgraçada* locates Guta in the most vulnerable emotional position from which to engage with the past, especially when compared to the characters in *Esperando al italiano*. The evening's devastating events coupled with childhood memories cause Guta to contemplate suicide, a prospect she considers and rejects for religious reasons in the opening minutes of the play, but then reconsiders once she decides that *Deus não existe* [God does not exist] (39). Rather than die in vain as a vengeance against Maribel and the others (40), Guta stages an elaborate ritual of purification and preparation in which she opens and uses up the Christmas gifts she purchased for her co-workers (42–43), and the seven presents for Maribel (45). She plays the record of Gounot's *Ave Maria*, waits for the doorbell to ring and then picks up the scissors and heads over to the door. The play ends with the voice of a news announcer coming through the wall from the neighbor's television set reporting on the murder of Maribel Vergari Chiafarello by Guta Mello Santos (48).

This overly melodramatic ending represents the transformation of the protagonist Guta from a passive victim, like Mariazinha of *Fala baixo*, into an active avenger. As an active avenger, Guta stops the negative spiral of the evening's events by assuming the morally superior position of God. Mariangela Alves de Lima calls it *deteriorização mental* (mental deterioration) and its groundwork was prepared in the characterization of Guta as an angry and envious person whose religious conservatism requires a *castigo* (punishment) for Maribel. Certainly when Guta begins singing

> "Vamos lavar Senhor . . . a alma do pecador" [Let us cleanse oh God . . . the soul of the sinner] (44)

as she makes her preparations for Maribel's arrival, she confirms that she will no longer wait for God to effect a punishment. Guta believes she can attain sainthood by acting for God and she carries out her mission to punish Maribel for her sins. The television news announcer gives a similar account as a motive for the killing in his news report (48).

As an avenger Guta is driven to commit a violent act. However, unlike other modern performances of women's anger that usually end in suicide, Guta turns against another, rather than against herself (Wiles 1998, 113–16). It could be argued that Guta's murderous action was meant to help her achieve subjectivity, but it is a highly questionable performance of self-liberation in which another person's life is lost. As a desperate woman who made too many sacrifices of self for "goodness" in exchange for too little gain, Guta finally empowers herself to do something on her own behalf in order to try to gain her lost self back. When Guta cuts free from friends and from God, she liberates herself from obligations and dependence on God's justice and decides for herself what kind of action is appropriate. Guta responds to a lifetime of "goodness" by performing "badly." In her push to gain autonomy and identity by saying no to her own goodness and no to her rival (121), Guta oversteps the boundary of reasonable behavior. Certainly she perceives Maribel to be the symbol for all her unfulfilled desires. When Maribel returns for a visit, she will once again invade and upstage Guta's mediocre life. Since Guta cannot accept Maribel as a model to follow or as a temporary release from her own world, she acts to destroy her.

The theatrical devices of monologue and role-playing work together to communicate Guta's actions as an avenger. Monologue is a theatrical convention with disruptive power, as witnessed in the first plays discussed in this chapter where, like Guta, the protagonists struggle to contest social expectations that they cannot meet. Soliloquy also serves as stylistic expression of both guilt and madness, in which it retains an alliance with demonic (or unconscious) powers, according to Frieden (119, 127). Guta's monologue uncovers her internal battle between self-control and rage that eventually leads her to take drastic action. In her final act of murder, she even assumes the powers of God, a move that could be read as both madness and demonic. Guta's role-playing of three versions of herself and of Maribel changes course after she receives Maribel's letter listing her accomplishments and successes. Faced with the upbeat news about Maribel's life, Guta can no longer enact her own imagined versions of Maribel's punishment. She assumes only one mask, that of the *trágica*, signaling to herself and the audience that she has no imagined options left. As she sets out her ritual of purification, Guta joins her present situation with the tragic version of her past in a misguided effort to find liberation.

Adorável desgraçada makes evident that the socialization of girls into categories of "good" and "bad" not only limits their development, it also hampers their aging. Guta is dangerous not only because she is needy, but also because she is handicapped. Her upbringing stunted her ability to find a true sense of herself and her femaleness, including her sexual expression. Assunção presents Guta and Maribel as the unhealthy boundaries for feminine sexuality, implying that there is a need to create a better option that lies between the two. Neither "good girls," "saints," or "bad girls" represent fully the human experience of being young and female. Likewise, none of these categories are useful to women who are aging. Through her creation of these extreme and marginal versions of womanhood, Assunção persists with her critique of traditional Brazilian society and its repressive, small-town values that deny women the wholeness of self. Assunção's *Adorável desgraçada* speaks from the margins of women's experiences about the ongoing search for a model of aging authentically.

Esperando al italiano and *Adorável desgraçada* demonstrate that aging women need more outlets for expressing themselves as they age than the worn out models society has provided them from their youth. The protagonists of *Esperando al italiano* take precautions and experiment with solutions for aging, especially the formation of a like-minded community. Without that solidarity, it is possible that one day they could find themselves in the same lonely and desperate situation as Guta from *Adorável desgraçada*. Nonetheless, the danger for the protagonists of both plays is the same, because they are needy and in search of the totality of their femaleness, including their sexual expression. Clearly the women in *Esperando al italiano* hope to find a solution for this expression through the co-op and remain optimistic about their chances. The same cannot be said of Guta in *Adorável desgraçada*. Yet, these two plays advocate for the acceptance of sexuality as an expression of humanity in the midlife woman. In addition, the plays show the importance of memories as a reservoir of potential resources that can help midlife women begin the search for new models for themselves, as Bertram J. Cohler noted in his study on reminiscence in middle- and old-age (1993, 120). Finally, these two plays communicate the dilemma of searching for an adequate representation for midlife women by enacting traditional social roles. It is in this bringing to life of models that no longer fit the wearers that the audience can best understand the characters' and their own needs to discover new identities for their aging selves.

Cuesta abajo by Gabriela Fiore, and Parque para dos by Teresa Marichal address the search for new expressions of female sexual desire and sexuality in examples of the ritual of sexual attraction as performed by male and female characters on benches in public parks. The aging characters are searching for romantic connection and understanding, but what they find are only temporary, superficial solutions. Cuesta abajo layers old movie scenarios, songs, and aging movie actors enacting roles from the past to comment on that past as a trap that immobilizes the aging, while Parque para dos critiques the conflict between generations over sexuality.

Cuesta abajo by Argentine Gabriela Fiore, is a one-act play that deals with the disguises that two individuals adopt in their search for love.[8] It dramatizes a chance encounter in the park between two aging characters, Gardel, viejo, teñido, gordo (old, dyed hair, fat) and Rita, fingida sensualidad, igual de grotesco (faked sensuality, equally grotesque) [25], who are waiting for someone else. During the one-act play, the characters meet, engage in a short-lived romance that then leads to conflict and finally to Rita's departure. Cuesta abajo presents a fantasy in which two former movie stars attempt to relive the plots from their most famous movies, but as aging versions of their former attractive selves. In yet another example of theatrical game-playing, as outlined by Catherine Larson (1991, 77–78), in which characters assume roles and stage plays, Cuesta abajo relives the romantic world of nostalgia and desire created by musical comedies from the 1930s and 1940s. During the play, the characters Rita and Gardel represent Rita Hayworth, the World War II era sex goddess, and Carlos Gardel, the carousing Argentine tango singer and dandy. Their conversations make reference to Hayworth's hit film Gilda (1946) and Gardel's musical Cuesta abajo (1934) that also serves as the title of the play. The meeting in the park bring Rita and Gardel together as they wait for their lost loves Glenn (Ford), romantic co-star of Gilda and Margarita, who shares the character traits of the homespun waitress Rosa in the film Cuesta abajo.

Beyond their similarity as musical comedies, Gilda and Cuesta abajo revolve around a common plot line in which an evil temptress bewitches the leading man. Whereas he eventually is rescued by an old friend, she falls on hard times. In the film *Cuesta abajo*, Carlos Gardel falls in love with Raquel and travels with her in Europe and the United States after abandoning his sweetheart Rosa. He finally is rescued by an old buddy to whom he vows in the song "Mi Buenos Aires Querido" (My Beloved Buenos Aires) to return to the capital and his true love. Rita Hayworth plays the evil temptress of *Gilda*, who first appears as the wife of the jealous owner of a casino, Ballin Mundson, and later after the owner's death, to his faithful employee Johnny Farrell (played by Glenn Ford) with whom she resumes a previous affair.

Cuesta abajo, the play, weaves together the movie plot lines, the music, and dance numbers from both movies, and biographical information about the movie stars Hayworth and Gardel into an anachronistic theatrical representation. The events on stage could not have taken place either on or off the movie set. Even though both movies take place in Buenos Aires, Gardel's *Cuesta abajo* was released one year before his tragic death in an airplane crash in 1935 and twelve years before the Hayworth movie *Gilda*. Nonetheless, the play ignores this historical information in order to study a hypothetical relationship between two of the movie world's greatest sex symbols, now in their later years, as Luiz Ordaz confirms in his notes on the play (1992, 94). Fiore's play picks up the action where the movie of the same name ended, with Gardel hoping to regain the lost love he had abandoned.

Cuesta abajo shares features with *Esperando al italiano* in its staging of games and reenacting of movies. Both plays employ movies and memories as vehicles for severing connections with the past and beginning the search for new models for aging. In each play, the characters must decide between change or stasis and, for the female characters, change is a necessary step towards independence and satisfying personal needs. Similar to Antonia, Rosalba and Teresa of *Esperando al italiano*, Rita longs for a romantic relationship. Yet, all these female protagonists are engaged in abandoning past feminine roles that tie them to men in traditional romantic and subservient ways. Whereas *Esperando al italiano* relies on an unconventional plot line in which the women protagonists boldly organize their search for sexual satisfaction, *Cuesta abajo* employs the commonplace romantic plot line of the two musical comedies that serve as its backdrop. Also in contrast to Romero's bawdy atmosphere, *Cuesta abajo* adopts an ironic and wistful stance with regard to its aging movie stars who attempt to hide from the passage of time by reliving worn-out movie roles and plots.

In *Cuesta abajo* the character Gardel has developed a routine that keeps him busy while he waits in the park. When Rita walks into the park, she encounters him already occupying one bench with a large suitcase full of props, a phonograph player and records, and his guitar. His props and his form of speaking, described as *Habla de manera recitativa* (He speaks in a rehearsed manner) [27], suggest that he comes to the park regularly looking for someone. Since he has repeated this action so many times, even the nuances of his technique have become as worn as his suit. During the course of the play, he asks for the time of day, cowers at the sound of planes flying overhead, recites and forgets the lines to famous tangos, wonders about how time might have changed his true love, prepares and offers Rita mate tea, and grabs his head in desperation. Through his frantic actions and conversation Gardel betrays that he is working to retain his memory of the past by repeating the same sentences and the same actions.

Rita and Gardel engage in a series of three games that bring them together as romantic partners and then separate them again. Each game highlights the distance between the past, in this case the protagonists' frozen movie image, and the present. The first game involves recognition in which each primps and poses as if for a publicity photo so that the other will see and recognize him/her. Gardel wants to be recognized as the tango composer Carlos Gardel and he wants to discover his beloved Margarita in the faces of the women who come to the park. At first Rita resists his game and then she joins in by pretending to be Margarita. For his part, Gardel engages in a ritual of beautifying himself, posing, and then asking Rita if she recognizes him. His mirror is actually a framed picture of the real Gardel when he was *joven y hermoso* (young and handsome), which does not reflect back the actor's image, but does constantly remind him of whom he is trying to impersonate (25). When Rita tells him it is not important that she recognize him, he objects stating:

> "Siempre es bueno saber que alguien se acuerda de uno" [It's always good to know that someone remembers you] (28).

Being seen as someone young and famous gives meaning to Gardel's life and thus he repeats the primping scene several times, making small adjustments such as putting on a cap or holding his guitar in a particular way. Rita encourages his efforts to continue the game by looking at him carefully, then suggesting that she might know him, and then stating that she is sure she does not recognize him.

For her part, Rita also dresses up, applying more layers of makeup, adjusting her wig, and putting on a pair of high heels in order to walk in a more sensual manner (32). Germaine Greer has pointed out that "The fifty-year-old woman, if she wishes to remain in the sex race, has got to make herself visible by some such means"(294). Indeed, the excessive makeup does make Gardel notice her as does Rita's provocative manner of walking, talking, and staring at him. Just as Gardel needs Rita to make him feel important, Rita needs Gardel to fall for her seduction. In both cases attracting the other means imitating youthful models; for Gardel it is assuring himself that he looks just like the framed picture of Carlos Gardel and for Rita it is asking Gardel to tell her she is beautiful. With a little prompting Gardel complies to her request and hails her as *hermosa* and *joven* (beautiful and young) [35].

This game of recognition draws the audience's attention to the passage of time that eventually changes the appearance and importance of everyone, even the most handsome of movie stars. By pretending to be movie stars Rita and Gardel attempt to escape the aging of their own bodies and restore themselves to the more youthful and desirable movie versions. The songs from the movies intervene to accompany them on their fantastic journey, inspiring them to relive key cinematic scenes reinforcing the association between the screen and life. For example Rita, in order to seduce Gardel, imitates the provocative dance scene from *Gilda* to the song "Put the Blame on Mame" and then repeats the famous quotation attributed to Rita Hayworth about how her lovers confuse her with her movie role: *Es que los hombres se acuestan con Gilda, pero despiertan junto a Rita Hayworth* (It's that men go to bed with Gilda, but they wake up with Rita Hayworth) [35]. This confusion between the real world and the movie world, also operates in the play *Cuesta abajo* where theatrical actors play characters who are pretending to be movie actors from the past, thus blending theatrical and movie roles, present and past. However, unlike the movies in which the ages of the characters are frozen in time, the individuals on stage, like those in the audience, must cope with the changes wrought by the passage of time.

Romance is the second game that the two play as they converse on the park bench. Gardel's longing for his Margarita and Rita's desire to have Glenn back replay the losses in the movie story lines that also draw the characters together in their loneliness. Gardel convinces himself that Rita must be his long lost Margarita, and Rita finally agrees to go along. Thus, each finds a reason to make a play for the other and for a short moment they become a couple like those in the movies: *Quedan enfrentados. Se frenan. En un arrebato Gardel abraza y besa a Rita. Ella se entrega. Es un beso apasionado. De verdad* (They stand facing each other. They stop. Suddenly Gardel grabs Rita and kisses her. She gives in to the moment. It is truly a passionate kiss) [35]. But their passionate embrace is more illusion than emotional connection, and their promises for eternal youth, beauty, and happiness are unrealizable dreams (35). Gardel criticizes Rita for her appearance:

"Sí, estás cambiada, Margarita, ¿eh? Más gordita, a lo mejor" [Yes, you have changed Margarita, isn't that so? A little fatter, possibly] (36),

and she complains about the misogyny of his songs:

"Usted canta cosas tristes; si no está muerta lo abandonó, si no lo abandonó está vieja, fea, usada por los hombres. Nada de eso me gusta" [You sing sad songs; if she isn't dead he abandoned her, if she hasn't been abandoned, then she is old, ugly and used by men. I don't like any of that] (38).

The final game that Rita and Gardel play and that changes the course of events in the play revolves around an envelope. In a theatrical moment, an envelope falls to the ground during a snow storm providing the protagonists with one last opportunity to connect with their lost loves. Both associate the envelope with their missing lover and both are simultaneously frightened away and drawn to the envelope's contents. In a duel of wills, Rita wants Gardel to open the letter but he delays by trying to distract her. His excuses and inactivity are explained by his fear that the letter will bring about a change (42). But Rita's frustration and anxiety represent her desire for change which leads her to pick up and open the letter:

"[(*Explotando.*) Es que yo quiero que cambie, ¿no se da cuenta? Quiero que cambie todo. Quiero poder descansar. Quedarme quieta. No se puede escapar toda la vida. El espejo persigue, la memoria persigue, la historia persigue, y yo corro y me disfrazo y me cuento mentiras, y todo, ¿para qué? ¿Para qué?" (*Toma el sobre*)]. [(*Exploding.*) It's that I want a change, don't you see? I want everything to change. I want to rest. Stay quiet. You can't escape for all of your life. The mirror pursues me, memory pursues me, history pursues me, and I run and I disguise myself and I tell myself lies, and for what? For what? (*She takes the envelope*)] (42).

Not surprisingly, when Rita finally manages to open the envelope it is as empty as its false theatrical pose of providing a deus ex machina solution to the play. This game of lost possibilities produces two distinct outcomes: for Gardel it is a relief that nothing has changed, but for Rita it is a disappointment (43). Thus, Gardel can return to his normal routine of waiting, but for Rita it inspires her to act:

"Lo que no puedo es esperar más. Me cansé. Tengo que retirarme" [I can't wait any longer. I am tired. I have to move on] (44).

The games of *Cuesta abajo* focus on how Gardel and Rita accept or rework the existing romantic scripts from their movie musicals. Gardel insists on rejecting the bold and evil woman who seduced him in order to wait for his true and loyal love. In so doing he rejects the passage of time. He even declares that he is immune to aging:

"No, a mí me hicieron perfecto, tan perfecto que ni envejecer me dejaron" [No, I was made perfect, so perfect that they won't even let me age] (43);

he asserts that he will resist the passage of time just as the real Carlos Gardel does in the song "Volver" (To Return) in which *veinte años no es nada* [twenty years is nothing]. In his statement of faith, he announces:

"Al fin y al cabo, todavía puedo volver..." [In the end, I can always return] (45).

The dramatic irony of his position, of course, can be seen in the contrast between his words and his appearance. While he may downplay the passage of twenty years (or more), that amount of time has changed his appearance, increased his age, and worn out his suit. In addition, that amount of time brings into question his belief that after twenty years of waiting Margarita will appear. Gardel hopes to hide his aging by waiting in the park where he can pretend to be the youthful and vigorous Carlos Gardel.

Rita also rejects the role of the evil temptress Gilda and the role of the good girl Margarita as well. Then she begins to reckon with the distance between herself and these roles:

> "Uno no puede ser personaje toda su vida y toda su muerte. Uno tiene que ser persona alguna vez" [You can't be a character all your life and all your death. You have to be a person sometime] (44).

It is the empty letter, a marker that signals the futility of waiting and pretending that provides the impetus for Rita to leave. While Gardel clings to the past, Rita moves toward liberating herself from it. As the stage directions indicate, Rita changes her clothes and shoes, removes all her makeup and finally pulls off her wig (43–44). In the final moments of the play, she gives Gardel the satisfaction of acknowledging him as Carlos, and she ends her wait for Glenn by asking Gardel for a *cachetada* (a slap on the cheek) [44], a reference to the movie scene with Hayworth's co-star Glenn Ford that she mentions earlier, in which he slaps her for flirting with other men.

Rita's punishment for flirting with Gardel, the *cachetada*, and her change of dress point to her preparation to leave the park. She seeks liberation from the stereotypical movie roles of sex goddess or good girl that make her dependent on her youthful body to win the protection of men. Like the protagonists of *Esperando al italiano,* who searched for a means to express themselves as desiring older women, Rita removes her past image in order to leave the park in search of a new one. Thus, she manages to save herself from the trap of waiting that keeps Gardel in the park. Her exit means life, but Gardel's immobility leads to his death. As the curtain closes, the audience sees Gardel's frozen image and hears the sounds of the tango *Cuesta abajo* and of an airplane that finally crashes (45). In that moment, the history of Carlos Gardel the tango composer who died in a plane crash in 1935 is merged with the figure of Gardel on the stage in a picture of loss— lost love, lost life. Thus, it is Gardel who has gone downhill, as the play's title suggests, while Rita has walked away.

In its treatment of aging *Cuesta abajo* posits the role of movie star as a mask that seduces its own wearer. For Gardel the songs, the image in the picture frame, the memories, and the wait for Margarita suffice for proof that time can stop and that it is possible to go back as the song "Volver" suggests. But for Rita the artifices of makeup, of seductive posturing, and of trying to fulfill everyone else's dreams don't agree with her age anymore, they belong to the past. In her efforts to stop being a character (*personaje*) and start becoming a person (*persona*), Rita assumes her status as an aging woman, frees herself from her past, the public park, and Gardel. The contrast between the two characters can be seen in this citation in which Gardel commits to staying in the park but Rita declines by contradicting a line from the song "Volver."

Gardel: Vuelva cuando quiera. Yo voy a estar acá, esperando. Siempre voy a estar esperando. (*Con miedo*). Hasta que me vengan a buscar. (*Mira hacia arriba.*)

Rita: *No creo que pueda volver, Carlos, ni siquiera con la frente marchita.* (44).

[Gardel: Come back whenever you want. I will be here, waiting. I will always be here waiting. (*With fear.*) Until they come to get me. (*He looks up at the sky.*)

Rita: I doubt I will return, Carlos, not even with a wrinkled face.]

Rita's afternoon of games in the park with Gardel liberates her from *Gilda*, the beautiful and tempting evil woman, a role and a costume that no longer adjust themselves to her aging body. By removing them and freeing herself from Gardel, she begins to focus on her own needs and her search for a new version of her aging self. Like the protagonists in *Esperando al italiano*, she is looking for a model that will acknowledge her sexuality, but not in the old roles. Her search began when she walked into the park to wait for Glenn, and it continues when she walks out of the park looking for herself.

By playing the roles of Margarita and Rita for Gardel, Rita makes a conscious choice that is "capable of affecting, for good or ill, the totality of the person and his *milieu*" as Eugene L. Moretta observes in reference to other role-playing Latin American plays (1980, 22). Further, Moretta notes that this role-playing can serve as a discovery that allows the character to participate in a reencounter with self that is a necessary first step toward a more profound identity (27–28). Indeed, Rita's willingness to play along with Gardel allows her to see herself from a new perspective and to leave those former versions behind.

Lovers meeting in the park also describes *Parque para dos* by Puerto Rican Teresa Marichal. However, this play employs both humor and satire to comment on the conflict between generations as staged in an encounter between lovers in the park that is observed and jeered by an audience of the elderly.[9] The play transforms a commonplace event, lovers meeting on a park bench, into a satire on sexuality and aging. The park bench becomes the stage and the lovers the center of attention for an audience seated in lawn chairs. The characters, identified only by gender and age, are Mujer (Woman), a prostitute of thirty, and her male client of forty five, Hombre (Man) who meet in a public park to become acquainted before their evening together and a group of elderly people, Viejo (Old Man, 68 yr.), Vieja (Old Woman, 75 yr.) and Abuela (Grandmother, 60 yr.), plus her granddaughter of sixteen, Muchacha (Girl), who arrive with lawn chairs to watch.

Parque para dos sets these two groups in opposition when the elderly audience appears in the park to watch the lovers, thus turning them into entertainment. The play opens with the meeting of Hombre and Mujer on the park bench to make their introductions. As they become more affectionate with each other the elders arrive and set up their chairs. After the lovers have engaged in some prolonged displays, they leave the bench and the elders move to occupy it. From their new position the elderly and Muchacha discuss their reasons for returning to the park each day. The tension between these two worlds rises as the physical actions of the lovers become more passionate and provocative to their audience and then falls after the couple leaves. For the elderly, the park bench is the site for a free sex show while for the prostitute Mujer it is the site for her sex business. In either case, the park bench is transformed from a neutral public place into a sexually charged entertainment space, a similar function as that in *Cuesta abajo*.

The behavior of the elderly, who make the lovers their entertainment, and the suggested regularity with which the performances on the park bench are given by lovers, clearly point to the metatheatricality of *Parque para dos*. The assembled group of elderly demonstrate through their actions and conversation that they know each other, that is, they are a community that frequents this venue. They pass judgment on the lovers, evaluate their performance, and function like an audience—approving by applauding the couple and disapproving by throwing trash at them. In response to the audience, the lovers become more than mere individuals engaged in the story of their sexual encounter, they become actors who acknowledge the audience and bow for it (9). Second, the actors and the audience imply that they go to the park regularly to perform or watch the performance. Mujer comments that she often meets her customers in the park, and the elderly remark that they enjoy coming to the park to watch lovers. In the following passage, the three elderly audience members list the same reasons for going to the park that many give for attending the theater—there is always something interesting to watch, it offers a change of pace, and it is an escape.

Viejo:	Ven como todos los días pasa algo diferente.
Vieja:	Sí, tiene razón.
Abuela:	Por eso es que me gusta tanto el parque . . . porque uno se divierte.
Viejo:	Sí, aquí uno si que se divierte.
Vieja:	Sí, uno se olvida de todo lo demás. (11)
[Old man:	Do you see how every day something different happens.
Old woman:	Yes, you're right.
Grandmother:	That's why I like the park so much, because one always has such a good time.
Old man:	Yes, here one really does have a good time.
Old woman:	Yes, one forgets everything else.]

Each group of characters establishes their own space in which to act and observes the general rules for being in the theater. The lovers occupy the center of attention sitting on the park bench, their embraces and kisses attract and keep the audience watching, and they meet the traditional physical requirements for actors with their handsome looks, costuming, and youthfulness. Mujer is described as *todo un modelito 'Dior'* (like a Dior model) and Hombre as *muy elegante* (very elegant) [1]. As good actors they remain focused on each other, seemingly oblivious to the spectators, except for one moment when the actors acknowledge their audience. The elderly function as an audience in that they are physically separate from the park bench and engaged in observing and reacting to them. They read the newspaper, gossip, and complain but they are always aware of the lovers and quick to note any change in their actions toward each other. They react approvingly or not to the actors but they do not challenge them directly. As audience they observe the rules of watching but not entering into the action.

Muchacha is the fourth member of the audience and at the other end of the age spectrum from the elderly as a retarded adolescent of sixteen. She cannot participate in the conversation of the elderly except to provoke her grandmother with questions about the couple. She is both excited and curious about the lovers, as revealed in the following questions:

> "(*Suspira*) Abuelita, ¿cuándo yo tenga novio, vamos a hacer eso?,"
> "(*Suspira*) Abuelita, ¿por qué besan tanto?" [(*Sighs.*) Granny, When I have a boyfriend, will we do that too? (*Sighs.*) Granny, why do they kiss so much?] (5).

Like many adolescents, Muchacha is anxious to know how to act with the opposite sex, an interest that leads her grandmother to command her not to watch.

By building a theatrical relationship between the lovers and the elders, Marichal reshapes an awkward and embarrassing moment into a funny comment on generational power. None of the characters have engaging personalities, yet each has a place and a role to perform. The lovers, a lonely widower and a prostitute, claim to know each other, because they have been screened and then advised by the agency that arranged their meeting. But each is full of preconceived notions about the other. Hombre is a powerful businessman surprised at the attitudes of the prostitute about her profession. He laughs at her interest in studying philosophy, because it is incongruous with her life, which he characterizes in negative and demeaning terms as immoral and lonely (3). Mujer is equally condescending towards him, laughing about the death of his wife of a broken neck from a car accident because, as a student of philosophy,

> "Me encanta reírme de la seriedad ajena" [I love to laugh at other people's pain] (4,2).

She defends her career choice without moral compunction, describing her work as simple, impersonal, and without trauma (3).

Similarly, the elderly audience members are whiners that reinforce the commonly held view of the aged and adolescents as grouchy and contrary. They complain about their own difficulties of aging, but they also enjoy condemning the young for their failings. The Vieja complains about her ill health, the Viejo of the high prices, and all of them yearn for the good old days, regret birthing their ungrateful children, and look forward to death. They long to escape to the past or to watch the lovers in order to forget about their problems and to recoup a sense of importance. In addition, the grandmother grumbles about the burden of caring for her retarded granddaughter that her own children abandoned:

"me tiraron a mi ésta" [they left this one with me] (9).

She fulfills her responsibility by taking her granddaughter with her but berating her constantly for her curiosity. As the curtain falls, Muchacha finally reacts to this abuse by speaking the words that the younger generation often thinks about its elders:

Muchacha:	Abuela cuando tú te mueras, ¿podré levantar la cabeza?
Abuela:	Sí, cuando yo muera, podrás levantar la cabeza.
Muchacha:	Abuela.
Abuela:	¿qué?
Muchacha:	Pues, muérete pronto. (11)
[Girl:	Grandmother, when you die, may I raise my head?
Grandmother:	Yes, when I die you may raise your head.
Girl:	Grandmother.
Grandmother:	What?
Girl:	Well, die soon then.]

In *Parque para dos*, sexual desire is the magnet that pulls the widower toward the prostitute and that pleases and disgusts the elderly so that they are drawn back to the spectacle on the park bench each day. As an audience, they are openly hostile towards displays of sexual desire but ultimately they approve since they continue to observe and comment even as they condemn. The strongest response that they muster is throwing cans, a satisfying outburst for them that provides a small sense of power at the same time that it rewards the couple for the intensity of its display. The prostitute and her client, players who perform a sexual transaction, defy the audience's values but gratify their voyeurism with their physical intimacy. Both groups exaggerate their reactions as can be seen in the following dialogue in

counterpoint in which the couple speaks in the romantic terms of
soap opera lovers while the audience decries their actions as indecent,
inappropriate for public places, and immoral. When the scene comes
to a climax the couple leaves the park bench.

Mujer:	Sí, creo que la vamos a pasar muy bien.
Vieja:	¡Pecaminosos!
Hombre:	Por toda la eternidad. . . .
Viejo:	¡Indecentes!
Mujer:	Por toda la eternidad, hasta que la muerte nos separe. . . .
Abuela:	¡Inmorales! (10)
[Woman:	Yes, I think we will get along very well.
Old woman:	You're sinners!
Man:	For all of eternity . . .
Old man:	You're indecent!
Woman:	For all of eternity, until death separates us. . . .
Grandmother:	You're immoral!]

As performers of sexuality and desire the couple represents the unattainable for the elderly and for Muchacha. However, at the ages of
forty-five and thirty they are approaching the point at which their
ages will surpass the acceptability of a public display, according to the
elderly. That their credibility depends on age is supported by the
following exchange in which the Vieja comments that

"La pareja de ayer era más entretenida" [The couple yesterday was
more entertaining] and Abuela explains that "Eran más jóvenes" [They
were younger] (10).

In her staging of age Marichal makes fun of both generations.
The elders invade the private moment of the lovers looking for cheap
thrills and a small moment of power to criticize their excesses. Even
under the spotlight of the elders, the lovers go to the park to show off
their sexual desires. All the characters are unsympathetic no matter
what their age: the self-centered adults who own the world yet treat
each other poorly, the bitter and frustrated elderly who criticize and
demean others, and the young who wish the old would die to make
room for them. When Mujer tells her client that the park is

"el lugar ideal . . . para conocer a alguien" [the ideal place to get to
know someone] (3)

she refers to her customer and to the audience watching the play. In this play about role-playing and performance, the park is not a place for only two, a contradiction to the play's title. By casting the lovers and the elders in a theatrical relationship Marichal laughs at human behavior and at the illusory nature of age, which moves individuals on and off the center stage of sexual desire and into and out of important, influential roles. That the Muchacha longs to be grown-up, that the powerful flaunt their desire, and that the elders find relief criticizing the younger generation, only draws more attention to the disconnection that culture has constructed for the stages of aging.

In the four plays on midlife at the postmenopausal marker, Latin American women dramatists tackle theatrical and cultural givens that have dominated the late twentieth century stage. They rework the conventions of the Theater of the Absurd by adding new meanings to the existing repertoire. For example, a closed space does not always represent suffocation or inhumanity, but can indicate protection and nurture. The repetition of activities does not necessarily lead to loss of meaning but rather can indicate a search to gain new meaning. Games and role-playing do not comprise a substitute for real action, but serve as methods for rehearsing or training for change. Games and reenactments are not simply hierarchical models of power distribution between men and women as Larson has contended in reference to other Latin American plays (78), but rather vehicles to self-understanding and improvement. More often than not these games free women from past gender-inscribed behavior.

In cultural terms, the plays present an inventory of roles that the women characters played and the relationships that they participated in during their youth. The movement of the plays depends on the ability of the characters to understand those old roles and their efforts to fashion new ones. In *Esperando al italiano* and *Cuesta abajo*, we see female characters actively engaged in discussing the past and rescuing from it the powers (sexual and/or emotional) to help them move into the future. In both plays, the characters decide to move on and to experiment with new models for being older. In contrast, *Adorável desgraçada* and *Parque para dos* reveal less productive reactions to the problem of how to age with grace. Both are cautionary tales that warn of the problems society creates for women by limiting the roles that they are allowed to play in their youth (good versus bad), and then further restricting those possible for them as elders. In both plays the characters react angrily and violently to those limitations. All four plays propose that as women age they can begin to take greater responsibility for developing their full human potential, that is their femaleness. In the worst scenario, *Adorável desgraçada*, it is the lack of a healthy life force and of companionship that deprives the protagonist of her full self. In the best scenario, *Esperando al italiano*, it is the appreciation of that sexuality and the support of others that drives the characters to begin to discover who they ought to be as elders.

Final Acts

The characters in the last two plays are the oldest and the most like the traditional image of grandmothers of all the protagonists discussed in this chapter. Like the elders in the play *Parque para dos*, they complain about their problematic relations with their children and their declining health. However, unlike the characters from Marichal's satire, these characters are described in the more respectful and dignified terms accorded to grandmothers in Latin America. The protagonist of *A assaltada* by Isis Baião is identified as *anciã* (venerable old woman) in the stage directions (113) while señorita Clara, the main character in *Que Dios la tenga en la gloria* by Carlota Martínez, is described in similar terms as *anciana señorita de 75 años* (elderly single woman of 75 years) [7].[10] Both plays present their characters in comfortable domestic settings, that are usually run by helpful companions or servants, and where they are protected from the bustle of the big city around them.

The ages and/or health of the protagonists locate them beyond the realm of midlife and into the final stage of life, that time most closely linked to death. Robert Kastenbaum has observed that "Although more elders are surviving longer than ever before, the association between old age and death has become stronger" and that "most people die of old age, rather than any other reason" ("Exit," 79). This inevitable association between old age and death is reflected in both plays by the physical condition of the protagonists and the events dramatized, and is implied in one title. *A assaltada* [The robbery victim] is a short sketch in which a burglar forces his way into a grandmother's apartment to steal her money. However, during the conversation the elder reveals that she is struggling with worse things in her life than the appearance of a robber at the door. As the assaulted person mentioned in the title, her list of affronts includes that she is being robbed, but also that she has been deprived of the emotional support of her children, of her companion—a pet cat that died recently, and soon of her own life from cancer. In a surprising turn of events, she offers her entire fortune to the thief who declines and runs away fearful that she must be the devil. *Que Dios la tenga en la gloria* [That God watch over her in Heaven] also represents generational conflict. The title echoes the phrase used when remembering those who have died, and in this play there are more dead people remembered than characters alive on the stage. The play moves between the present and the past to explain the life of the protagonist, señorita Clara, her niece Cándida, and the conflict over sexual behavior that has ruined their affective bonds. The description printed on the back cover of Martínez's work states: "cuenta el choque ético entre la anciana señorita Clara y su sobrina-nieta Cándida, quien aparentemente ha incurrido en el pecado de mantener relaciones prenuciales" [tells of the ethical conflict between Miss Clara and her great niece Cándida who apparently has committed the sin of having sexual relations before marriage]. This summary fails to mention, however, that the play retraces the history of that relationship before it broke down.

In spite of the negative connotations of the titles, I will argue that the protagonists of these two plays are engaged in final acts of affirmation that many elders perform as they approach death. According to Mary Bray Pipher, as they face death the elderly often make a final gesture to sustain themselves and others. For example, they may perform a noble act before death, or perform heroically in their dying moments, or voice and acknowledge regrets in order to reconcile with self and family, or find acceptance (1999, 205, 215–16). Life review is one method for settling accounts that was described by Robert Butler in the early 1960s based on his research with the aged. Individuals making a life review tend to recall, examine, and order their memories for the purpose of giving meaning to their lives. Such affirming acts of elders who face death with dignity inform the readings of the two plays studied here. *A assaltada* presents a final noble act from a dying grandmother while *Que Dios la tenga en la gloria* employs a structure similar to that of a life review in order to enable its protagonist to lay the conflicts and disappointments of the past to rest.

A assaltada is the third short sketch by actress and playwright Isis Baião studied here and like its predecessors it demonstrates what

Brazilian theater scholar Fred M. Clark identifies as Baião's "incisive and irreverent humor" (1998, 89). As in the earlier sketch in this chapter, *Espelho, espelho meu*, the characters are identified only in generic terms by gender and profession. The antagonist, identified as Assaltante (Robber), forces his way into the apartment of a well-to-do elder woman called the Assaltada (Robbery victim). Rather than responding in fear to the robber's aggressive language and handgun, the protagonist acts calmly and generously toward her intruder offering him dessert, cool water to calm his nerves, and the obligatory coffee. This role reversal surprises the robber who accepts these acts of hospitality, but maintains his guard and continues to threaten his victim:

> "A senhora num tem medo de morrer?" [Lady, aren't you afraid to die?] (115).

The shocking revelation in her answer explains her courage and unnerves the intruder:

> "Estou quase morrendo, meu filho. Os médicos me deram dois meses de vida. Câncer!" [I almost am dying, my son. The doctors gave me two months to live. Cancer!]

It appears that the Assaltada has won over her intruder when she explains to him how her disrespectful children already are arguing over the inheritance. But the solution that the Assaltada has chosen to resolve the conflict between her children goes far beyond the comprehension of the thief:

> . . . "Se perderem a minha herança, pode ser que aprendam a viver. É por isso que vou deixar tudo para o senhor" [. . . If they lose their inheritance, maybe they will learn to live. That is why I am going to leave everything to you] (115).

No matter how the grandmother argues for the benefits her money could provide the robber and his family, he believes her actions are inspired by evil forces and runs away (116). The grandmother's audacious proposal takes on even greater proportions when she complains in her closing comment that this was her third failed attempt to give away her inheritance:

"Mas o qué que eles querem? É o terceiro que foge!" [But, what more
do they want? That's the third one who has run away] (116).

This humorous encounter demonstrates one manner of waiting
and then acting with a sense of purpose. It also challenges the gen-
eralized assumptions about elderly women as "sweet little old ladies,"
that is, as harmless individuals, possibly disconnected from reality, and
old-fashioned. This grandmother defies those expectations with what
Pipher calls "a final request with great power" (203). Rather than
being forced to decide how to distribute her resources between her
children, the Assaltada makes an unexpected move to attempt to
donate the money to someone who would have more appreciation for
it, thus hoping to teach her children one final lesson. The fact that
she has failed three times with her wish not only comments on the
supposed regularity with which the wealthy are robbed in Brazil's
unequal society, but also on the unusual nature of her request. It so
defies the traditional behavior of both grandmothers and upper-class
society, that all three robbers interpret the bequest as evil rather than
as a windfall. But the Assaltada persists, waiting for each new robber
in the hope that he will be an appreciative beneficiary, that is, someone who will take her seriously and take her money. The stage directions describe her sense of failure after she calls to the fleeing robber
Anciã, sozinha, joga-se numa cadeira, arrasada [Alone, the elderly woman
throws herself into a chair, devastated] and she speaks her last line of
incredulity *desesperada* (desperately) [116].

The humor of the sketch derives from the unexpected nature of
the elder's actions that invert her relationship with the Assaltante.
There is some evidence that the grandmother's actions might be
motivated by revenge. For example, she mentions the disappointments in her life, the losses she has suffered, her loneliness, and the
unexpected sadness that her children have caused her (115). She
contrasts her poor mother-child relationships with the loyalty that the
robber declares for his mother, and she tells him that her inheritance
will help him honor his mother as he has promised (116). These
statements imply that the grandmother appreciates the simple values
of loyalty that the burglar demonstrates but that her own financially
secure children do not have. The positive outcomes that the grandmother hopes to encourage through the donation of her inheritance,
a form of social work for thieves and moral instruction for her chil-

dren, and the stage directions about her emotions and intentions tend to suggest that she is not looking for revenge but for a creative solution. The Assaltada's behavior is described with adjectives such as *calma e distinta* (calm and refined), *finíssima* (very elegant), *tranquilamente* (peacefully), and *indiferente, gentil* (indifferent, kind), and her solicitous and understanding manner when confronted by an individual described as *paranóico, olhando pra todos os lados* (paranoid, looking all around) [114] imply that she is acting with courage and that her actions point to a higher, if unusual, moral ground.

In speaking about performances by older women, Anne Davis Basting has noted their importance in reallocating cultural capital to older women and in untangling the association between old age and old-fashioned principles that reinforce the desire to remain young (1998, 132). The protagonist of *A assaltada* accomplishes both goals by demonstrating her own version of genteel heroism rather than fear in her meeting with the robber and by choosing the unexpected rather than the usual in her plans to disburse her income. Her actions provoke admiration for the generosity of the request, but also surprise for the difficulty in seeing the request granted. As an old woman's story *A assaltada* reinvigorates the passive feminine image of old age and dying, turning it into an image of grandmotherly wisdom and spunk.

Que Dios la tenga en la gloria begins with the image of death communicated in the mourning clothes worn by the protagonist señorita Clara and her companion Rosaura as they return home after mass, but the play ends in an image of harmony between señorita Clara and her sister Paulina as they participate in an imaginary concert. Between the darkness of the opening and the lightness of the closing this two-act play in fourteen scenes retraces key moments in señorita Clara's life and relationship with her niece Cándida. As an unmarried woman Clara followed the tradition of her culture by serving in the house of her married sister Cristina until her decision to leave following the marriage of her niece Cándida. Now living in her deceased parents' home with her older sister Misia Paulina, Clara spends most of her time waiting for her niece to visit. Señorita Clara has lost all of her family connections except Cándida and Paulina, but Cándida never comes to visit and Clara rarely goes to Paulina's room.

The play presents a patchwork of scenes from the present and past of Clara's life as a seventy-five year old. The movement in the play tells the story of the creation and breaking of the emotional bonds between Clara and her niece in act 1, and Clara's eventual acceptance of that break in act 2. In its disjointed episodes from Clara's past and her life in the present, the play constructs a life review for Clara that allows her to gain insight into her relationship with Cándida.

Robert Butler's idea of a life review as a "reorganization of past experiences" in which the past "marches in review, is surveyed, observed, and reflected upon by the ego" theorizes a time in an elder's life when the awareness of death is so great as to provoke a reconsideration of past conflicts for the purpose of reconciliation and resolution (qtd. in Merriam 1995, 8). According to Butler, life review is "prompted by the realization of approaching dissolution and death" that is a response to the "biological and psychological fact of death" or it may be a response to "crises of various types." Thus, life review involves working with memories, much like the activities of the protagonists discussed above in plays such as *Esperando al italiano, Adorável desgraçada,* or *Cuesta abajo* but for a different purpose. Rather than searching for ways to confront the future, life review means making preparations for the end of life by settling past accounts.

Señorita Clara lives in a climate of loss and death in which she has outlived most of her family and her best friend Francia. The play opens immediately following the mass for the one year anniversary of the death of Clara's best friend. It is through memories of that deceased friend that Clara begins to reconstruct her memories of her beloved niece Cándida. This opening sequence highlights Clara's decision years earlier to become Cándida's primary caregiver and establishes the frame of the play in which Clara's memories of the past have the power to transform her present. The anniversary of Francia's death triggers this conversation between past and present, in a similar manner to that described by Butler above. Clara's life as an old woman is constantly being interrupted by memories from the past that appear when Clara dozes off or when she is sleeping. She lives in a dialogue with the past, replaying key moments of her younger self in conversation and conflict with her family members.

During act 1, the scenes from the past explain how Cándida became more than a beloved member of the extended family, but actually a de facto daughter for Clara. In the present, Clara looks at family photos and remembers her younger days with her sisters and parents. In the flashbacks she relives those days during the courtship and marriage of Cándida's parents and later in her role as a substitute mother for Cándida after the death of her parents. For Clara these emotional connections of a mother-daughter relationship explain the importance of Cándida in her life and why she continues to wait for her to visit. When Cándida does not arrive as expected, Clara finds comfort playing with a doll that she keeps hidden in a suitcase in her room.

The key scene in act 1 presents the conflict that caused the separation of the mother-daughter dyad. In this scene, Clara and Cándida argue over the importance of virginity before marriage. Cándida defends her sexual activity as a necessary strategy against her aunt's rigid opposition to all her suitors and as a means to guarantee her engagement. But for Clara it is an unpardonable sin. In an act that serves to harm her own interests, Clara condemns her niece for her actions and shows her anger by refusing to have anything to do with her, even refusing to be a grandmother to Cándida's children:

"Ahí va a estar tu castigo, ni abuela ni nada, no te lo perdono" [This will be your punishment, don't expect me to be a grandmother or anything else, I cannot pardon you] (25).

These strong words from the past that cut Clara off from the only family she has, provoke her in the present to visit her sister Paulina in her room.

Clara's mixing of memories from the past with events in the present clouds her sense of the passage of time. She waits for Cándida without really knowing how long she has been waiting or how long it has been since Cándida came. Her companion Rosaura and the maid Marina never challenge her belief that Cándida will come and never state clearly how long it has been since anyone visited. Thus, Clara keeps her hope alive by waiting. But when she finally goes to her sister Paulina in scene 1 of act 2, she is forced to confront the facts. Clara takes her sister a guayaba fruit treat that has gotten moldy. The moldy treat reveals that Clara has not received any visitors for a long time. Paulina draws that conclusion even though Clara refuses to accept it, as the following citation demonstrates:

Misia Paulina: Y para qué quiero yo arreglar nada. No espero a nadie. Allá tú guardando bocadillos que se vuelven mohosos porque ya nadie viene a verte.

La señorita Clara: (*Con la voz ahogada a punto de llorar*): No digas eso. No
                            vuelvas a repetirlo. Ellos siempre me llaman por
                            teléfono cuando no pueden venir. Iban a un viaje muy
                            largo de donde me van a traer muchas cosas . . . (30)
[Misia Paulina: And why should I straighten up anything. I don't
                            expect anyone. And you there, saving up goodies
                            that then turn moldy because nobody comes to see
                            you anymore.
La señorita Clara: (*With her voice choking, almost to the point of crying.*)
                            Don't say that. Don't repeat that again. They al-
                            ways call me on the phone when they can't come.
                            They were going on a long trip from which they
                            will bring me many things . . .]

The events that finally manage to help Clara reconcile her waiting
in the present with her actions in the past are a nightmare and a
flashback of a conversation about death. While in a death-like faint
Clara dreams of a decadent and surrealistic nightclub where Cándida,
her husband Angel, and another woman act out Clara's fears of her
niece as a morally loose woman who drinks, smokes, and talks of trips
to Miami to buy expensive watches (31). Immediately following this
scene, a flashback retells a conversation between Clara and a house
servant named Eufrasia. In her nightmare, Eufrasia sees corpses protesting the way in which the living have abandoned them by leaving
their graves in a protest march (33). These nightmares speak to Clara
about her longing for her niece and turn her toward a reconciliation
with her only remaining family member Paulina. When she finally
awakes Clara has been transformed. She gives up waiting for Cándida
stating that her niece will not come to visit anymore. Then she declares herself to be in excellent health and prepares to return to visit
her sister to participate in a concert (36).

The closing scene between Clara and Paulina, in which each
pretends to play an instrument as part of a concert to which an
imaginary audience has convened, emphasizes that Clara has left her
world of waiting to inhabit the world of her sister. The stage instructions state: (*Paulina toma un imaginario violín. Otro tanto Clara con su
clarinete. Afina. Inician una hermosa pieza. Se apagan las luces*) (Paulina
picks up an imaginary violin. Clara does the same with a clarinet. She
tunes the instrument. They begin a lovely piece. The lights go down)
[37]. This heavenly image of music supports the idea that Clara is

better off in her sister's room than waiting for her niece to arrive. In her dreams and reminiscences Clara has felt the separation, acknowledged her loss of Cándida, and reconciled with her older sister. Rather than waiting for someone that she has realized will not come, Clara finds companionship and music with her older sister. In a life-affirming conclusion, she ends her relationship with the past by achieving an understanding of her own place within it and turns her attention toward the present.

Even though the protagonists of both Baião and Martínez's plays appear to represent the comforting presence of grandmothers, neither is totally at ease with her own life nor engaged in ministering to family, common stereotypes for older women. Instead, both are seeking answers and relationships that will define their remaining moments on Earth. The enigma of death looms much closer to these characters and the idea of waiting for a resolution is too passive for them. Each woman is living fully in the present, Clara in harmony and the Assaltada in frustration. But neither wishes to escape into the past or refuses to confront the concerns of the day. Thus, their representations of old age, while humorous and fragile, contain the essence of active aging.

The eight plays studied in this chapter portray the nuances of aging by offering alternatives to its traditional plot line. Neither passive nor plump nor grandmotherly, the protagonists of these plays actively contest the stereotypes and prejudices that society has constructed. By asserting their rights to sexual expression and/or their rights to make decisions about their lives, these characters counteract the notions that aging women must acquiesce to the desires of others. Most of the women characters studied in this chapter demonstrate that there is meaningful life after youth even though it requires a conscious effort to struggle against society's efforts to erase and devalue them.

Many of the plays emphasize not only the continuity of life that requires changing and adapting, but also maintaining the true essence of self, especially that spark of feminine desire. The midlife characters and the elders have many resources at their disposal to help them search for a sense of self over time, or their "age identity." By reenacting the youthful past and comparing it to their aging in the present, the characters show the layering of their identities over time. In most cases the protagonists are not mourning their past identities nor regretting leaving youthfulness behind. Neither are they escaping into the past as a way of hiding from the present. They have not been totally brainwashed by the incantations about loss that comprise their cultural context and constitute "age lore." Rather they are mining the past and honoring their sexuality as a life force for the future. Many of these women protagonists are making the idea of "being of age" into an activity.

Loneliness appears as a common characteristic in these plays. Not only do the protagonists appear on stage alone, but they often feel alone and resentful of a culture that pushes them to one side. The protagonists from *Soliloquio, Espelho, espelho meu, Cuesta abajo*, and *Esperando al italiano* engage in a constant battle of repeating culture's degrading messages and then affirming their own vitality. Much like the negotiations between mothers and daughters in chapter 2, the midlife and elder women characters of this chapter are most successful when engaged with each other in community-building and reciprocity. Thus, the network of friendships in *Esperando al italiano* functions as a good model for reinforcing the worth of aging women.

The most common bond that marks women's lives, that all important relationship to family and children, proves to be a poor substitute for an internal sense of meaning and contentment with life. Children and grandchildren in these plays do not provide a community of support for these elder characters, but rather a source of disappointment and obligation. For example, they echo the values of a youth culture and attempt to control and limit their elders' opportunities. Children and grandchildren also demand services and financial benefits from their female elders in order to guarantee their own security and freedom. Only one play, *Que Dios la tenga en la gloria*, portrays a caring and sympathetic family member, also an elder, who provides understanding and respect. Those characters with problematic family relations relish being away from their burdens. Yet all the characters, even those who are left alone, chose action over passivity. None are willing to simply give in to society's self-defeating messages about aging.

In assessing the impact of these plays on aging by Latin American women dramatists, it is useful to consider Richard Hornby's observation: "Drama is not a mirror held up to nature, but rather a gauge" (1986, 27). These plays register one important measurement on the cultural gauge. At least half of the plays studied in this chapter have been performed and rewarded as meaningful cultural contributions. Therefore, some audiences in large cities in Venezuela, Brazil, and Puerto Rico have been privileged to witness the testimony of older women's voices and bodies. On the cultural gauge, the topic of aging, and in particular feminine aging, has just begun to attract the attention of writers and audiences. The visibility of aging women will only grow over time due to the greater longevity of the aging members of the post-World War II generation. The search for femaleness will only increase as women live longer, providing the theater with more opportunities to explore the relationship and meaning of aging and sexuality. In the future, it will be important to provide as many images of aging as possible to help audiences reflect on the passage of their own lives and to help them formulate new layers of identity for the future.

CONCLUSION

Beyond the Footlights

"Porque creo que ya la tarea de que la mujer tenga un lugar
protagónico en escena, está hecho. O por lo menos encaminado."
[Because I think that the task of putting women into a protagonist's
role on stage is complete. Or at least on its way.]

—Susana Torres Molina, "Conversaciones."

In this panoramic and introductory study of twenty-four plays from
seven countries by eighteen Latin American women playwrights
I have assembled a sample of a generation of writers united by
shared historical and cultural traditions, gender, social class, and a
feminist critique. They are the ones who have found the means to
make female experience visible on the stage. In presenting these writers as a part of an artistic group, I am claiming a space for them within
a tradition of literary history that declares they don't exist. In fact,
their plays give testimony to others and to themselves that as a body
of writers they are building a presence for women on Latin America's
stages, as Susana Torres Molina suggests in the epigraph. This study
proposes that neither women playwrights nor women's experiences
are exceptions to dramatic art. They may have been devalued and
disappeared from the official record and even restricted from appearing on the stage, but such exclusion can no longer persist. This recov-
ery of the contributions of women from the recent past intends to
document what this generation of dramatists has said about female
experiences in Latin America, so that both dramatists and women can
be acknowledged as participants in the life of the *casa patriarcal*. In
some small way, this study proposes to help open the doors of the
theater and welcome more women into a place where they can begin
to feel at home.

The comparative approach employed here creates conversations
between these plays that never would have taken place in a more

traditionally oriented approach, since neither the specificity of women's lives nor plays written by women are common topics in Latin American theater criticism. When one dramatist studies women's lives, she pursues a personal interest. However, when a large group of playwrights compose more than one hundred plays on the topic in the span of only twenty years, then their work can become a new area of study in Latin American theater scholarship. Such an argument can be supported by more than wishful thinking given the impressive number of performances and the publication of these plays. Of the corpus studied in this book, over 60 percent have been performed and all but three of the twenty-four plays examined have been published. Thus, this method of associating plays thematically and according to gender not only is warranted, but also uncovers new topics and authorizes further investigation and analysis.

There are two broad conclusions that can be drawn from this study of the stages of women's lives as portrayed in drama. First, the search for female identity can be understood as a process that is often represented as a ritual or a journey. In their relationships with lovers, husbands, daughters, and a youth-oriented society, women characters are constantly negotiating with existing stereotypes and values. Rituals are employed in these plays to help the protagonists disconnect themselves from previous versions of themselves, from imposed expectations for them, and/or from unhealthy liaisons with others. Journeys also appear as processes that women characters assume in the hope of discovering better alternatives. The choice of a journey or a ritual locates women as seekers who explore and experiment. Thus, they are initiators of action who engage our interest as they engage in conflict with others. Even though conflict does not always produce successful alternatives, it functions to disrupt and question the status quo. Second, female identity is not a rigid, preconceived construction that must be repeated without room for improvisation. Rather it is an activity that collects many layers as it develops in response to social and biological demands. In healthy women identities change over time, just as bodies grow. Contrary to traditional representations of women on stage as predictable and static, these plays present a fascinating range of interpretations of the female experience. They restore vitality, creativity, and energy to the dramatic image of Latin American women, bringing the women on stage more into agreement with the women in the audience.

Yet no matter what the stage of life, all these protagonists are linked to the nucleus of the human experience, family life. Family life occupies the central space and focus of the women's lives in these twenty-four plays. As already noted, family life also retains an important and honored place in Latin American society. Yet, none of the plays studied here locate women within the bustling and cluttered context of family life, even though all but five of the plays take place within the home. Thus, the traditional ideals of extended family life that reign off the stage are not echoed on stage in these plays. The women dramatists in this corpus isolate their protagonists and focus solely on their testimony about the female condition. The majority of the plays present only two characters, a number that is particularly appropriate for the one-act format preferred by most. By placing female protagonists alone on the stage the playwrights focus attention on them and announce the importance of the words and issues they address. The isolation of female protagonists on stage also points to the changing shape of family life in Latin America where fewer people occupy the home, where the economic situation for many is precarious, and where the cost of sociopolitical unrest and dictatorship may have reduced the family size involuntarily.

Isolation on stage also communicates the need that all the female characters express for an emotional connection between individuals that transcends the narrowly defined roles women and men are allowed to play within the home and beyond it. The feminist critiques made in these plays not only expose the problems of male power and dominance, but they also demonstrate this yearning for new models of human relations. Many of the plays reveal how patriarchy separates and manipulates wives and daughters and the aging for its own benefit, yet several provide alternatives. Staging new versions of family life that emphasize egalitarian and humanitarian models of relationship stimulates audiences to reconsider their own ideas and ideals about private life.

The new examples of relationship offered in these plays take the shape of caring and respectful attachments between women and a small circle of loved-ones. The characters find the greatest emotional health in equitable and reciprocal relationships committed to mutual obligation and support. Couples who incorporate democratic and egalitarian principles into their marriages, such as the one in *Boca molhada de paixão calada*, remake the centuries-old hierarchy that separates women and men. Mothers who negotiate with and learn to support daughters, such as those in *La partida* and *Madre nuestra que estás en la tierra*, help to formulate and bring to life new techniques for raising children. Aging women who use all their energies, including their sexuality, to create new opportunities for themselves, such as those in *Esperando al italiano*, legitimize each other's needs and build bonds that can endure the changes in times and bodies.

The setting for most of these plays, the home, is presented as a problematic space with both positive and negative functions in women's lives. On the one hand, the home serves as the traditional site for women and the domain for women's duties as housewives and mothers. Thus, it protects them and provides them with a refuge from the outside world or even from other family members. The home offers women an identity and role, that is, it secures women's traditional status through her association with men and family. Women characters appear authentic when placed in the context of their homes. At the same time, the home also confines women, limiting their freedom to leave and interact with others. The expectations of family members require that women must always be at home ready to receive guests or welcome returning workers and students. From this perspective, the home becomes a trap that impinges on the female sense of self. Therefore, the plays reveal that the home is not necessarily a haven to all its inhabitants and that its values are not always beneficial. Like the other givens of female life addressed in these plays, the home contains contradictory messages that must be exposed to audience consideration.

Within the walls of the homes represented in these plays most of the properties stand as markers for the common activities of the family. Bedroom, living room, and kitchen furniture, wall decorations, and windows and doors remind the audience of the routines of the characters who inhabit these plays. More importantly, many of the plays utilize the association between the characters and their space to reinforce the dramatic action. Female characters interact with their spaces in a meaningful manner either to contest the ways in which they are suffocated by them or to defend them from invaders. Both standing and hand-held mirrors play important roles in all three chapters. They are symbols of how women have been defined in outward and visual terms by society, as Jenijoy LaBelle has remarked (1988, 14).

Mirrors offer a multiplicity of references for the female characters in these plays. In *Amantíssima*, the mirror represents a form of self-absorbed vanity, the traditional association for it, as LaBelle has pointed out (14). However, in other mother-daughter plays and in the plays of romance, the mirror functions as a tool for imposing social norms (LaBelle, 151). Mirrors remind the female characters of the importance of their looks and they assist women in a rigorous comparison of self-perception with physical reality. Rarely are mirrors perceived to be friends to women characters, who may seek solace in the glass, but not find it. As women age, mirrors indicate how and where women's bodies and beauty are changing (99). For example, in *Espelho, espelho meu*, the protagonist engages in a verbal battle with her mirror in an effort to defend herself against societal demands for youth and beauty. Finally, the mirrors stand for the theater itself, reflecting back to the public an image of family life and social values that the playwrights have crafted to challenge existing views and practices.

The plays in this corpus partake of techniques from both the realistic/naturalist theater and the modernist, or nonrealistic theater. Roughly one-half of the plays examined here stage women's lives as a realistic drama, a serious narrative meant to be taken seriously. By choosing to write drama about women, even in the short format preferred by many, the dramatists confirm that women's lives offer both interest and significance for this noble theatrical form. Since drama engages its audience and invests it in the character's situation, it creates an emotional connection with its audience. As a result, drama has been a favorite for many socially conscious Latin American dramatists attempting to portray social inequality and injustice. The women dramatists studied here have extended both the meaning of politics and the place it is practiced by moving their dramas into the most intimate spaces of the home and into the personal lives of its female characters.

The remaining half of the plays in this corpus employ comedy, metatheater, and parody to shed light on life in the home. Not surprisingly the most common form of metatheater found in these plays is role-playing since it raises questions about human identity and social roles, as Richard Hornby has pointed out (1986, 68). Calling attention to the constructedness of the theater's world serves these women dramatists as a vehicle to question the construction of social roles. Role-playing contributes an important function to the plays by reminding the audience that human roles and identities are not innate but learned (72). Thus, metatheater provides a format in which women playwrights can explode and undermine commonly held views about women, gender roles, and aging. In these plays, the women protagonists question and shock their audience by performing outside the molds of gender roles programmed by family and society. Parody operates in a similar manner as role-playing and in several plays the two appear simultaneously. Through exaggeration and distortion, parody produces a world that is disconnected from the realm of the real. In this other world, humor can tackle subjects and behavior that would be too threatening to the existing social structure. Parody distances its audiences from the real world in order to provide a new context in which to evaluate behaviors and values taken for granted. Instead of offering a catharsis through emotion and identification, parody offers a connection through the laughter of recognition.

The title for this chapter, "Beyond the Footlights," refers to the powerful impact these plays can have in real women's lives. In her essay on the trends in twentieth century feminine literature in Brazil, critic Nelly Novães Coelho refers to the period of the 1960s through 1980s as a time of feminist awareness or *conscientização*. She explains the work of fiction writers this way: "por volta dos anos 60, já a 'imagem tradicional da mulher' está irremediavelmente superada, na literatura em geral, como padrão a ser seguido (O que não impede que, ao nível do Sistema Social vigente e no âmbito das famílias, ela continue sendo exigida e se tornando cada vez mais difícil de ser conservada pelas mulheres, sem questionamento)." [during the sixties, the 'traditional image of woman' has already been surpassed, in women's literature in general, as a model to be followed (although that didn't prevent it from being required by the dominant social system and by the family, which made it all the more difficult for women to maintain without question)] (1989, 10). In this passage, the Brazilian critic delineates the problematic distance between the enlightened lives of fictional characters and the day-to-day lives of real women in Brazil's traditional society. During the years Novães Coelho cites, 1960s–1980s, Latin America experienced tremendous social upheaval, some of which was reflected in the works of women dramatists that were staged at the same time. Plays by women occupied an important place then as a reinforcement to women's fiction, helping to span the great divide between the creative portraits of women represented in novels and the real conditions of struggle in their lives. At a time when theater attracted a popular audience, many of the plays studied here contributed to promoting new versions of womanhood. As mentioned in chapter 1, Leilah Assunção's *Roda cor de roda*, was acknowledged to be one of the reasons behind changes to Brazil's constitution and thus contributed directly to improving women's legal status there.

Now that more women than ever before are writing and staging their plays in Latin America, the potential impact of theater on society could be even greater if these plays can help diminish the distance between fictional opportunities and real ones. Imagining women's theater as a medium engaged in transforming the feminine condition in Latin America through the representations of women's lives, returns the theater to its traditional role as a social conscience in society. Both the critiques of existing conditions and the ideals of relationship expressed in the plays can contribute in important ways to the goal of achieving social justice for women by presenting examples that challenge women and men to think and act differently both within the home and beyond it.

APPENDIX 1

Plays by Chapter

Chapter 1

Ana Istarú, *El vuelo de la grulla* (performed and published 1984)
Inés Margarita Stranger, *Cariño malo* (performed and published 1990)
Consuelo de Castro, *À prova de fogo* (performed 1993, published 1977)
Leilah Assunção, *Boca molhada de paixão calada* (performed 1984, published 1988)
Estela Leñero, *Casa llena* (performed and published 1986)
Thais Erminy, *Whisky & Cocaína* (performed and published 1984)
Leilah Assunção, *Roda cor de roda* (performed 1975, published 1977)
Sabina Berman, *Uno/El bigote* (performed 1986, published 1985)

Chapter 2

Isis Baião, *Marcadas pela culpa* (published 1989)
Ana Istarú, *Madre nuestra que estás en la tierra* (performed 1988, published 1989)
Thais Erminy, *En un desván olvidado* (published 1991)
Rebecca Bowman, *De compras* (published 1995)
Pilar Campesino, *La partida* (published 1989)
Maria Adelaide Amaral, *Querida mamãe* (performed 1994, published 1995)
Susana Torres Molina, *Amantíssima* (performed 1988)
Diana Raznovich, *Casa matriz* (performed 1991, published 1989)

Chapter 3

Lidia Rebrij, *Soliloquio de la gorda* (performed 1987, published 1992)
Isis Baião, *Espelho, espelho meu* (published 1989)
Mariela Romero, *Esperando al italiano* (performed and published 1988)
Leilah Assunção, *Adorável desgraçada* (performed 1994)
Gabriela Fiore, *Cuesta abajo* (performed 1988, published 1990)
Teresa Marichal, *Parque para dos* (performed 1980s)
Carlota Martínez, *Que Dios la tenga en la gloria* (performed 1983, published 1994)
Isis Baião, *A assaltada* (published 1989)

APPENDIX 2

Dramatists by Country

Argentina

Marta Degracia
Cristina Escofet
Amancay Espíndola
Gabriela Fiore
Susana Freire
Andrea Garrote
Adriana Gente
Susana Gutiérrez Posse
María Inés Indart
Lucía Laragione
Beatriz Mosquera
Alicia Muñoz
Susana Poujol
Cecilia Propato
Diana Raznovich
Irene Ruderman
Beatriz Seibel
Hebe Serebrisky
Susana Torres Molina
Mariana Trajtenberg
Adriana Tursi
Patricia Zangaro

Bolivia

Maritza Wilde

Brazil

Regiana Antonini
Maria Adelaide Amaral
Leilah Assunção
Isis Baião
Consuelo de Castro
Vera Karam
Noemi Marinho

Chile

Macarena Baeza
Sandra Cepeda
Verónica Duarte
Francisca Imboden
Lucía de la Maza
Inés Margarita Stranger

Colombia

Fanny Buitrago

225

Costa Rica

Leda Cavallini
Ana Istarú
Lupe Pérez

Cuba

Carmen Duarte
Malena Espinosa

Dominican Republic

Chiqui Vicioso

Mexico

Leonor Azcárate
Sabina Berman
Carmen Boullosa
Rebecca Bowman
Pilar Campesino
Ángela Galindo
Estela Leñero
María Luisa Medina
Sylvia Mejía
Carmina Narro
Gilda Salinas
Teresa Valenzuela

Puerto Rico

Teresa Marichal
Aleyda Morales
Guanina Robles

Peru

Estela Luna

Venezuela

Thais Erminy
Carlota Martínez
Mónica Montañes
Xiomara Moreno
Inés Muñoz
Lídia Rebrij
Mariela Romero
Ana Teresa Sosa

Notes

Introduction

1. All translations of citations in Spanish and Portuguese are my own in this and all remaining chapters of the book.

2. See for example Gabriela Inclán and Felipe Galván, ed. *Teatro, mujer y latinoamérica* (Puebla, Mexico: Tablado Iberoamericano, 2000); and Julia Elena Sagaseta, ed. *Dramaturgas* (Buenos Aires: Editorial Nueva Generación, 2001).

3. The first conference about women's drama from the Spanish- and Portuguese-speaking worlds was held in Cincinnati, Ohio in 1994. "Un escenario próprio" was dedicated to Spanish, Latin American and United States Latina playwrights. A collection of the conference papers relating to Spain, *A Stage of Their Own* edited by Kirsten Nigro and Phyllis Zatlin was published (Ottawa: Girol Books, 1998). Cádiz, Spain has hosted at least two conferences on Iberoamerican women in the theater in 1997 and 1999. The conference papers from the 1997 event were edited by Laura Bores Canstanyer and published with the title *Reescribir la escena* (Madrid: Fundación Autor, 1998).

4. In a recent interview, Susana Torres Molina notes the contribution of her generation of dramatists to change the masculine orientation of the theater. She states ". . . y pienso que fue importante que nuestra generación empezara a escribir mucho teatro desde una perspectiva de la mujer"[I think it was important that my generation began to write a lot of theater from the woman's perspective]. María Claudia André, "Conversaciones sobre vida y teatro con Susana Torres Molina." *Latin American Theatre Review* 35, no. 2 (2002): 94.

5. Two anthologies of Spanish women dramatists also point to the preference for short plays. These are Fernando Doménech, ed. *Teatro breve de mujeres, siglos 17–20* (Madrid: Asociación Directores de Escena, 1996);

and Patricia W. O'Connor, ed. and trans., *Mujeres sobre mujeres, teatro breve español, a bi-lingual edition* (Madrid: Editorial Fundamentos, 1998).

Chapter 1: Reclaiming the Home

1. In this category, these titles also are noteworthy: *Bodas de papel* (1976), *Intensa magia* (1996), and *De braços abertos* (1984) by Maria Adelaide Amaral (Brazil); *Louco circo do desejo* (1989) and *Script-tease* (1989) by Consuelo de Castro (Brazil); *Lua nua* (1990) by Leilah Assunção (Brazil); *El vendedor* (1981) by Mariela Romero (Venezuela); *La casa chica* and *La pistola* (1984) by Sabina Berman (Mexico); *Solas en la madriguera* (1988) and *Las que aman hasta morir* (1995) by Cristina Escofet (Argentina); and a collection of three plays *Teatro herético* (1987) by Carmen Boullosa (Mexico).

2. Other plays of note in this category are *Estela y la geografía política* (1982) by Teresa Valenzuela (Mexico); *Octubre terminó hace mucho* (1974) by Pilar Campesino (Mexico); *Entre Villa y una mujer desnuda* (1993) by Sabina Berman (Mexico); *Adjetivos* (1990) by Maritza Wilde (Bolivia); and *Oldies* (1994) by Aleyda Morales (Puerto Rico).

3. In addition there are these plays: *La tercera mujer* (1982) and *Chismes nocturnos de señoras decentes* (1996) by Thais Erminy (Venezuela); *Margarita resucitó* (1988) by Leonor Azcárate (Mexico); and three short plays by Isis Baião (Brazil), *A vingança histórica ou As mulheres vão à luta*; *Mulher Maravilha X Super-Homem*, and *O amestrador e o mágico* (1989). The other role-playing works are two by Argentine Susana Torres Molina, *Extraño juguete* (1977) and . . . *Y a otra cosa mariposa* (1981).

4. Feminist educator Tatiana Acurio directed a project in Lima, Peru among lower-class women who had been involved in community organizations. Her conclusions about relations between these wives and their husbands reflect similar needs for open discussion as those of the editors Gonzalbo Aizpuru and Rabell. Acurio states: "Notamos que hay una casi institucionalizada carencia de diálogo" [We noticed that there is an almost institutionalized lack of dialogue] (94).

5. Brazilian anthropologist Roberto da Matta describes this crucial division between the home and the world beyond it in several important studies of Brazilian culture, most notably *Casa e rua: espaço, cidadania, mulher e morte no Brasil* (São Paulo: Brasiliense, 1985), and *O que faz o brasil, Brasil?* (Rio de Janeiro: Rocco, 1986).

6. For example, see Phyllis A. Harrison's "Overview" in her book *Behaving Brazilian* (Rowley, MA: Newbury House, 1983), for more information.

7. Ana Istarú received her B. A. in Dramatic Arts from the University of Costa Rica in 1981. She is an actress by profession, as well as a creative writer and author of several books of poetry. She has won awards as

an actress, poet, and dramatist. In addition to this play, she has also written *Madre nuestra que estás en la tierra* that will be discussed in chapter 2, *Babyboom en el paraíso* (1995), and *Hombres en escabeche* (2000).

8. The title is taken from a waltz by Palmenia Pizarro. *Cariño malo* has participated in international festivals in Manizales and Cali, Colombia, Buenos Aires, and in several other Latin American cities. Inés Margarita Stanger's work with Teatro La Magdalena has had at least four fruitful productions: *Cariño malo* (1990), *Malinche* (1993), an adaptation of Herman Hesse's *Siddhartha*, and *Tálamo* (1997). Efforts similar to those of Stranger's in collective creation, an egalitarian framework for drama development particularly congenial to women, are these two from Colombia— Marta Cecilia Ruiz and Beatriz Marín, *Tardes abrasadas* (1992), and Pilar Restrepo, *La máscara, la mariposa y la metáfora* (1998).

9. Héctor Bonaparte notes that women going into the public world gain space and stature in society while men who assume more responsibility at home lose their masculinity (1997, 73). If this is true, then what María Luísa wants for herself will improve her status, while in the eyes of society what she wants for Esteban will emasculate him.

10. Leilah Assunção (also spelled Assumpção), and Consuelo de Castro participated in the rebirth of Brazilian theater following the military overthrow of 1964. Assunção's most famous play is *Fala baixo senão eu grito* (1969), which has been performed internationally. Recently she has written and staged *O momento de Mariana Martins* (1999), and *Intimidade indecente* (2001). Many of Conseulo de Castro's plays were published in *Urgência e ruptura* (1989). Since then she has written *Medéia: memórias do mar aberto* (1997), and *Making-Off* (1999), which were performed as readings and *Only You*, which was staged in 2000 and published in 2001.

11. This decree turned the military coup into a dictatorship. It increased existing censorship rules on public performances, limited the ability to congregate in public, and increased the conditions under which politicians and others could lose their rights as citizens. Yan Michalski refers to 1968 as "Talvez o ano mais trágico de toda a história do teatro brasileiro" [Possibly the most tragic year in all the history of Brazilian theater] (1985, 33).

12. During the historical moment when the play was to have been performed, this audience involvement with the events on stage did exist since many theaters staged plays of resistance and critique of the military regime for audiences of like-minded intellectuals and students.

13. Thais Erminy, like many of the dramatists studied in this book, is both an actress and a dramatist. Her play *En un desván olvidado* will be studied in chapter 2. In addition to the play examined here, which was staged in 1984 and won an honorable mention, she has written and staged *La cárcel* (1981), which also won an honorable mention, and *La tercera*

mujer (1982). Her plays *Chismes nocturnos de señoras decentes* (1995), and *La deci$ión* (1995), are in manuscript form. Estela Leñero, daughter of the distinguished novelist and playwright Vicente Leñero, is the author of *Las máquinas de coser* (1985), which received an honorable mention in the UNAM's Rodolfo Usigli competition, *Tooodos los dias* (1988), *Habitación en blanco* (1989), which was awarded the "Premio nacional de teatro" from the Instituto Nacional de Bellas Artes, *Insomnio* (1991), and *Paisaje interior* (1995).

14. Examples of female revenge movies in the United States are *Lipstick* with Margaux Hemingway (1976), and *The Burning Bed* with Farrah Fawcett (1985).

15. *Roda cor de roda* was revived in a performance in Brasília in January 1988 and again in São Paulo in July 2002.

16. Leilah Assunção's choice of Amélia for the name of the traditional, saintly wife was based on a national myth established in the 1940s samba *Ai que saudade da Amélia* [Oh, how I miss Amélia]. Marta Alvim reports that Amélia refers to "a former lover—Amélia, '*a mulher de verdade*' (the real woman)—who had stuck by her partner faithfully under the most excruciating circumstances." According to Alvim, "That samba so accurately mirrored society's entrenched view on the 'proper' role of females that before long, *Amélia*, was unofficially incorporated into the (Brazilian) Portuguese vernacular. According to the *Aurélio Dictionary*, Amélia is synonymous with "a woman who accepts all sorts of afflictions and/or abuse, without complaining, for the love of her man" (11).

17. Sabina Berman is one of the best known playwrights working in Mexico today. She has a substantial body of work, including *Yankee* (1979), *Aguila o sol* (1984), *Muerte súbita* (1989), and *Krisis* (1996). Her most famous piece to date is *Entre Villa y una mujer desnuda* [Between Villa and a Naked Woman] which was both a play (1994) and a film (1995) and has been translated and performed outside of Mexico.

18. See Roberto Reis "Muita Serventia" in *Cultural and Historical Grounding for Hispanic and Luso-Brazilian Feminist Literary Criticism* (Minneapolis, MN: Institute for the Study of Ideologies and Literature, 1989), for more on the literary portrait of wives.

19. The debate about how to create equal marriage has not been resolved in the United States either. For example, the lead article in the women's supplement *Sage* (November 2002) of the *Albuquerque Journal* featured an article with the headline "Balancing Act." It opens with the question "Is equality in marriage ever possible?" While the article notes, somewhat optimistically, that traditional models have been thrown out, it asks if there are new models to replace the old ones (8).

Chapter 2: Questioning Motherhood

1. Recent mother-daughter plays by women dramatists in the United States include Marsha Norman's Pulitzer Prize winner '*night, Mother* (1983), and Julie Jensen's *Last Lists of my Mad Mother* (1999). Recent plays on the topic from Latin America include Argentina's Griselda Gambaro, *De profesión maternal*, performed in 2000 and from the exiled Cuban writer Malena Espinosa, *¿Cero, cero . . . ? bolero para un eterno retorno* performed in Spain and in Kansas in 2003.

2. According to LiesbethWoertman: "We can describe the 1970s and 1980s as a period in which individual experiences of women with regard to maternity were revealed in all their ambivalences by feminist women. The 1980s were also a time when motherhood as an institution was criticized, but the insight that mothers are made within a social context had to wait for the 1990s" (1993, 59).

3. A history of the adoration of the Virgin Mary and the doctrine of Theotokos, that Mary is the mother of God, is developed by Jaroslav Pelikan in *Mary Through the Centuries*. Linda B. Hall's new book, *Mary, Mother & Warrior: The Virgin in Spain and the Americas* (2004), is particularly helpful in recognizing the importance of Mary as a cultural and religious icon in Latin America.

4. See Sandra Messinger Cypess, *La Malinche in Mexican Literature*, and Beth Miller, *Women in Hispanic Literature* (Berkeley, CA: University of California Press, 1983). The topic of Mexican myths of motherhood has gained scholarly and creative attention since the early 1980s.

5. A National Public Radio report in December 2002, "Educating Latinos," examines some of the same issues that Ruth Wodak and Muriel Schulz studied in 1986. In particular the NPR report outlined an effort in El Paso, Texas to bring mothers and daughters together to encourage the young women to stay in school until graduation. Rather than follow in their mothers' footsteps, the program helps mothers reinforce their daughters' efforts to be successful in education, even as new mothers.

6. *Madre nuestra que estás en la tierra* was first performed by the Compañià Nacionael de Teatro of Costa Rica in 1988 and published in *Escena* vol. 20/21 in 1989. *El vuelo de la grulla* was studied in chapter 1. Ana Istarú's *Babyboom en el paraíso* (1995), winner of the "María Teresa León" prize for Iberoamerican theater is a one woman show that almost could have figured in this chapter since it represents the story of a woman's efforts to conceive, carry her child, and give birth. During the play, the mother converses with all the interested family members and friends who accompany her journey, including the fetus. Brazilian Isis Baião has only a collection of

short plays in print, *Em cenas curtas*, even though many of her plays have been performed. She has also written and staged *Instituto Naque de Quedas e Rolamentos* (1978), *Cabaret da crise: As da vida também votam* (1982), and *Essas mulheres ou She by Three of Them* (1993). Like Baião and Istarú, the Venezuelan Thais Erminy is both actress and dramatist. Her play *Whisky & Cocaína* was examined in chapter 1.

    7. Pilar Campesino published four plays in the collection *Teatro* (1980). They are *Los objetos malos*, staged in 1967; *Verano negro*, staged in 1968; *Octubre terminó hace mucho tiempo* staged in 1974, and *eSe 8*. *Octubre terminó hace mucho tiempo* has been performed in the United States. Since then she has published *Del corazón a la palabra*, the children's play *Mi pequeño Tristán tú eres el amo* (1996), and *La madeja o esto es nosotros* (2000). Maria Adelaide Amaral began writing and staging her plays in the late 1970s. Among her most famous staged plays are *A resistência* (1975), *Bodas de papel* (1976), *Ossos d'ofício* (1980), *De braços abertos* (1984), and *Intensa magia* (1995). *Querida mamãe* opened in Rio in 1994 and ran in São Paulo from 1995–96. Susana Torres Molina is a prolific writer of plays, prose, and film scripts. Her plays are *Extraño juguete*, performed in 1977 and published in 1978, . . . *Y a otra cosa mariposa*, staged in 1981 and published in 1988, *Espiral de fuego* produced in 1985 and *Canto de sirenas* staged in 1995 were both published in the same volume in 2002, and *Lo que no se nombra* performed in Madrid and published there as well in 2002. Diana Raznovich has staged and published *Buscapiés* (1968), *Plaza hay una sola* (1969), *El desconcierto* (performed in 1981, published in 1992), *Jardín de otoño* (1985), and *Objetos personales* (published in English translation in 1996). *Casa matriz* orignally was published in 1989, revised and republished in 1997, and then included in a bilingual collection in 2002. It was first performed in Italy in 1991, in the United States in 1992, Buenos Aires in 1993, and in Berlin in 1996. The first translation of *Casa matriz* appeared in *Women Writing Women* in 1997. It was published in a second translation along with three other Diana Raznovich plays in the bi-lingual collection *Defiant Acts: Four Plays* from Bucknell Press (2002). It also has been published in Spain by Casa de América (2001) in a collection of three plays by Raznovich. Other plays include *Máquinas divinas* (1996), *Fast Food a la velocidad de la muerte* (2001), *De la cintura para abajo*, and *De atrás para adelante* (2002).

    8. Carla Olson Buck has shown the importance of motherhood to Campesino's identity as a dramatist and mentions the poem in tribute to Campesino's mother that opens her collection of plays and the dramatist's own words regarding the status of women and mothers in Mexican society.

    9. In his insightful discussion of Maria Adelaide Amaral's play that shares several points with my own, David George notes that lesbianism has been a taboo subject in Brazilian theater. Amaral's character Helô, according

to George, is "one of the few protagonists in Brazilian theater to represent lesbianism as a positive experience" (2000, 89).

10. Other women dramatists listed in the article are Marta Degracia, Irene Ruderman, Adriana Gente, Patricia Zangaro, Susana Poujol, and Susana Freire.

11. In a recently published interview, Susana Torres Molina mentions her interest in dance theater, especially Butoh, a contemporary Japanese style that influenced her work on *Amantíssima* "Es una técnica muy expresiva, fuerte, conmociante. Los cuerpos desnudos, o casi, totalmente maquillados de blanco se mueven como seres que están más allá de la vida y de la muerte" [It is a very expressive technique, strong and moving. The bodies are almost naked, the makeup is white and the movement is like beings that are beyond life and death] (91).

12. This and all future citations refer to the second version of *Casa matriz* published in 1997.

13. Like Raznovich, humorist Erma Bombeck made reference to both feminine roles in her book *Motherhood: The Second Oldest Profession* of 1983.

14. The topic of mother-daughter relations also attracted the attention of Brazilian dramatist Leilah Assunção whose works are studied in chapters 1 and 3. She published a collection of memoirs about mothering and her relationship with her adolescent daughter titled *Na palma da minha mão* in 1998.

Chapter 3: Staging Age and Sexuality

1. Recent plays in English about aging women include *Driving Miss Daisy* (play and film) of 1988 by Alfred Ulry, *Three Tall Women*, Edward Albee's Pulitzer Prize winner of 1994, and Margaret Edson's 1999 Pulitzer Prize winner *Wit*. Other plays in Spanish on aging are Chiqui Vicioso, *Trago amargo/O Wish-ky Sour* (Dominican Republic, 1996); Mónica Montañes, *El aplauso va por dentro* (Venezuela, 1997).

2. Information on Isis Baião was presented in chapter 2. Lidia Rebrij's play is part of the collection *Fastos y oropeles da la carne*. The other play, *Discurso de la soledad*, features a solitary man on stage waiting for his paid visitor to come keep him company. The two monologues were performed in 1987. Rebrij, who is originally from Argentina, has also published short stories and most recently the novel *Más frágil que el cristal* (2000).

3. *Esperando al italiano* was written in 1987, performed by the New Theater Group of Caracas in 1988; it was given the Venezuelan Critics Award in 1989. It first appeared in print in 1988, then was reprinted in the collection *Las risas de nuestras medusas* in 1992, and in English translation in the collection *Women Writing Women* in 1997. Mariela Romero's earlier plays

are *Algo alrededor del espejo* (1967), the award-winning piece *El juego* (1976), *El inevitable destino de Rosa de la noche* (1980), *El vendedor* (1981), and *Tania en 5 movimientos* (1998).

4. *Las viejas vienen marchando* by Argentine Cristina Grillo tells a similar story. Five elder women friends gather to celebrate the seventy-fifth birthday of one of the group. The friends are determined to treat the honoree to her request of a young lover who will help her lose her virginity and have an orgasm. The play ran for three years in Buenos Aires at the turn of the twenty-first century, was performed in Chile and Perú, and opened in Mexico City in the fall of 2002.

5. *Adorável desgraçada* opened first in Rio de Janeiro (1992) under the title *Quem matou a baronesa?*[Who killed the baroness?] and then in São Paulo (1994) with its current title where it won several awards. A portion of the play has been translated into English and published in *Fourteen Female Voices from Brazil* (2002). Assunção has written numerous plays and television scripts. Her plays *Roda cor de roda* and *Boca molhada de paixão calada* were discussed in chapter 1.

6. See articles by Anita Stoll, "Playing a Waiting Game," in *Latin American Women Dramatists*, ed., Catherine Larson and Margarita Vargas (Bloomington, IN: Indiana University Press, 1998); Jacqueline Eyring Bixler, "For Women Only," in *Latin American Women Dramatists*; Catherine Larson, "Playwrights of Passage," *Latin American Literary Review* 19, no. 38 (1991): 77–89; Joseph Chrzanowsky, "El teatro de Mariela Romero," *Revista Canadiense de estudios hispánicos* 7, no. 1 (1982): 205–11.

7. See articles by Susana Castillo in *Latin American Theatre Review*, 14, no. 1 (1980): 25–33; Severino João Albuquerque, *Violent Acts* (Detroit: Wayne State University Press, 1991); Eugene L. Moretta, "Spanish American Theatre of the '50s and 60's, *Latin American Theatre Review* 13, no. 2 (spring 1980): 5–30.

8. *Cuesta abajo* opened in Buenos Aires in October of 1988 and later was published in the collection of plays *Otro teatro después de Teatro Abierto* in 1990. It was performed at the 1992 Manizales Theater Festival in Colombia representing Argentina. Gabriela Fiore has also written *Paso doble*.

9. *Parque para dos* forms part of the trilogy *El parque más grande de la ciudad* (1979). It was performed in Puerto Rico in the 1980s under the direction of Rosa Luisa Márquez. Teresa Marichal has written over twenty plays, of which only a few have been published: *Paseo al atardecer* (1986), *Vlad* (1991), and *Rejum-reja-mujer-rejum* (2003).

10. *Que Dios la tenga en la gloria* was performed in 1983 at the VI National Festival of Theater where it won an award. It was published in 1994 together with the play *Ultima recta final* from 1988. Carlotta Martínez, who began her career in the theater as an actress, has also written the play *Padre Nuestro que estás en la casa*.

Bibliography

Acurio, Tatiana. *Con el permiso de mi esposo.* . . . Lima, Peru: Asociación de Comunicadores Sociales Calandria, 1994.

Adler, Heidrun and Kati Röttger, eds. *Performance, pathos, política—de los sexos.* Madrid and Frankfurt: Vervuert & Iberoamericana, 1999.

Aguirre, Isidora. "Respuestas al cuestionario." In *Dramaturgas latinoamericanas contemporáneas: antología crítica.* Eds. Elba Andrade and Hilde F. Cramsie, 71–75. Madrid: Editorial Verbum, 1991.

Alarcón, Norma. "La literatura femininsta de la chicana: una revisión através de Malintzin o/ Malintzin: devolver la carne al objeto." In *Esta puente mi espalda: voces de mujeres terceromundistas en los Estados Unidos.* Eds. Cherríe Moraga and Ana Castillo, 230–41. San Francisco: Ism, 1988.

Albuquerque, Severino João. *Violent Acts: A Study of Contemporary Latin American Theatre.* Detroit: Wayne State University Press, 1991.

Alvear, Inmaculada. "Dramas de mujeres II: exploración y búsqueda." In *Dramas de mujeres.* Ed. Halima Tahan, 23–36. Buenos Aires: Ediciones Ciudad Argentina, 1998.

Alvim, Marta. "Turning the Tide." *Brazzil* 12, No. 178 (December 2000): 11–15.

Amaral, Maria Adelaide. *Cherish Thy Mother (scenes 6–8).* Trans. David S. George. In *Fourteen Female Voices from Brazil.* Ed. Elzbieta Szoka, 175–206. Austin: Host, 2002.

———. "Interview." In *Fourteen Female Voices from Brazil.* Ed. Elzbieta Szoka, 166–74. Austin: Host, 2002.

———. *Querida mamãe.* São Paulo: Editora Brasiliense, 1995.

Andrade, Elba and Hilde F. Cramsie, eds. *Dramaturgas latinoamericanas contemporáneas: antología crítica.* Madrid: Editorial Verbum, 1991.

André, María Claudia. "Conversaciones sobre la vida y teatro con Susana Torres Molina." *Latin American Theatre Review* 35, No. 2 (spring 2002): 89–95.

———. "Más allá del bien y del mal: Conversación con Diana Raznovich." *Gestos* 18, No. 35 (April 2003): 153–60.

Apter, Terri. *Secret Paths: Women in the New Midlife*. New York: W. W. Norton, 1995.

Arizpe, Lourdes. "Foreword: Democracy for a Small Two-Gender Planet." In *Women and Social Change in Latin America*. Ed. Elizabeth Jelin, xiv–xx. London: Zed, 1990.

Azor, Ileana. "La mujer como sujeto corporal y reflexivo en el teatro mexicano actual. Dos experiencias, dos miradas, un nuevo sistema." *Latin American Theatre Review* 36, No. 2 (Spring 2003): 63–71.

Assunção, Leilah. "Adorável desgraçada," unpublished play, 1994.

———. "Boca molhada de paixão calada." In *3 Contemporary Brazilian Plays in Bilingual Edition*. Eds. Elzbieta Szoka and Joe W. Bratcher III, 293–361. Austin: Host, 1988.

———. "Interview." In *Fourteen Female Voices from Brazil*. Ed. Elzbieta Szoka, 139–45. Austin: Host, 2002.

———. *The Passion of Miss Congeniality (excerpt)*. Trans. David S. George. In *Fourteen Female Voices from Brazil*. Ed. Elzbieta Szoka, 146–63. Austin: Host, 2002.

———. Personal interview. São Paulo, Brazil. 12 June 1982; 27 May 1994.

———. "Roda cor de roda." *Da Fala ao Grito*. 185–282. São Paulo: Símbolo, 1977.

Aston, Elaine. *An Introduction to Feminism and Theatre*. London: Routledge Press, 1995.

Austin, Gayle. *Feminist Theories for Dramatic Criticism*. Ann Arbor: University of Michigan Press, 1990.

Bahamón Vargas, Berenice, Jairo Duque, Claudia Duque, Douglas Quirós and Oswaldo Montferrand. Consejo Episcopal Latinoamericano. *El liderazgo del anciano en América Latina*. Bogotá, Colombia: Documentos CELAM No. 133, 1994.

Baião, Isis. "A Assaltada." *Em cenas curtas*. 113–16. Rio de Janeiro: Achiamé, 1989.

———. "A mulher en-cena." In *A transgressão do feminino*. Ed. Maria Helena Kühner, 24–28. Rio de Janeiro: Projeto Mulher/Projeto Anna Magnani/PUC, RJ: 1989.

———. "Espelho, espelho meu." *Em cenas curtas*. 131–35. Rio de Janeiro: Achiamé, 1989.

———. "Marcadas pela culpa." *Em cenas curtas*. 13–20. Rio de Janeiro: Achiamé, 1989.

Balderston, Daniel and Donna J. Guy, eds. *Sex and Sexuality in Latin America*. New York: New York University Press, 1997.

Barbosa, Maria José. *Clarice Lispector: Spinning the Webs of Passion*. New Orleans: University Press of the South, 1997.

Barreca, Regina. *Perfect Husbands (& Other Fairy Tales)*. New York: Harmony, 1993.

Basting, Anne Davis. *The Stages of Age: Performing Age in Contemporary American Culture*. Ann Arbor: University of Michigan Press, 1998.

Bepko, Claudia and Jo-Ann Krestan. *Too Good For Her Own Good*. New York: Harper and Row, 1990.

Berg, Eliana Goulart. "The Discourse of Cruelty and the Absurd and the Representation of Difference in the Theatre of Women Playwrights in Latin America." Ph.D. diss., University of Wisconsin, 1998.

Berman, Sabina. "El suplicio del placer: uno/el bigote." *Teatro de Sabina Berman*. 161–78. México: Gaceta, 1994.

———. *The Theatre of Sabina Berman: 'The Agony of Ecstasy' and Other Plays*. Trans. Adam Versényi. Carbondale: Southern Illinois Press, 2003.

Bissett, Judith. "La revolución y el papel de la mujer en el teatro de Consuelo de Castro y Pilar Campesino." *Latin American Theatre Review* 33, No. 1 (fall 1999): 45–53.

———. "Leilah Assunção: Marginal Women and the Female Experience." In *Latin American Women Dramatists: Theater, Texts, and Theories*. Eds. Catherine Larson and Margarita Vargas, 202–14. Bloomington, IN: Indiana University Press, 1998.

Bixler, Jacqueline Eyring. "For Women Only?: The Theatre of Susana Torres Molina." In *Latin American Women's Drama: Theater, Texts, and Theories*. Eds. Catherine Larson and Margarita Vargas, 215–33. Bloomington, IN: Indiana University Press, 1998.

———. "Games and Reality on the Latin American Stage." *Latin American Literary Review* 12 (1984): 22–35.

Boling, Becky. "Reenacting Politics: The Theater of Griselda Gambaro." In *Latin American Women Dramatists: Theater, Texts and Theories*. Eds. Margarita Vargas and Cathy Larson, 3–22. Bloomington, IN: Indiana University Press, 1998.

Boorman, Joan Rea. "Contemporary Latin American Women Dramatists." *Rice University Studies* 64, No. 1 (1978): 69–80.

Bonaparte, Héctor. *Unidos o dominados: mujeres y varones frente al sistema patriarcal*. Rosario, Argentina: Homo Sapiens, 1997.

Bonilla, María and Stoyan Vladich. *El teatro latinoamericano en busca de su identidad cultural*. San José, Costa Rica: Cultur Art, 1988.

Bose, Christine E., and Edna Acosta-Belén. "Introduction." In *Women in the Latin American Development Process*. Eds. Christine E. Bose and Edna Acosta-Belén, 1–11. Philadelphia: Temple University Press, 1995.

Bowman, Rebecca. "Trilogía: De compras. La laguna. Desayuno." *Tramoya* 44 (julio–septiembre 1995): 133–51.

Brandão, Ruth Silviano and Lúcia Castello Branco, eds. A mulher escrita. Rio de Janeiro: Casa-Maria Editorial/Livros Ténicos e Científicos, 1989.

Brown, Janet. Taking Center Stage: Feminism in Contemporary U.S. Drama. Metuchen, NJ: Scarecrow Press, 1991.

Brown-Guillory, Elizabeth. Women of Color: Mother-Daughter Relationships in 20th-Century Literature. Austin: University of Texas Press, 1996.

Buck, Carla Olson. "Power Plays/Plays of Power: The Theater of Pilar Campesino." In Latin American Women's Drama: Theater, Texts, and Theories. Eds. Catherine Larson and Margarita Vargas, 55–73. Bloomington, IN: Indiana University Press, 1998.

Burgess, Ronald D. "Sabina Berman's Undone Threads." In Latin American Women Dramatists: Theater, Texts, and Theories. Eds. Catherine Larson and Margarita Vargas, 145–58. Bloomington, IN: Indiana University Press, 1999.

Butler, Judith. Bodies That Matter. London: Routledge Press, 1993.

———. Gender Trouble. London: Routledge Press, 1990.

———. "Performative Acts and Gender Constitution: An Essay in Phenomenology and Feminist Theory." In Performing Feminisms: Feminist Critical Theory and Theatre. Ed. Sue-Ellen Case, 270–82. Baltimore: Johns Hopkins, 1990.

Butler, Robert N. "The Life Review: An Intrerpretation of Reminiscence in the Aged." Psychiatry: Journal for the Study of Interpersonal Processes 26 (February 1963): 65–76.

Butto, Andréa. "Gênero, família e trabalho." In Mulher e política: gênero e feminismo no Partido dos Trabalhadores. Eds. Ángela Borba, Nalu Faria, and Tatau Godinho, 71–84. São Paulo: Fundação Perseu Abramo, 1998.

Canstanyer, Laura Bores, ed. Reescribir la escena. Madrid: Fundación Autor, 1998.

Campesino, Pilar. "La partida." Doce a las doce: teatro breve. 38–57. Mexico City: Obra Citada, 1989.

Castellanos, Gabriela, Simone Accorsi, and Gloria Velzaco, eds. Discurso, género y mujer. Cali, Colombia: Facultad de Humanidades, 1994.

Castello Branco, Lúcia. "A (im)possibilidade da escrita feminina." In A mulher escrita. Eds. Ruth Silviano Brandão and Lúcia Castello Branco, 111–22. Rio de Janeiro: Casa-Maria Editorial/Livros Técnicos e Científicos, 1989.

Castillo, Debra. Talking Back: Toward a Latin American Feminist Criticism. Ithaca: Cornell University Press, 1992.

Castillo, Susana. "Fantasías textuales: el mundo dramático de Mariela Romero." In Las risas de nuestras medusas: teatro venezolano escrito por mujeres. Ed. Susana Castillo, 37–43. Caracas: Fundarte, 1992.

———. "*El juego*: textro dramático y montaje." *Latin American Theatre Review* 14, No.1 (fall 1980): 25–33.

———. ed. *Las risas de nuestras medusas: teatro venezolano escrito por mujeres*. Caracas: Fundarte, 1992.

Castro, Consuelo de. Personal interview. São Paulo, Brazil. 12 June 1982; 19 May 1994.

———. *Á prova de fogo*. São Paulo: Hucitec, 1977.

Castro-Klarén, Sara. "Introduction." In *Women's Writing in Latin America*. Eds. Sara Castro-Klarén, Sylvia Molloy, and Beatriz Sarlo, 3–26. Boulder, CO: Westview Press, 1992.

Chodorow, Nancy. *The Reproduction of Mothering: Psychoanalysis and the Sociology of Gender*. Berkeley, CA: University California Press, 1978.

Chrzanowsky, Joseph. "El teatro de Mariela Romero." *Revista canadiense de estudios hispánicos*. 7, No. 1 (1982): 205–11.

Cicerchia, Ricardo. "The Charm of Family Patterns: Historical and Contemporary Change in Latin America." In *Gender Politics in Latin America: Debates in Theory and Practice*. Ed. Elizabeth Dore, 118–33. New York: Monthly Review Press, 1997.

Cixous, Hélène. "Aller à la mer." Trans. Barbara Kerslake. *Modern Drama* 27 (December 1984): 546–48.

Clark, Fred M. "Theater, Actress, Woman: Isis Baião's *As da vida também votam* and *Essas mulheres*." *Luso-Brazilian Review* 35, No. 2 (1998): 87–97.

Coan, Olair. "Leilah festeja 25 anos de negro." *Diário Popular,* n.p., n.d.

Cohler, Bertram J. "Aging, Morale, and Meaning: The Nexus of Narrative." In *Voices and Visions of Aging: Toward a Critical Gerontology*. Ed. Thomas R Cole, et. al. 107–33. New York: Springer, 1993.

Constantino, Roselyn. "El discurso del poder en *El suplício del placer*." In *De la colonia a la postmodernidad: teoría teatral y crítica sobre teatro latinoamericano*. Eds. Peter Roster and Alexandro Martínez Camberos, 245–52. Buenos Aires: Galerna, 1992.

Copper, Baba. *Over the Hill: Reflections on Ageism Between Women*. Freedom, CA.: Crossing Press, 1988.

Cramsie, Hilde F. "La marginación lingüística y social de la mujer en dos obras de Ana Istarú." In *Mujer y sociedad en América: VI Simposio Internacional*. Eds. Juana Arancibia, Adrienne Mandel, and Yolanda Rosas, 43–58. Buenos Aires: Instituto Literario y Cultural Hispánico, 1990.

Croft, Susan. *She Also Wrote Plays: An International Guide to Women Playwrights from the 10th to the 21st Century*. London: Faber and Faber, 2001.

Cuesta abajo. 1934. Dir. Louis Gasnier. Exito Producciones.

Cypess, Sandra Messinger. "Dramaturgia femenina y transposición histórica." *Alba de América*. 12–13 (1989): 283–304.

————. "From Colonial Constructs to Feminist Figures: Re/Visions by Mexican Women Dramatists." *Theatre Journal* 41, No. 4 (December 1989): 492–504.

————. "La dramaturgia femenina y su contexto socio-cultural." *Latin American Theatre Review* 13, No. 2 (spring 1980): 63–68.

————. *La Malinche in Mexican Literature.* Austin: University Texas Press, 1991.

Daly, Brenda O., and Maureen T. Reddy, eds. *Narrating Mothers: Theorizing Maternal Subjectivities.* Knoxville: University of Tennessee Press, 1991.

Dauster, Frank. "Raising the Curtain: Great Ladies of the Theater." In *Performance, pathos, política—de los sexos.* Eds. Heidrun Adler and Kati Röttger, 23–40. Madrid and Frankfurt: Vervuert and Iberoamericana, 1999.

Davidson, Cathy N., and E. M. Broner, eds. *The Lost Tradition: Mother and Daughters in Literature.* New York: Frederick Ungar, 1980.

Debold, Elizabeth, Marie Wilson, and Idelisse Malave, eds. *Mother Daughter Revolution: From Betrayal to Power.* New York: Addison-Wesley, 1993.

del Río, Marcela. "Especificidad y reconocimiento del discurso dramático femenino en el teatro latinoamericano." In *Performance, pathos, política—de los sexos.* Eds. Heidrun Adler and Kati Röttger, 41–54. Madrid and Frankfurt: Vervuert and Iberoamericana, 1999.

Devor, Holly. *Gender Blending.* Bloomington, IN: Indiana University Press, 1989.

Dinnerstein, Dorothy. *The Mermaid and the Minotaur: Sexual Arrangements and the Human Malaise.* New York: Harper and Row, 1976.

Dixon, Penelope. "Mothering Today: A Brave New World." In *Mothers and Mothering: An Annotated Feminist Bibliography.* Ed. Penelope Dixon, 3–9. New York: Garland Press, 1991.

Doménech, Fernando, ed. *Teatro breve de mujeres, siglos 17–20.* Madrid: Asociación de Directores de Escena, 1996.

Dolan, Jill. *The Feminist Spectator as Critic.* Ann Arbor: University Michigan Press, 1988.

Dore, Elizabeth. "The Holy Family: Imagined Households in Latin American History." In *Gender Politics in Latin America: Debates in Theory and Practice.* Ed. Elizabeth Dore, 101–17. New York: Monthly Review Press, 1997.

Doria, Ola Martha Peña. "Tres generaciones de dramatrugas mexicanas: censura y autocensura." *Conjunto* 104 (1996): 47–55.

Durham, Eunice R. "Family and Human Reproduction." In *Family, Household and Gender Relations in Latin America.* Ed Elizabeth Jelin, 40–68. London: Kegan Paul, 1991.

Echevarría, Ana M. "Performing Subversion: A Comparative Study of Caribbean Women Playwrights." Ph.D. diss., Cornell University, 2000.

Eidelberg, Nora and María Mercedes Jaramillo, eds. *Voces en escena: antología de dramaturgas latinoamericanas.* Medellín, Colombia: Universidad de Antioquia, 1991.

Esslin, Martin. *The Theatre of the Absurd.* Garden City, New York: Anchor Books, 1969.

Erminy, Thais. *En un desván olvidado.* Caracas: Fundarte, 1991.

———. *Whisky & Cocaína.* Caracas: n. p., 1984.

Faria, Nalu. "Sexualidade e feminismo." In *Mulher e política: gênero e feminismo no Partido dos Trabalhadores.* Eds. Angela Borba, Nalu Faria, and Tatau Godinho. São Paulo: Fundação Perseu Abramo, 1998.

Ferris, Lesley, ed. *Crossing the Stage: Controversies on Cross-Dressing.* London: Routledge Press, 1993.

Fiore, Gabriela. "Cuesta abajo." In *Otro teatro después de Teatro Abierto.* Ed. Jorge A. Dubatti, 24–45. Buenos Aires: Libros del Quirquincho, 1990.

Flax, Jane. "Mothers and Daughters Revisited." In *Daughtering and Mothering: Female Subjectivity Reanalysed.* Eds. Janneke van Mens-Verhulst, Karlein Schreurs, and Liesbeth Woertman, 145–56. London: Routledge Press, 1993.

Flores, Yolanda. *The Drama of Gender: Feminist Theater by Women of the Americas.* New York: Peter Lang, 2000.

Foster, David William. "Recent Argentine Women Writers of Jewish Descent." In *Passion, Memory, Identity.* Ed. Marjorie Agosín, 35–58. Albuquerque: University of New Mexico Press, 1999.

Foster, David William and Roberto Reis, eds. *Bodies and Biases: Sexualities in Hispanic Culture and Literature.* Minneapolis: University of Minnesota Press, 1996.

France, Anna Kay and P. J. Corso, eds. *International Women Playwrights.* Metuchen, NJ: Scarecrow, 1993.

Franco, Jean. *Plotting Women: Gender and Representation in Mexico.* New York: Columbia University Press, 1989.

———. "From the Margins to the Center: Recent Trends in Feminist Theory in the United States and Latin America." In *Gender Politics in Latin America: Debates in Theory and Practice.* Ed. Elizabeth Dore, 196–208. New York: Monthly Review Press, 1997.

Friedan, Betty. *The Fountain of Age: Intimacy Beyond the Dreams of Youth.* New York: Touchstone, 1993.

Frieden, Ken. *Genius and Monologue.* Ithaca: Cornell University Press, 1985.

Freuh, Joanna. "Monster/Beauty: Midlife Bodybuilding as Aesthetic Discipline." In *Figuring Age: Women, Bodies, Generations.* Ed. Kathleen Woodward, 212–26. Bloomington, IN: Indiana University Press, 1999.

Galvão, João Cândido. "Review of *Boca molhada de paixão calada*." In *3 Contemporary Brazilian Plays in Bilingual Edition*. Eds. Elzbieta Szoka and Joe W. Bratcher III, 215–16. Austin: Host, 1988.

Gambaro, Griselda. "¿Es posible y deseable una dramaturgia específicamente femenina?" *Latin American Theatre Review* 13, No. 2 (summer 1980): 17–21.

———. "Respuestas al cuestionario." In *Dramaturgas latinoamericanas contemporáneas: antología crítica*. Eds. Elba Andrade and Hilde F. Cramsie, 147–58. Madrid: Editorial Verbum, 1991.

Gann, Myrna S. "Masculine Space in the Plays of Estela Leñero." In *Latin American Women Dramatists: Theater, Texts, and Theories*. Eds. Catherine Larson and Margarita Vargas, 234–42. Bloomington, IN: Indiana University Press, 1998.

García Lorenzo, Luciano. *Autoras y actrices en la historia del teatro español*. Murcia, Spain: Universidad de Murcia, 2000.

Garner, Shirley Nelson. "Constructing the Mother: Contemporary Psychoanalytic Theorists and Women Autobiographers." In *Narrating Mothers: Theorizing Maternal Subjectivities*. Eds. Brenda O. Daly and Maureen T. Reddy, 76–93. Knoxville: University of Tennessee Press, 1991.

Geis, Deborah R. "Wordscapes of the Body: Performative Language as *Gestus* in Maria Irene Fornes's Plays." In *Feminist Theatre and Theory*. Ed. Helene Keyssar, 168–88. New York: St. Martin's Press, 1996.

George, David. *Flash and Crash Days: Brazilian Theater in the Post-Dictatorship Period*. New York: Garland Press, 2000.

Gilbert, Lucy and Paula Webster. *Bound By Love: The Sweet Trap of Daughterhood*. Boston: Beacon Press, 1982.

Gilda. 1946. Dir. Charles Vidor. Columbia Pictures.

Gilligan, Carol. "Remapping the Moral Domain: New Images of Self in Relationship." In *Mapping the Moral Domain*. Eds. Carol Gilligan, Janie Victoria Ward, and Jill McLean Taylor, 3–13. Cambridge: Harvard University Press, 1988.

Gladhart, Amalia. *The Leper in Blue: Coercive Performance and the Contemporary Latin American Theater*. Chapel Hill: North Carolina Studies in the Romance Languages and Literatures, 2000.

Gleen, Evelyn Nakano, Grace Chang, and Linda Rennie Forcey, eds. *Mothering: Ideology, Experience, and Agency*. London: Routledge Press, 1994.

Glickman, Nora. "Parodia y desmitificación del rol femenino en el teatro de Diana Raznovich." *Latin American Theatre Review* 28, No. 1 (fall 1994): 89–100.

———. "El teatro del absurdo de Diana Raznovich." In *Antología crítica del teatro breve hispanoamericano. 1948–1993*. Eds. María Merecedes

Jaramillo and Mario Yepes, 188–94. Medellín, Colombia: Editorial Universidad de Antioquia, 1997.

Gonzalbo Aizpuru, Pilar and Cecilia Rabell. "Diálogo abierto sobre la familia iberoamericana." In *La familia en el mundo iberoamericano*. Eds. Pilar Gonzalbo Aizpuru and Cecilia Rabell, 9–40. Mexico: Universidad Nacional Autónoma de México, 1994.

González, Maria. "Love and Conflict: Mexican American Women Writers as Daughters." In *Women of Color: Mother-Daughter Relationships in 20th-Century Literature*. Ed. Elizabeth Brown-Guillory, 153–71. Austin: University of Texas Press, 1996.

Greer, Germaine. *The Change: Women, Aging and Menopause*. New York: Knopf, 1992.

Griffin, Gariele. "Turning on the Mother: The Dramatization of Anxiety Concerning 'the Mother' in Plays from the 1890s to the 1980s." *Forum Moderns Theater* 6, No. 1 (1991): 25–40.

Guimarães, Carmelinda. "Dramaturgia feminina." *Revista de Teatro*, No. 493–494 (setembro 1995): 18–21.

———. "Mariazinha mudou de nome e já amadureceu." *A Tribuna*, 3 Sept. 1994, E–2l.

Gullette, Margaret Morganroth. *Declining to Decline: Cultural Combat and the Politics of the Midlife*. Charlottesville: University of Virginia Press, 1997.

Gutmann, David. "Beyond Nurture: Developmental Perspectives on the Vital Older Woman." In *In Her Prime: A New View of Middle-Aged Women*. Eds. Judith K. Brown and Virginia Kerns, 198–211. South Hadley, MA: Bergin & Garvey, 1985.

Guzik, Alberto. "Adoravelmente sádica." *Jornal da Tarde*, 16 Sept. 1994, 8–A.

———. "Apresentação: essa difícil humanidade." In *Querida Mamãe*. Maria Adelaide Amaral, 7–11. São Paulo: Editora Brasiliense, 1995.

———. "Boca molhada de paixão calada: uma frágil emoção corroída pelo tempo." In *Nossos autores através da crítica*. São Paulo: Museu Lasar Segall, 1997. 27–28.

Hahner, June E. *Emancipating the Female Sex: The Struggle for Women's Rights in Brazil, 1850–1940*. Durham: Duke University Press, 1990.

Harrison, Phyllis A. *Behaving Brazilian: A Comparison of Brazilian and North American Social Behavior*. Rowley, MA: Newbury House, 1983.

Hart, Lynda. "Introduction: Performing Feminism." In *Making a Spectacle: Feminist Essays on Contemporary Women's Theatre*. Ed. Lynda Hart, 1–21. Ann Arbor: University of Michigan Press, 1989.

Hegstrom, Valerie and Amy R. Williamsen, eds. *Engendering the Early Modern Stage: Women Playwrights in the Spanish Empire*. New Orleans: University Press of the South, 1999.

Hendricks, Jon., ed. *The Meaning of Reminiscence and Life Review*. Amityville, NY: Baywood, 1995.

Hirsch, Marianne. "Mothers and Daughters." *Signs* 7, No. 1 (1981): 200–22. Reprint in *Ties that Bind*. 177–99. Chicago: University of Chicago Press, 1990.

———. *The Mother/Daughter Plot: Narrative, Psychoanalysis, Feminism*. Bloomington, IN: Indiana University Press, 1989.

Holte, Matilde Raquel. "Teatro contemporáneo judeo-argentino: una perspectiva feminista bíblica." Ph.D. diss., Catholic University of America, 2002.

Hormigón, Juan Antonio, ed. *Autoras en la historia del teatro español*. 4 vols. Madrid: Publicaciones de la Asociación de Directores de Escena de España, 1996.

Hornby, Richard. *Drama, Metadrama, and Perception*. Lewisburg, PA: Bucknell University Press, 1986.

Hurtado, María de la Luz. "La experimentación de formas dramáticas en las escrituras femeninas/escrituras de la mujer en Chile." *Latin American Theatre Review* 31, No. 2 (spring 1998): 33–43.

Inclán, Gabriela and Felipe Galván, eds. *Teatro, mujer y latinoamérica*. Puebla, Mexico: Tablado Iberoamericano, 2000.

Issacharoff, Michael. "Space and Reference in Drama." *Poetics Today* 2, No. 3 (spring 1981): 211–24.

———. *Discourse as Performance*. Stanford, CA: Stanford University Press, 1989.

Istarú, Ana. "The Flight of the Crane." Trans. Timothy J. Rogers. *Latin American Literary Review* 17, No. 33 (1989): 97–117.

———. "Madre nuestra que estás en la tierra." In *Dramaturgas latinoamericanas contemporáneas*. Eds. Elba Andrade and Hilde F. Cramsie, 231–59. Madrid: Verbum, 1989.

———. "Madre nuestra que estás en la tierra." In *Drama contemporáneo costarricense*. Eds. Carolyn Bell and Patricia Fumero, 265–306. San José, Costa Rica: Editorial de la University de Costa Rica, 2000.

———. "Respuestas al cuestionario." In *Dramaturgas latinoamericanas contemporáneas: antología crítica*. Eds. Elba Andrade and Hilde F. Cramsie, 225–30. Madrid: Editorial Verbum, 1991.

———. "El vuelo de la grulla." *Escena* 5, No. 11 (1984): 15–19.

Jabif, Nora Lía. "Las hijas de Griselda Gambaro." *Teatro2* 3, No. 4 (julio 1993): 48–51.

———. "Entrevista con Griselda Gambaro." *Teatro2* 3, No. 4 (julio 1993): 53–54.

Jaramillo, María Mercedes, Betty Osorio de Negret, Ángela Inés Robledo, eds. *Literatura y diferencia: escritoras colombianas del siglo XX*. 2 vols. Medellín, Colombia: Ediciones Uniandes, 1995.

Jay, Julia de Foor. "(Re)claiming the Race of the Mother." In *Women of Color: Mother-Daughter Relationships in 20th-Century Literature*. Ed. Elizabeth Brown-Guillory, 95–116. Austin: University of Texas Press, 1996.

Jelin, Elizabeth. "Introduction: Everyday Practices, Family Structures, Social Processes." In *Family, Household and Gender Relations in Latin America*. Ed. Elizabeth Jelin, 1–5. London: Kegan Paul, 1991.

———. "Introduction." In *Women and Social Change in Latin America*. Ed. Elizabeth Jelin, 1–11. London: Zed, 1990.

———. "Citizenship and Identity: Final Reflections." In *Women and Social Change in Latin America*, 184–207. London: Zed, 1990.

Kaminsky, Amy K. *Reading the Body Politic: Feminist Criticism and Latin American Women Writers*. Minneapolis: University of Minnesota Press, 1993.

Kastenbaum, Robert. *Defining Acts: Aging as Drama*. Amityville, NY: Baywood, 1994.

———. "Exit and Existence: Society's Unwritten Script for Old Age and Death." In *Aging, Death, and the Completion of Being*. Ed. David D. Van Tassel, 69–94. Philadelphia: University of Pennsylvania Press, 1979.

Keith, Pat M., and Robert B. Schafer. *Relationships and Well-Being Over the Life Stages*. New York: Praeger, 1991.

Keyssar, Helene, ed. *Feminist Theatre and Theory*. New York: St. Martin's Press, 1996.

Kintz, Linda. *The Subject's Tragedy: Political Poetics, Feminist Theory, and Drama*. Ann Arbor: University of Michigan Press, 1992.

Kühner, Maria Helena. "A trajetória feminina dos anos 60 aos 90." *Revista de Teatro* 481 (1992): 7–9.

LaBelle, Jenijoy. *Herself Beheld: The Literature of the Looking Glass*. Ithaca, NY: Cornell University Press, 1988.

Larson, Catherine. "Playwrights of Passage: Women and Game-Playing on the Stage." *Latin American Literary Review* 19, No. 38 (1991): 77–89.

Larson, Catherine, and Margarita Vargas, eds. *Latin American Women's Drama: Theater, Texts, and Theories*. Bloomington, IN: Indiana University Press, 1998.

Lavrin, Asunción. "Introducción: el escenario, los actores y el problema." In *Sexualidad y matrimonio en la América hispánica siglos XVI–XVII*. Ed. Asunción Lavrin, 13–40. Mexico: Grijalbo, 1989.

Leira, Halldis and Madelien Krips. "Revealing Cultural Myths on Motherhood." In *Daughtering and Mothering: Female Subjectivity Reanalysed*. Eds. Janneke van Mens-Verhulst, Karlein Schreurs, and Liesbeth Woertman, 83–96. London: Routledge Press, 1993.

Leñero, Estela. "Casa llena." In *La pareja*. 45–92. Puebla, Mexico: Universidad Autónoma de Puebla, 1986.

Leonard, Candyce and Iride Lamartina-Lens, eds. *Nuevas manatiales: dramaturgas españolas en los noventa*. Vol. 1. Ottowa: Girol Books, 2001.

———. *Nuevas manatiales: dramaturgas españolas en los noventa*. Vol. 2. Ottowa: Girol Books, 2002.

Lerner, Gerda, ed. *The Female Experience:An American Documentary*. Indiannapolis, IN: Bobbs-Merrill, 1977.

Lima, Mariangela Alves de. "Monólogo acentua o drama da solidão." *O Estado de São Paulo*, 25 August 1994, Caderno 2, D–5.

Lindstrom, Naomi. *The Social Conscience of Latin American Writing*. Austin: University of Texas Press, 1998.

Lombardi, Alicia. *Entre madres e hijas: acerca de la opresión psicológica*. Buenos Aires: Ediciones Noe, 1986.

Magaldi, Sábato. "Um documento exemplar." In *À prova de fogo*. Consuelo de Castro, ix–xi. São Paulo: Editora Hucitec, 1977.

Magnarelli, Sharon D. "Authoring the Scene, Playing the Role: Mothers and Daughters in Griselda Gambaro's *La malasangre*." *Latin American Theatre Review* 27, No. 2 (spring 1994): 5–27.

Marichal, Teresa. "Parque para dos." unpublished play, 1979.

Martínez, Carlota. *Que Díos la tenga en la gloria*. Caracas, Venezuela: Fundarte, 1994.

Masiello, Francine. *Between Civilization & Barbarism: Women, Nation, and Literary Culture in Modern Argentina*. Lincoln: University of Nebraska Press, 1992.

Matta, Roberto da. *A casa e a rua: espaço, cidadania, mulher e morte no Brasil*. São Paulo: Brasiliense, 1985.

———. *O que faz o brasil, Brasil?* Rio de Janeiro: Rocco, 1986.

Melhuus, Marit and Kirsti Anne Stølen, eds. *Machos, Mistresses, Madonnas*. London: Verso, 1996.

Mercer, Ramona T., Elizabeth G. Nichols, and Glen Caspers Doyle, eds. *Transitions in a Woman's Life: Major Life Events in Developmental Context*. New York: Springer, 1989.

Merriam, Sharan B. "Butler's Life Review: How Universal is it?" In *The Meaning of Reminiscence and Life Review*. Ed. Jon Hendricks, 7–19. Amityville, NY: Baywood, 1995.

Michalski, Yan. *O teatro sob pressão*. Rio de Janeiro: Jorge Zahar, 1985.

Miller, Beth, ed. *Women in Hispanic Literature: Icons and Fallen Idols*. Berkeley, CA: University of California Press, 1983.

Miller, Nancy K. "The Marks of Time." In *Figuring Age: Women, Bodies, Generations*. Ed. Kathleen Woodward, 3–19. Bloomington, IN: Indiana University Press, 1999.

Miller, Yvette E. and Charles M. Tatum, eds. *Latin American Women Writers: Yesterday and Today*. *Latin American Literary Review*. Pittsburgh, PA: Carnegie-Mellon University, 1977.

Milleret, Margo. "Acting Radical: The Dramaturgy of Consuelo de Castro." In *Latin American Women Dramatists: Theater, Texts, and Theories.* Eds. Margarita Vargas and Cathy Larson, 89–109. Bloomington, IN: University of Indiana Press, 1998.

———. "Daughters vs. Mothers on Latin American Stages." In *Todo ese fuego: Homenaje a Merlin Forster.* Eds. Mara L. García and Doug Weatherford, 135–47. México: Universidad Autónoma de Tlaxcala, 1999.

———. "Lessons from Students about the Brazilian Dictatorship." *Hispania* 85, No. 3 (2002): 658–64.

———. "Staging Sex and the Midlife Woman in Mariela Romero's *Esperando al italiano.*" *Revista de estudios hispánicos* 34 (2000): 247–60.

———. "Teatro feminino latino-americano."*Revista de Teatro,* No. 491–492 (1994): 62–67.

Montes, Consuelo Morel. *Identidad femenina en el teatro chileno.* Santiago, Chile: Ediciones "Apuntes," 1996.

Montilla, Lorena Pino. *La dramaturgia femenina venezolana.* Tomo 1. Caracas, Venezuela: Centro Latinoamericano de Creación e Investigación Teatral, 1994.

Moretta, Eugene L. "Spanish American Theatre of the 50's and 60's: Critical Perspectives on Role Playing." *Latin American Theatre Review* 13, No. 2 (spring 1980): 5–30.

Mota, Carlos Guilherme. "À prova de fogo: da memória." In *À prova de fogo.* Consuelo de Castro, xv–xvi. São Paulo: Editora Hucitec, 1977.

Nash, Jay Robert and Stanley Ralph Ross, eds. *The Motion Picture Guide.* Vol 3. Chicago: Cinebooks, 1985.

Neugebauer-Visano, Robynne. "Seniors and Sexuality? Confronting Cultural Contradictions." In *Seniors and Sexuality: Experiencing Intimacy in Later Life.* Ed. Robynne Neugebauer-Visano, 17–34. Toronto: Canadian Scholar's Press, 1995.

Nice, Vivien E. *Mother and Daughters: The Distortion of a Relationship.* New York: St. Martin's Press, 1992.

Nigro, Kirsten. "Breaking (It) Up is (Not) Hard to Do: Writing Histories and Women Theater Artists in Latin America." *Gestos* 14 (November 1992): 127–39.

———. "Inventions and Transgressions: A Fractured Narrative on Feminist Theatre in Mexico." In *Negotiating Performance: Gender, Seuxality, and Theatricality in Latin/o America.* Eds. Diana Taylor and Juan Villegas, 137–58. Durham: Duke University Press, 1994.

———. "Theatre, Women, and Mexican Society: A Few Exemplary Cases." *Bucknell Review* 40, No. 2 (1996): 53–66.

Nigro, Kirsten and Phyllis Zatlin, eds. *A Stage of Their Own.* Ottawa: Girol Books, 1998.

Novães Coelho, Nelly. "Tendências atuais da literatura feminina no Brasil." In *Feminino Singular*. Ed. Nelly Novaes Coelho, 4–13. Rio Claro de São Paulo: Edições GRD, 1989.

Núcleo de Estudos Sobre a Mulher. Working Paper. *Mulher: preconceito e casamento*. Rio de Janeiro: Pontifícia Universidade Católica, 1984.

Núñez Becerra, Fernanda. *La Malinche: de la historia al mito*. Mexico, D.F.: Instituto Nacional de Antropología e Historia, 1996.

O'Connor, Patricia W. "Women Playwrights in Contemporary Spain and the Male-Dominated Canon." *Signs* 15, No. 2 (1990): 376–90.

———. ed. and trans. *Mujeres sobre mujeres, teatro breve español*. Madrid: Editorial Fundamentos, 1998.

Olcoz, Nieves Martínez de. "Decisiones de la máscara neutra: dramaturgia femenina y fin de siglo en América Latina." *Latin American Theatre Review* 31, No. 2 (spring 1998): 5–16.

———. *Teatro de mujer y culturas del movimiento en América Latina*. Santiago, Chile: Editorial Cuarto Propio, 2000.

O'Quinn, Kathleen. "Hold Your Applause: Uncovering Plays by Spanish American Women, 1839–1930." Paper presented at the A Stage of Their Own Conference and Festival, Cincinnati, Ohio, October 1994.

Ordaz, Luis. *Aproximación a la trajectoria de la dramática argentina*. Ottawa: Girol, 1992.

Pallottini, Renata. "A mulher na dramaturgia brasileira." In *Feminino singular*. Ed. Nelly Novaes Coelho, 102–24. Rio Claro de São Paulo: GRD, 1989.

Pavanetti, P. Eduardo. *La madre educadora en un mundo que cambia*. Montevideo: Don Bosco, 1975.

Pelegrini, Sandra de Cássia Araújo. "A sociabilidade feminina nos palcos brasileiros: um destaque à produção de Leilah Assunção." *Estudos Históricos* 28 (2001): 87–102.

Pelikan, Jaroslav. *Mary Through the Centuries*. New Haven: Yale, 1996.

Pellettieri, Osvaldo. *El teatro y su crítica*. Buenos Aires: Galerna, 1998.

Peña Doria, Olga Martha. "Tres generaciones de dramaturgas mexicanas: censura y autocensura." *Conjunto*, No. 104 (octubre–diciembre 1996): 47–54.

Phillips, Shelley. *Beyond the Myths: Mother-Daughter Relationships in Psychology, History, Literature and Everyday Life*. London: Penguin Press, 1996.

Pianca, Marina, ed. "La mujer en el teatro latinoamericano." *Diógenes: anuario crítico del teatro latinoamericano*. 9–10 (1993–1994): 273–397.

Pipher, Mary Bray. *Another Country: Navigating the Emotional Terrain of Our Elders*. New York: Riverhead Books, 1999.

———. *Reviving Ophelia: Saving the Self of Adolescent Girls*. New York: Ballantine Books, 1994.

Prado, Décio de Almeida. "Prefácio." In À prova de fogo. Consuelo de Castro, xiii–xiv. São Paulo: Editora Hucitec, 1977.

Quinlan, Susan Canty. The Female Voice in Contemporary Brazilian Narrative. New York: Peter Lang 1991.

Rathbun, Jennifer. "The Dramatic Feminine Discourse of Cristina Escofet." Ph.D. diss., University of Arizona, 2002.

Ravetti, Graciela, and Sara Rojo. "Comentario." In Antología bilingüe de dramaturgia de mulheres latinoamericanas. Eds. Graciela Ravetti and Sara Rojo, 121–24. Belo Horizonte, Brazil: Armazém de Idéias, 1996.

———. "Maria Adelaide Amaral ou a crise da classe média brasileira." Latin American Theatre Review 30, No. 1 (fall 1996): 43–54.

Raznovich, Diana. "Casa matriz." In Antología crítica del teatro breve hispanoamericano. 1948–1993. Eds. María Merecedes Jaramillo and Mario Yepes, 159–87. Medellín, Colombia: Editorial Universidad de Antioquia, 1997.

———. "Casa matriz." In Salirse de madre. Ed. Hilda Rais, 163–86. Buenos Aires: Croquiñol, 1989.

———. "Casa matriz: Simulacros afectivos, resoluciones brechtianas." Teatro al Sul 3, No. 4 (1996): 11–13.

———. "Casa matriz." Colección teatro americano actual. Vol. 7. Madrid: Casa de América, 2001.

———. "Dial-a-Mom." In Women Writing Women: An Anthology of Spanish American Theater of the 1980s. Ed. and Trans. Teresa Cajiao Salas and Margarita Vargas, 215–41. Albany, NY: State University of New York Press, 1997.

———. "MaTRIX, Inc." In Defiant Acts: Four Plays. Trans. Diana Taylor and Victoria Martínez, 99–127. Lewisburg, Penn.: Bucknell University Press, 2002.

Rebolledo, Tey Diana. Women Singing in the Snow: A Cultural Analysis of Chicana Literature. Tucson: University of Arizona Press, 1995.

Rebrij, Lidia. "Fastos y oropeles de la carne: Soliloquio de la gorda." In Las risas de nuestras medusas: teatro venezolano escrito por mujeres. Ed. Susana Castillo, 101–04. Caracas: Fundarte, 1992.

Reis, Roberto. "Muita Serventia." In Cultural and Historical Grounding for Hispanic and Luso-Brazilian Feminist Literary Criticism. Ed. Hernán Vidal, 567–80. Minneapolis: Institute for the Study of Ideologies and Literature, 1989.

Restrepo, Pilar. La máscara, la mariposa y la metáfora. Cali, Colombia: Teatro La Máscara, 1998.

Rice, Susan. "Sexuality and Intimacy for Aging Women: A Changing Perspective." In Seniors and Sexuality: Experiencing Intimacy in Later Life. Ed. Robynne Neugebauer-Visano, 55–71. Toronto: Canadian Scholar's Press, 1995.

Rich, Adrienne. *Of Woman Born: Motherhood as Experience and Institution.* New York: W. W. Norton, 1976.

Rizk, Beatriz J. "El arte del performance y la subversión de las reglas del juego en el discurso de la mujer." *Latin American Theatre Review* 33, No. 2 (spring 2000): 93–111.

———. "Hacia una poética feminista: la increíble y triste historia de la dramaturgia femenina en Colombia." In *Literatura y diferencia: escritoras colombianas del siglo XX.* Eds. María Mercedes Jaramillo, Betty Osorio de Negret, Ángela Inés Robledo, 233–66. Vol. 2. Medellín, Colombia: Ediciones Uniandes, 1995.

Rodríguez B., Orlando. *Teatro venezolano contemporáneo: antología.* Madrid: Sociedad Estatal Quinto Centenario, 1991.

Rogers, Timothy J., trans. "Introduction to 'The Flight of the Crane' by Ana Istarú." *Latin American Literary Review* 17, No. 33 (1989): 96.

Rojas, Margarita, and Flora Ovares. "Genealogía de mujeres: *Madre nuestra que estás en la tierra.*" In *Drama contemporáneo costarricense.* Ed. Carolyn Bell and Patricia Fumero, 307–16. San José: Editorial de la Universidad de Costa Rica, 2000.

Rojo, Sara. "La mujer en el teatro chileno: del texto al público." Ph.D. diss., State University of New York at Stony Brook, 1991.

Romero, Mariela. "Esperando al italiano." In *Las risas de nuestras medusas: teatro venezolano escrito por mujeres.* Ed. Susana Castillo, 65–99. Caracas, Venezuela: Fundarte, 1992.

———. *El teatro de Mariela Romero.* Caracas: FUNDARTE, 1998.

———. "Waiting for the Italian." In *Women Writing Women: An Anthology of Spanish-American Theater of the 1980s.* Ed. and trans. Teresa Cajiao Salas and Margarita Vargas, 245–307. Albany, NY: State University of New York Press, 1997.

Röttger, Kati. "El poder de la mascarada." In *Performance, pathos, política— de los sexos.* Eds. Heidrun Adler and Kati Röttger, 101–23. Madrid and Frankfurt: Vervuert and Iberoamericana, 1999.

———. "Introducción." In *Performance, pathos, política—de los sexos.* Eds. Heidrun Adler and Kati Röttger, 9–21. Madrid and Frankfurt: Vervuert and Iberoamericana, 1999.

Ruiz, Marta Cecilia and Beatriz Marín. *Tardes abrasadas.* Medellín, Colombia: Asociación Taller de Teatro El Chisme, 1992.

Sagaseta, Julia Elena, ed. *Dramaturgas/1.* Buenos Aires: Editorial Nueva Generación, 2001.

Salas, Teresa Cajiao and Margarita Vargas, eds. and trans. *Women Writing Women: An Anthology of Spanish-American Theater of the 1980s.* Albany, NY: State University of New York Press, 1997.

Sayers, Janet. "Maternal and Phallic Power: Fantasy and Symbol." In *Daughtering and Mothering: Female Subjectivity Reanalysed.* Eds. Janneke van Mens-Verhulst, Karlein Schreurs, and Liesbeth Woertman, 62–69. London: Routledge Press, 1993.

Schutte, Ofelia. *Cultural Identity and Social Liberation in Latin American Thought.* Albany, NY: State University of New York Press, 1993.

Scolnicov, Hanna. *Women's Theatrical Space.* London: Cambridge University Press, 1994.

Seda, Laurietz. "Consumismo, maternidad y representación en *Casa matriz* de Diana Raznovich." *Itaca* 1, No. 6–7 (1996): 22–27.

———., ed. *La nueva dramaturgia puertorriqueña.* San Juan, Puerto Rico: Editorial Lea, 2003.

Seibel, Beatriz. *De ninfas a capitanas.* Buenos Aires, Argentina: Editorial Legasa, 1990.

Seminar on Feminism and Culture in Latin America. "Introduction." In *Women, Culture, and Politics in Latin America.* 1–9. Berkeley, CA: University of California Press, 1990.

Senelick, Laurence. *The Changing Room: Sex, Drag and Theatre.* London: Routledge Press, 2000.

———. "The Illusions of Sex." *American Theatre* 12, No. 9 (November 1996): 12–16.

———. ed. *Gender in Performance: The Presentation of Difference in the Performing Arts.* Hanover, MA: Tufts University Press, 1992.

Shaw, Deborah. "Problems of Definition in Theorizing Latin American Women's Writing." In *Gender Politics in Latin America: Debates in Theory and Practice.* Ed. Elizabeth Dore, 161–74. New York: Monthly Review Press, 1997.

Shedd, Sally H. "Gender Traders/Gender Traitors: Staging Non-Traditional Gender Roles and Alternative Sexualities." Ph.D. diss., University of Kansas, 1998.

Skidmore, Thomas E. *Brazil: Five Centuries of Change.* Oxford: Oxford University Press, 1999.

Soares, Vera. "Muitas faces do feminismo no Brasil." In *Mulher e política: gênero e feminismo no Partido dos Trabalhadores.* Eds. Ángela Borba, Nalu Faria, and Tatau Godinho, 33–54. São Paulo: Fundação Perseu Abramo, 1998.

Solomon, Alisa. *Re-dressing the Canon.* London: Routledge Press, 1997.

Souto-Maior, Valéria Andrade. *Índice de dramaturgas brasileiras do século XIX.* Florianópolis: Mulheres, 1996.

———. *O florete e a máscara: Josefina Alvares de Azevedo, dramaturga do século XIX.* Florianópolis: Mulheres, 2001.

Stoll, Anita. "Playing a Waiting Game: The Theater of Mariela Romero." In *Latin American Women Dramatists: Theater, Texts, and Theories*. Eds. Catherine Larson and Margarita Vargas, 41–52. Bloomington, IN: Indiana University Press, 1998.

Stranger, Inés Margarita. "Cariño malo." In *Antologia bilíngüe de dramaturgia de mulheres latino-americanas*. Eds. Graciela Ravetti and Sara Rojo, 125–38. Belo Horizonte, Brazil: Armazém de Idéias, 1996.

Suleiman, Susan Rubin. "Daughters Playing: Some Feminist Rewritings and the Mother." In *Subversive Intent: Gender, Politics, and the Avant-Garde*. 163–69. Cambridge: Harvard University Press, 1990.

———. "Writing and Motherhood." In *The (M)other Tongue*. Eds. Shirley Nelson Garner, Claire Kahane, and Madelon Sprengnether, 352–77. Ithaca: Cornell University Press, 1985.

Suplicy, Marta. *De Mariazinha a Maria*. Petrópolis: Vozes, 1985.

Surrey, Janet. "The Mother-Daughter Relationship: Themes in Psychotherapy." In *Daughtering and Mothering: Female Subjectivity Reanalysed*. Eds. Janneke van Mens-Verhulst, Karlein Schreurs, and Liesbeth Woertman, 114–24. London: Routledge Press, 1993.

Szoka, Elzbieta, ed. *Fourteen Female Voices from Brazil*. Austin: Host, 2002.

Szoka, Elzbieta and Joe W. Bratcher III, "Introduction to *Boca Molhada de Paixão Calada*." In *3 Contemporary Brazilian Plays in Bilingual Edition*. Eds. Elzbieta Szoka and Joe W. Bratcher III, 211–12. Austin: Host, 1988.

Tahan, Halima. "Introducción." In *Dramas de mujeres*. Ed. Halima Tahan, 11–22. Buenos Aires: Ediciones Ciudad Argentina, 1998.

Taylor, Diana. "The Theater of Diana Raznovich and Percepticide in *El desconcierto*." In *Latin American Women Dramatists: Theater, Texts, and Theories*. Eds. Catherine Larson and Margarita Vargas, 113–25. Bloomington, IN: Indiana University Press, 1998.

Taylor, Diana, and Roselyn Constantino, eds. *Holy Terrors: Latin American Women Perform*. Durham, NC: Duke University Press, 2003.

Taylor, Diana, and Juan Villegas, eds. *Negotiating Performance: Gender, Sexuality, and Theatricality in Latin/o America*. Durham, NC: Duke University Press, 1994.

Tindó Secco, Carmen Lucia. *Além da idade da razão: longevidade e saber na ficção brasileira*. Rio de Janeiro: Graphia, 1994.

Torres Molina, Susana. "Amantíssima," unpublished play, 1988.

Trevizan, Liliana. *Política/sexualidad: nudo en la escritura de mujeres latinoamericanas*. Lanham, MD: University Press of America, 1997.

Vaitsman, Jeni. *Flexíveis e plurais: identidade, casamento e família em circunstâncias pós-modernas*. Rio de Janeiro: Rocco, 1994.

Verséñyi, Adam. "Translator's Introduction." In *The Theatre of Sabina Berman: The 'Agony of Ecstasy' and Other Plays*. xi–xix. Carbondale: Southern Illinois University Press, 2003.

Villani, Sue Lanci and Jane E. Ryan. *Motherhood at the Crossroads: Meeting the Challenge of a Changing Role*. New York: Insight Books, 1997.

Vincenzo, Elza Cunha de. *Um teatro da mulher*. São Paulo: Editora Perspectiva, 1992.

Wandor, Michelene. *Carry on, Understudies: Theatre and Sexual Politics*. London: Routledge Press, 1986.

Web, Ruth B. "Physiology and Sexuality in Aging." In *Sexuality and Aging*. Ed. Irene Mortenson Burnside, 7–17. Los Angeles: University of Southern California Press, 1975.

Wehling, Susan Rita. "Feminist Discourse in Latin American Women Playwrights." Ph.D. diss., University of Cincinnati, 1992.

Wexman, Virginia Wright. *Creating the Couple: Love, Marriage, and Hollywood Performance*. Princeton: Princeton University Press, 1993.

Wiles, Timothy. "Suicide and Self-Annihilation: Marsha Norman's *'night, Mother* and Karen Finley's *The Constant State of Desire*." In *Staging the Rage: The Web of Misogyny in Modern Drama*. Eds. Katherine H. Burkman and Judith Roof, 112–23. Madison: Associated University Presses, 1998.

Willard, Ann. "Cultural Scripts for Mothering." In *Mapping the Moral Domain*. Eds. Carol Gilligan, Janie Victoria Ward, and Jill McLean Taylor, 225–43. Cambridge: Harvard University Press, 1988.

Witte, Ann. *Guiding the Plot: Politics and Feminism in the Work of Women Playwrights from Spain and Argentina, 1960–1990*. New York: Peter Lang, 1996.

Wodak, Ruth and Muriel Schulz. *The Language of Love and Guilt: Mother-Daughter Relationships from a Cross-Cultural Perspective*. Amsterdam: John Benjamins, 1986.

Woertman, Liesbeth. "Mothering in Context: Female Subjectivities and Intervening Practices." In *Daughtering and Mothering: Female Subjectivity Reanalysed*. Eds. Janneke van Mens-Verhulst, Karlein Schreurs, and Liesbeth Woertman, 57–61. London: Routledge Press, 1993.

Woodward, Kathleen, ed. *Figuring Age: Women, Bodies, Generations*. Bloomington, IN: Indiana University Press, 1999.

———. "Inventing Generational Models: Psychoanalysis, Feminism, Literature." In *Figuring Age: Women, Bodies, Generations*. Ed. Kathleen Woodward, 149–68. Bloomington, IN: Indiana University Press, 1999.

Wyatt-Brown, Ann M., and Janice Rossen, eds. *Aging and Gender in Literature: Studies in Creativity*. Charlottesville: University Press of Virginia, 1993.

Xavier, Elódia. *Tudo no feminino: a mulher e a narrativa brasileira contemporânea*. Rio de Janeiro: Francisco Alves, 1991.

Zachman, Jennifer A. "El placer fugaz y el amor angustiado: metateatro, género y poder en *El suplício del placer* de Sabina Berman y *Noches de amor efímero* de Paloma Pedrero." *Gestos* 16, No. 31 (April 2001): 37–50.

Zayas de Lima, Perla. "Susan Torres Molina, la mujer y el mito." In *Dramas de mujeres*. Ed. Halima Tahan, 327–45. Buenos Aires: Ediciones Ciudad Argentina, 1998. 327–45.

Index

255